GAY AND LESBIAN PARENTS

GAY AND LESBIAN PARENTS

Edited by

FREDERICK W. BOZETT

PRAEGER

Westport, Connecticut
London

Library of Congress Cataloging-in-Publication Data

Gay and lesbian parents.

    Bibliography: p.
    Includes index.
    1. Homosexual parents—United States. 2. Children of
homosexual parents—United States. I. Bozett,
Frederick W., 1931–
HQ76.3.U5G37 1987   306.8'74   87-13852
ISBN 0-275-92370-3 (alk. paper)
ISBN 0-275-92541-2 (pbk. : alk. paper)

Library of Congress Catalog Card Number: 87-13852
ISBN 0-275-92370-3
ISBN 0-275-92541-2 pbk.

First published in 1987

Praeger Publishers, 88 Post Road West, Westport, CT 06881
An imprint of Greenwood Publishing Group, Inc.

Printed in the United States of America

The paper used in this book complies with the Permanent
Paper Standard issued by the National Information Standards
Organization (Z39.48-1984).

10 9 8 7 6 5 4 3 2

This Book is Dedicated

To all gay and lesbian parents and their children.

And to the memory of:

Bob
Jon Patrik
Grady

With love.   F.W.B.

CONTENTS

IV: Psychosocial Implications and Legal Issues

V: Epilogue

FOREWORD

The present work raises all of the contemporary issues surrounding discussions of gay and lesbian parenthood. These issues are directly related to policy deliberations dealing with child custody, foster and adoptive homes by gays and lesbians, and therapy. The chapters of this work attempt to marshall the admittedly limited research on these issues and provide answers. However, it is notable that most of these issues are negative ones in the form of charges that have been made against the adequacy of gay/lesbian parenting. Hopefully, these issues can be settled in near future research so that the study of gay/lesbian parenthood can move on to other issues.

Bozett argues that for gay/lesbian parents, and especially custodial ones, bonds to children are almost invariably given primacy over bonds to lovers. He sees this as a sometime problem for such parents who are faced with conflicting loyalties. It should be noted, however, that such conflicts are endemic to stepfamilies of whatever sexual orientation and whatever marital status. For example, gay/lesbian stepfamilies seem most similar to common-law stepfamilies in which the status of the nonlegal stepparent is ill defined in the family. Such ambiguity of commitments can then easily give rise to disagreements over the priority of obligations. Presumably, that ambiguity is most characteristic of stepfamilies in their early stages and either greater clarity is reached over time or the family dissolves.

Bozett also raises the question of how well custodial gay or lesbian parents can relate to the gay/lesbian worlds that are typically populated by single persons. This is a real problem since many lesbian and gay parents come to feel socially isolated and left out by the homosexual worlds with which they identify. But again, this problem is not unique to gay/lesbian parents. Social worlds are nearly totally segregated by singleness and parenthood regardless of sexual orientation. Heterosexual couples almost never invite single persons with or without children to social occasions due to potential problems of jealousy, someone feeling left out of a conversation, incompatibility of interests, or the need to relate to others as a couple rather than as an individual. The gay/lesbian worlds seem to operate according to similar principles of homophily and segregation. However, since the gay and lesbian worlds are very largely unisex worlds, the barriers between couples and others may be less than in the heterosexual world, that is, there is no person placed in a minority by virtue of gender.

As noted by Bozett, there are difficulties in a custodial gay/lesbian parent finding a partner. Potential partners may be reluctant to assume obligations toward children. This reluctance is also present in the heterosexual world and limits the remarriage possibilities for parents without partners. Potential heterosexual husbands may prefer to father their own children rather than inherit someone else's. However, an alternative possibility is that being a gay/lesbian parent could make one an attractive potential partner for other homosexuals who are interested in having children but for whom most of the alternative avenues to parenthood are difficult. Such positive possibilities should not be ignored.

An issue invariably raised in discussions of homosexual parenthood is whether children raised by homosexuals will also be homosexual. This issue is always a concern in custody cases and foster or adoption matters. The authors of the present volume do a good job of presenting the extant research which shows that the sexual orientation of the parent seems to have absolutely no effect on the child's sexual orientation. They also note that virtually all homosexuals had heterosexual parents who did not succeed in raising children like themselves. Data such as these can be immensely useful in dispelling gratuitous, and seemingly ubiquitous, assumptions held by many persons. Since the data on this issue are to be found only in relatively unknown journals, volumes such as this can help give them wider circulation.

The reader may want to compare the chapter by Matteson on bisexual parents with that by Miller on gay fathers. Matteson argues for the viability of families in which one parent, usually the husband, is and acts bisexually. Miller suggests that such families are probably not viable and that the husband's homosexual needs will either result in marriage termination or in a marriage enduringly unsatisfying for all involved. It is unclear whether Matteson and Miller are both talking about the same kinds of fathers. Is Miller describing homosexual fathers while Matteson is describing truly bisexual partners? If so, they do not disagree. However, one can wonder whether the fathers whom Matteson is describing are truly bisexual. The most common case he describes is a father who loves his wife — "kinesthetically" — but is attracted — "visually" — to men. Do such fathers then find their love at home, their sex outside, and remain permanently on the periphery of the gay world by virtue of the division of their commitments? To Miller such men would be gays who cannot unite their love and their homosexuality. It would be interesting to see further dialogue between the two authors on this topic.

The need for external supports for lesbian mothers is repeatedly emphasized by McCandlish and Pennington. While partnerless heterosexual mothers can often fall back on the grandparents for assistance after the divorce/separation, this option is sometimes foreclosed for lesbian mothers. Homosexuals of both sexes are often alienated from their own parents or they may prefer to keep them at a distance. Also, a gay/lesbian parent is frequently reluctant to be "pushy" in seeking support from ex-husbands because of a possible custody case in which the former's sexual orientation is made an issue. However, lack of supports and social isolation is not unique to homosexual parents. Survey data have shown that partnerless parents are the most socially isolated of all types of households regardless of sexual orientation, have the least resources for housework and childcare, and have the lowest incomes compared to two-income households who are the financial elite among households.

In the excellent chapter on legal issues, Rivera describes how the ambiguity and abstractness of laws governing custody disputes — "best interests of the children" — have left decisions largely at the mercy of the knowledge/ignorance and prejudices of individual judges. This has had the effect that the outcomes of gay/lesbian custody disputes vary greatly by region of the country. In conservative regions such as the South, Southwest, and Intermountain states the homosexual parent rarely wins while in other regions the homosexual parent may often win custody. It could be argued that greater explicitness in the pertinent laws would narrow the freedom of judges to exercise their prejudices. However, it should be noted that, at least in conservative regions, attempts by legislatures to make the laws more concrete would probably result in a virtual abolition of the parental rights of homosexuals. Appeals from lower courts to either legislatures or appellate courts will often result in an explicit ban on the rights of homosexuals when the appellate body is conservative. This was clear in the *Hardwick* case (1986) where the U.S. Supreme Court rendered a sharply explicit and highly conservative interpretation of an area of law that had until then been ambiguous.

I briefly mention a topic not covered in the present volume. To what extent is there family violence among gay and lesbian households? To date there is no research. It is clear that almost all serious violence occurring in the gay world is precipitated by heterosexual males. Does the pacificity of the gay world also include the gay home? Do lesbian couples engage in little interpersonal violence, thus paralleling typical gender differences in violence whereby men are found to be much more pugnacious than women? Alternatively, does the considerable research on cross-gendering during the childhoods of homosexuals have implications for the extent of domestic violence during adulthood?

Foreword — *Joseph Harry*

ACKNOWLEDGMENTS

First, I want to thank all contributors for their participation in this undertaking. For most, writing their chapter involved conducting original research, or organizing knowledge gleaned over many years from their own professional experience. In more than one instance it meant writing the chapter on short notice, while in another it entailed gleaning data from across the country while on vacation. Not only do I appreciate the dedicated effort of which these examples are but illustrations, but I am also indebted to all contributors for the outstanding quality of their work.

In addition, I extend my gratitude to Ramona Mercer and Leonard Schatzman of the University of California, San Francisco and Phyllis Stern of Dalhousie University, Nova Scotia. If, years ago, they had not had faith in me and encouraged me as they did this book would not be a reality. I also want to thank Irene Elmer of Berkeley, California, who helped when it was needed most. Without Irene I would not have been able to undertake this project. I am also beholden to Charles T. Hendrix for his assistance and support.

Thanks are also due Professor Lorraine Singer, dean, and Dr. Constance Baker, associate dean and director, Graduate Program, both of the College of Nursing, University of Oklahoma, for their personal and administrative support of this undertaking. Likewise, I am deeply indebted to Loretta Leach, whose secretarial skills were critical to accomplishing this project. Last, I am grateful to Alison Podel Bricken, sociology editor at Praeger, for her encouragement, sage advice, and guidance throughout all phases of the process.

PREFACE

Gay men and lesbians form families. The families they establish often appear identical to the families of nongays. The homosexual parent may be legally joined with a spouse of the opposite sex and have one or more biological or adopted children. On the other hand, although less common, gay men and lesbians may adopt children as single parents with or without a lover who may serve in the stepparent role. Likewise, some gay men and lesbians choose to parent by providing foster care. Furthermore, lesbians, by the fortune of their biology, have the option of becoming parents through alternative fertilization. Increasingly, they are choosing to parent by this means (Pies, 1985). Other less common avenues to become a parent are through the use of surrogate mothers by single or coupled gay men, and communally whereby more than one gay man inseminates a lesbian and after birth they rear the offspring as if it were biologically related to them all (Schulenburg, 1985). There are other means by which parenthood can also be achieved. But the unions these gay men and lesbians form are unquestionably families. They are established groups of individuals who interrelate in order to satisfy their mutual needs for love and affection, both physical and emotional. They meet one another's survival needs by providing for food and shelter, and by assisting each other to maintain their social, spiritual, psychological, and physical health. They are interdependent economically, psychologically, and physically. They are committed to nurturing one another, they provide each other with a sense of identity, and they have a shared history, past and present, with the intention of a future. Moreover, the families discussed in this book also have children; thus, they have the additional responsibility of transmitting cultural and societal values to the next generation. Hence, without question, these social units formed by gay men and lesbians constitute families. They meet every qualification or criterion established to be a "family." Religious fundamentalists and political conservatives are indisputably wrong when they describe homosexuality and homosexuals as antifamily.

Thus, the purpose of this work is twofold. The first is to broaden the readers' thinking on homosexuality and homosexuals in general to include the dimension of children and parenting within the context of family. The vast majority of literature and research on homosexuality either ignores or pays scant attention to this facet of the subject. It is time for the lacunae to be filled to the extent possible although many gaps in our knowledge remain. The second purpose is to provide the reader with specific information. Thus, most of what is known about gay fathers and lesbian mothers who choose to parent is herein addressed. The content also includes data on the children of gay and lesbian parents, as well as a discussion of alternative forms of parenthood such as adoptive and foster parenthood, stepparent families, and gay men and lesbians in heterosexual family unions. Moreover, because of their special significance, there are separate chapters on legal issues, counseling needs, and social psychological concerns for gays and lesbians considering parenthood. The body of the last chapter constitutes a discussion of obstacles facing gay/lesbian families and the need for theory development and additional research.

There is no similar book. In 1985 Joy Schulenburg published *Gay Parenting*, the only other book on the subject. Although it is an excellent work, professionals are not its principal audience. The present work is conceived primarily for professionals, although laypersons will also find it of value. When I was creating the contents I envisioned a book that would synthesize the empirical, theoretical, and contemporary literature about gay men and lesbians as parents in the multiple contexts within which their parenting occurs. With that goal in mind I contacted experts whom I knew to be knowledgeable in the various content areas to be included. Because of the lack of literature on some of the subjects, on several occasions locating qualified authors constituted a serious problem. However, perseverance pays and ultimately suitable contributors were found for all chapters. In several instances I received more than I requested, the writer providing original, unpublished research. Also, in several instances it is the first time, to my knowledge, for more than just anecdotal data to be published on the subject.

Hence, this book is on the cutting edge of a new specialty in both gay studies and family science. It is one that begins to fill a much needed gap and serves to enrich our knowledge about homosexuality, fatherhood, motherhood, and parenting in general. I have found the contents to be both enlightening and thought provoking, and I anticipate the reader will also find it so.

L

GAY AND LESBIAN PARENTS

1

GAY FATHERS

Frederick W. Bozett

It may appear to the reader that the identities of gay and father are anomalous and at opposite extremes. Homosexuals as a group are often proclaimed to be antifamily. But the desire to parent is not the sole preserve of heterosexuals. Gays, like nongays, are often inclined toward parenthood. Gay adult love does not cancel out the desire or love for children (Marciano, 1985). Although one's desires to parent can often be satisfied through performing psychological father roles such as elementary school teacher or pediatric nurse (Giveans & Robinson, 1985), these surrogate roles are not sufficient for many gay men. Gay fatherhood can be achieved in a variety of ways. Probably most common is "heterosexual" marriage in which fatherhood is achieved through sexual union. Other, less common means, are out of wedlock impregnation through natural means or by artificial insemination. There is a trend for an increasing number of lesbians to choose parenthood, conception occurring through artificial insemination of sperm donated by a gay man of their choice (Pies, 1985). Gay male couples may become fathers by use of mother surrogates who are artificially impregnated with the mixed sperm of the couple. Other ways are to adopt children singly or as a couple, or to provide foster care (Harry, 1983; see also Chapter 6). However, because all research on gay fathers has been carried out on men who have married, it is these men specifically that this chapter refers to although much of its content may apply to gay fathers who have never married.

The purpose of this chapter is to review what is known about gay fathers based upon published research and other substantive accounts.

The chapter describes and explains the gay-father career in which the identity of gay father evolves. It includes a discussion of the management of both the gay identity and the father identity, and addresses the father-child relationship. Implications for professionals are also made. The chapter ends with recommendations for further study.

Although no statistics on most aspects of homosexuality can be stated with confidence, the number of gay fathers can be estimated. According to Kinsey, Pomeroy, and Martin (1948), Churchill (1971), and Kingdon (1979) approximately 10 percent of the population is gay. Also, in 1985 the U.S. Bureau of the Census estimated that the U.S. population in 1984 was 236.6 million. Thus, the gay population is estimated to be somewhat over 23 million. Moreover, about 20 percent of the gay male population has been married (Bell & Weinberg, 1978; Harry, 1983; Jay & Young, 1979; Spada, 1979). How many gay men have married more than once is unknown. Further, it is estimated that 20 to 50 percent of gay men who have married have one or more biological children (Bell & Weinberg, 1978; Miller, 1979a). How many gay men have adopted, foster, or stepchildren is unknown and cannot be estimated. Hence, it is likely that there are between 1 and 3 million gay men who are natural fathers. The combined number of children of gay men and lesbians has been estimated at 6 million by Schulenberg (1985) and 14 million by Peterson (1984). Thus, even without precise statistics, it is reasonable to assume that there are several million children of gay fathers.

THE GAY-FATHER CAREER

The concept of career is useful for detailing sequential development or stages of status passage (Miller, 1978). It has been found that gay fathers proceed through relatively predictable sequential stages typified by five marker events: dating, marriage, becoming a father, alteration in the spousal relationship (usually separation and divorce), and enactment of a gay lifestyle. These five benchmarks characterize what Lindesmith, Strauss, and Denzin (1977) refer to as the public or objective career, whereas the private, subjective career is typified by a gradual reformulation of sexual identity from heterosexual or bisexual to homosexual.

Developing a positive gay identity may be especially difficult for gay fathers because they have two identities that are at the extremes of social acceptance; fatherhood is highly socially sanctioned whereas the opposite is true for homosexuality. Because of their own social learning, gay fathers may believe the two identities are incompatible. Moreover, each identity tends to be unacceptable to the larger nongay society, and gay men who are fathers are often rejected by gays. Thus, the tendency is for gay fathers to be chameleon-like, living parallel lives portraying only one identity or the other depending upon the particular social milieu the man is in at the time. Living a dual biography in dichotomous worlds results in cognitive dissonance (Festinger, 1957) in which one's feelings and behavior are at odds. Thus, the task of the gay father is to achieve congruence of these two apparently disparate identities. A redefinition of the self is required whereby a cognitive restructuring (McCall & Simmons, 1966) of the self-image takes place so that the man's homosexuality is internalized as positive; there is a healthy "deviance avowal" (Ablon, 1981) in which the gay father gives up his counterfeit identity, and his self-conception and social interactions with gays and nongays become normalized and without strain.

There are two primary mechanisms by which the man achieves congruence between his two identities and his behavior. First is participation in the gay world over time. By this participation the father sees himself reflected in the person of other gays and learns that there is little basis in reality for the negative social stereotype of gay persons. Participation over time facilitates a gradual reconstruction of identity and attitudes toward gays, and thus toward the self as gay, so that ultimately identity reconciliation (Robinson & Barret, 1986) and adult sexual resocialization (Miller, 1978, 1986) occurs, and the man places himself in the cognitive category (McCall & Simmons, 1966) of gay. The second mechanism is disclosure of the gay identity to others. Although disclosures are difficult because of the fear of rejection and consequent stigmatization, rejections are rare. It appears that although gays collectively are rejected, individually they are not. Hence, as the gay father discloses to an increasing number of persons who are mostly approving, the man gradually introjects their acceptance, which further facilitates development of a positive gay identity.

Gay Fathers in the Heterosexual World

There are many reasons a gay man would marry, and most of them are the same as for nongays (Bozett, 1985). M. W. Ross (1983) identifies five categories of reasons. First is pressure from external sources such as family, friends, and the girlfriend. Second, marriage may be an attempt to deemphasize or "cure" one's homosexuality, or the man may believe it to be just a passing phase. Third is genuine love for a woman. In a study of lesbian and gay spouses, Wyers (1984) found this to be the most common reason for marriage among his gay male subjects. Fourth, companionship, stability, or relief from loneliness are given as reasons. Lastly, M. W. Ross (1983) itemizes unawareness of homosexuality as a reason. In addition to the reasons already enumerated, gay men may marry in order to have children, to hide their homosexuality, or they may think of themselves as bisexual, which justifies or explains a heterosexual union.

The initial period of the marriage appears to be no different than other marriages, and sexual relations are satisfactory. If the man had been sexually active with men before marriage he usually ceases after marriage. The man expects to maintain a monogamous relationship with his wife. However, after the first year or two of marriage sexual frequency with the wife often declines. Moreover, the man may fantasize sex with men during coitus with the wife. H. L. Ross (1972, 1978) reports that the men in his study explained that their wives had little need for sex, but this was disputed by the wives.

Eventually, most gay married men begin having clandestine homosexual liaisons either again or for the first time, and they gradually increase in frequency. These encounters usually occur in the impersonal and sleazy milieu of public restrooms, parks, pornographic bookstores, or gay baths. Because of the current epidemic of AIDS (Acquired Immune Deficiency Syndrome), these men may also fear acquiring the disease and transmitting it to their wives.[1] In addition to this worry, shame and guilt over the duplicity of their behavior is often felt. This was the situation of a father who had his first gay sexual experiences after his son was born. The internal conflict was so great that he attempted suicide twice. He stated:

> I was going through all sorts of guilt about being a bad father, and I felt, "Oh, I'm a terrible father; I can't hack it as a father." That was one of my biggest, worst fears. I didn't know how to be a gay father. I didn't think it was possible. Seemed like a contradiction of terms to me. I thought, "I can't." I was really hating myself for being a gay because I thought that it wouldn't work. I thought they were anathema[2] (Bozett, 1981a, p. 554).

Some men reduce the conflictual feelings by rationalizing gay sex as "therapy," since it relieves pent up tensions, or they justify it solely on the basis of sexual rather than affectional attraction.

It is worth noting that there seem to be differences between gay fathers who first begin homosexual activity after marriage as contrasted with those men who had experienced sex with men prior to marriage and who continued homosexual liaisons during marriage. It appears that men in the latter category manage the extramarital affairs with less guilt and conflict than do men who first begin after marriage (Bozett, 1981a). For men in the former group the duplicity is much more difficult to tolerate.

Miller (1978, 1979b, 1986), in his study of gay fathers, organizes his data along a four-point continuum to indicate the typical stages in gay fathers' moral careers. According to Miller, gay fathers at this stage of their career are at the "Covert Behavior" point on the continuum. The gay world is not perceived as a viable option because, due to limited experience within it, they hold society's stereotype of gay men as being effeminate, and they see no resemblance between themselves and the stereotype. Fathers in the "Covert Behavior" category remain married because of their children. Also, they commonly seek counseling.

Over time the gay father career progresses. These men gradually meet more gay men in a variety of social settings. Ultimately they are able to put themselves in the cognitive category of gay. Miller (1978, 1979, 1986) identifies these men as being at the "Marginal Involvement" point on the career continuum. Psychologically, fathers in the "Marginal involvement" category are more comfortable with their homoerotic feelings than are "Covert Behavior" fathers. Insufficient time spent at home creates guilt that is assuaged by showering the family with gifts. Fathers at the "Marginal Involvement" stage remain married because they fear permanent separation from their children, and because divorce would lower their standard of living. Albeit it is likely unsatisfying to remain in one of these two marginal and unhappy states (Cory, 1951; Miller, 1978), most gay fathers probably do because of their self-loathing (introjected homophobia), love for their family (especially their children), or for other reasons. Foreclosure of the gay father career frequently occurs here without further progression. For many gay fathers the inability to express themselves freely as the gay men they know themselves to be, combined with continual restriction of their full participation in the gay world, causes a buildup of tension and hostility that they eventually unleash on their families (Bozett, 1982). Moreover, they may be angry without really knowing why. At this time the family agonizes. Communication breaks down and eventually the relationship crumbles. If counseling is sought it is usually not effective in preventing separation. It is at this point when the family is in a state of almost total disrepair that many of these men will disclose their homosexual feelings and activities to their wives (Bozett, 1982).

However, not all families experience this kind of sharp conflict. Other couples may gradually grow apart, with limited communication and few common interests. At the same time the man experiences increasing frustration at not being able to freely actualize himself as the gay man he knows himself to be. Eventually, these feelings peak at which time he comes out to his wife.[3] There are likely other family scenarios that also lead to disclosure, but sharp conflict and gradual distancing are two that have been identified in the research literature (Bozett, 1982). Bozett (1982) also found that there was a direct relationship between extent of social-sexual activity in the gay world and the degree of overt family conflict: the less the sexual activity the greater the conflict.

Modes of adjustment in the marriage and the marital relationship after the man comes out to his wife vary, and depend on several factors. It appears that women who had knowledge of their husbands' homosexuality on some level prior to marriage were more understanding, or at least less upset, than wives who had no forewarning (Bozett, 1979, 1982). In the study by H. L. Ross (1972, 1978) a variety of adjustments in the marital relationship were made. One was the *double-standard marriage* in which the husband carried on overt homosexual liaisons that were resented but tolerated by the wife. The *innovative marriage* was one in which both partners consented to sexual relationships with others, with occasional menage-à-trois. The couples in the study by Ross who exemplified this adjustment mode were also sexually active with one another. In the research by Bozett (1979) one couple fit this mode but maintained a platonic relationship. They were, however, deeply committed to one another, and to their son. Moreover, the importance they attributed to *family* was especially intense. Another category of adjustment identified by H. L. Ross (1972, 1978) is the *platonic marriage* in which the marital pair do not have sexual relations, but the husband has casual sexual liaisons on the side. Lastly, the couple may adjust by separation. However, H. L. Ross found that couples tended to stay together if there were children.

All research on gay fathers has found that the primary mode of adjustment to the father's homosexuality is separation and divorce.[4] However, it is important to stress two additional points. First, efforts to maintain the marriage and thus the integrity of the family are usually made. Second, the man's homosexuality is not necessarily the cause of the divorce. For example, the wife may reject the husband's advances, or she may develop an outside relationship and be the one to initiate the marital dissolution. Gay fathers' marriages, like most other marriages, deteriorate for a variety of reasons (Hunt & Hunt, 1977; Jay & Young, 1979). In an interesting study of married homosexual men (not necessarily fathers), M. W. Ross (1983) reports that homosexuality per se does not necessarily cause marriages to break up. According to Maddox (1982), "Everything is possible in human arrangements, of course, but the prognosis for gay-straight marriages is poor. If the homosexuality of one does not pull the partner out of the marriage, the suppressed sexuality of the other will" (p. 72).

In sum, Bozett (1982) found that:

1) in most marriages in which the husband is homosexual and discloses his homosexuality to his wife, divorce is the usual outcome; 2) partial disclosure by the man of his homosexual inclinations before marriage appears to prepare the wife for his full disclosure during marriage; 3) gradual disclosure (partial to complete) correlates with a relatively amicable separation and divorce; 4) without partial disclosure before marriage, and thus no preparation for the wife, a highly antagonistic spousal relationship develops and the marriage ruptures; 5) wives who had some forewarning (i. e., partial disclosure before marriage) were more accepting of their husbands as homosexuals . . . 6) even though several wives of men in the study sample gave their husbands permission to have sex with men during marriage in an attempt to keep the marriage intact, all except one of the marriages failed. . . . Finally, 7) the wife who is approving reflects to the man that he is acceptable to her in spite of his homosexual disposition . . . the wife's disapproval makes it harder for the man to accept himself as gay. However, in order to meet his affectional and sexual needs he seeks out other homosexuals, thus increasing his exposure to the sexual and social aspects of the gay world. This in turn encourages him to begin to accept his own gay identity. Hence, from the point when the man discloses partially or completely to the point when the couple separates or divorces, most wives, no matter what posture they take regarding their husbands' homosexuality, appear to be enablers of their husbands' self-acceptance of their homosexuality and their transition toward a homosexual lifestyle (pp. 87–88).[5]

Although gay fathers may want to be free to explore their sexuality and to fully express their gay identity without the albatross of marital obligations, separation and divorce may nevertheless be difficult, primarily because they must also leave their children.

> Leaving home . . . brings the conflict between spousal and parental roles to center stage. That is, parents in a troubled marriage are likely to experience the clash of needing to leave as a spouse, but needing to stay as a parent. The impulse to stay as a parent can derive from the simple desire to be with one's child, or the conviction that even an unhappy marriage ought to be maintained for the sake of children. In either case, the same separation one may desire as a spouse, one may abhor as a parent (Rosenblum, 1986, p. 201).

Gay Fathers in the Gay World

Separation allows for much greater participation in the gay world. At this time most gay fathers will immerse themselves by attending gay social functions, having sexual experiences, and participating in other aspects of gay life. The number of gay friends also increases.

Gay fathers may discover, however, that their social acceptance by other gays is not as easily achieved as they thought it would be. The reason for this is because their parental obligations, whether or not their children live with them, conflict with certain characteristics of the gay world. The first of these characteristics is that the overt, visible gay culture these men most commonly enter is singles-oriented in which most of the participants are not committed to another man in a spouse-like relationship. Another characteristic is that unattached gay men are usually financially independent with economic commitments only to themselves. This kind of independence allows for mobility whereby they can come and go at will during their leisure because of limited obligations to others.

On the other hand, gay fathers do not have these freedoms unless they have given up their parenting obligations (which is rare), or unless their children are emancipated. It appears that most gay fathers accept these restrictions and obligations without objection. Research studies (Bozett, 1980; Miller, 1979a; Turner, Scadden, & Harris, 1985) bear out that most gay fathers are concerned about the quality of their parenting and relationships with their children, and that they willingly do what is necessary to continue parenting well regardless of their children's ages.

Not only must gay fathers disclose their homosexuality to nongays for their career to progress, they must also disclose their father identity to gays for which they may also be rejected (Bozett, 1981a,b). Fadiman (1983) refers to this as the "double closet." Whereas having children in the nongay world is a status passage, in the gay world it may be a stigma. "Everyone in my life that's close to me must welcome my son or they're not my friends. It's as simple as that" (Bozett, 1984, p. 65). Only when the children are adults or, in the apparently rare instance when a gay father abrogates his parental responsibilities, do other gay men's acceptance of gay fathers' children become less important (Bozett, 1984).

It is probable that most gay men who have never experienced fatherhood do not understand how important children are to gay fathers. According to Mager (1975):

> Gays in general should be more open and understanding of the special problems of gay parents (both faggot and lesbian). Children are not, after all, pets or toys, and I have grown weary of the attitude of some of my gay friends that it is cute that I have children — cute, but not very important (p. 132).

A custodial gay father supported this notion when he stated:

> For me, one of the most important aspects of my life is that I'm gay and another of the most important aspects is that I'm a father. And aside from a number of interests, those are the things around which my life revolves. And I think, and I suspect this is true of many gay fathers, that there is a significant alienation from other gays because of the fact that you're a father. And I suspect once again, that it arises from the idea of responsibility for another person (Bozett, 1981a, p. 556).

In the research by M. W. Ross (1983) it was found that men who first discovered their homosexuality after marriage were more likely to maintain more or less exclusively homosexual relationships which tended to last longer as compared to men who knew they were gay before marriage. One gay father said that he thought that

> Gay men who have been married know a lot more about what I call the stuffing of relationships than just plain gay men. . . . I feel that some gay people don't have any imagination beyond the immediacy of just what's happening (Bozett, 1981a, p. 556).

Coming out to gays as a father has a similar function and effect as does disclosing gay identity to nongays. It helps affirm the identity of gay father to the self, and other gays' approbations of the gay man as father further helps reduce cognitive dissonance, promoting identity validation. The two identities of gay and father begin to fuse, and a new cognitive category of gay father evolves.

Miller (1978, 1979b, 1986) designates gay fathers who separate from their families and enter the gay world as being at the "Transformed Participation" or "Open Endorsement" points on the moral career continuum. Men in the "Transformed Participation" category identify themselves as gay and come out to a limited extent publicly. Their gay involvement is social and emotional as well as sexual. According to Miller (1978, 1979b, 1986) this acculturation into the gay world involves four areas of concern: (1) disadvantages of advanced age and/or late arrival on the gay scene; (2) the necessity of learning new gay social definitions and skills; (3) the need to reconcile prior fantasies to the realities of the gay world; and (4) balancing and compartmentalizing their gay and father roles. Fathers at the "Open Endorsement" point on the continuum are proud of their gay identity and readily acknowledge it publicly. Their leisure time is often spent with their lover, their children, and a close network of gay friends and organizations, rather than in gay commercial establishments.

GAY FATHERS AND THEIR CHILDREN

Although many gay fathers remain married and keep their homosexuality hidden (Harris & Turner, 1986) many others do come out to their children (Bozett, 1980; Miller, 1979a). They do so because their gay identity is a deeply internalized and enduring aspect of their psyche. Miller (1978, 1979b, 1986) makes the point that in spite of increased public stigma, gay fathers achieve a sense of psychological well-being as their stigmatized careers progress.

Commonly, men at this stage of the gay father career can no longer tolerate the burden of secrecy. Don Clark (1977), a gay father and clinical psychologist writes:

> Generally speaking, it is important for the Gay person not to hide Gay identity from offspring, because they are too close to keep in ignorance. To hide it is to give yourself the message that you are ashamed and that there is

some cause for shame. To hide it is likely to give them the same message. And it is not such a good feeling to have a parent who is ashamed (pp. 133–134).

Although many fathers want their children to know they are gay, they do not disclose unless there is some compelling reason. The two most common circumstances that provoke disclosure are parental separation or divorce, and the development of a lover relationship (Bozett, 1981b; Miller, 1978). Children may find out about the father from the mother and father together telling them, they may overhear their parents discussing it, they may figure it out for themselves, or the father himself may tell them (Wyers, 1984).

The means by which the father discloses takes several forms. For example, with small children the father may disclose indirectly by taking children to a gay social event or by hugging another man in their presence. Both indirect and direct means may be used with older children in which the father also discusses his homosexuality with them. On the basis of reported research (Bozett, 1980, 1986; Miller, 1979a) children of all ages and both sexes almost always respond positively. There are several explanations for this. Both Bozett (1980) and Miller (1979a) found that many gay fathers had taught their children to accept variance in human behavior. In addition, it is unlikely that after coming out children would perceive their fathers negatively after years of having loving and nurturing fathers. It is also unlikely that they would abruptly discontinue loving a father with whom they had had a positive relationship for years. Moreover, disclosure may help relieve family tensions as the children may be less likely to blame themselves for problems in the home (Miller, 1979a).

Children indicate acceptance of their father as gay both verbally and behaviorally. One father reported that after disclosure to his children "they wanted to see what Dad's life was like. So, we'd go out dancing in gay bars. All three of us. They would dance, and I'd dance with each of them separately. I'd dance with my son. He's very understanding. He thinks it's fine" (Bozett, 1981b, p. 102). Another man described his adult daughter's reaction to his disclosure this way: "She said, 'I thought you'd been fighting it all this time. I feel so relieved.' And she reached over and grabbed my hand, and she just cried with great relief. She was feeling for me. Being compassionate with me — for my feelings. I didn't have to hold anything back" (Bozett, 1980, p. 177).

However, not all children are accepting (see Chapter 3). A major determinant seems to be the father's own acceptance. Schulenberg (1985) found that parents who were ashamed or confused about their homosexuality reported negative reactions from their children. Also, children who are told when they are younger appear to have fewer problems with acceptance than do older children (Schulenberg, 1985; Turner, Scadden, & Harris, 1985). This supports Berzon (1978) and Moses and Hawkins (1982) who write that children should be informed as early as possible. The foremost reason is that the longer the father waits the more time children have to take in society's homonegative viewpoint, which makes it much more difficult for the father to present a positive image of himself as gay (Moses & Hawkins, 1982). Also, some children may suspect their fathers are gay years before they are told and may resent not having been informed earlier.

Furthermore, it is not realistic to expect children who are old enough to understand the stigma of homosexuality, to accept immediately and approve of their father as gay. Few fathers have moved easily or accidentally from step to step in their career sequence. According to Miller (1986) each level is achieved by a painful searching process, negotiated with both the self and the larger world.

Not all gay fathers come out to their children. The reasons vary. One reason is because of the father's own homophobia. Another is fear of the ex-wife's vindictiveness if she were to find out. Other reasons for not coming out to children are fear that it will damage them, that it will be too upsetting, that it is not their business, and that they will not understand (Wyers, 1984).

AIDS is another area of concern for gay fathers. They may be concerned not only for themselves but they also worry that contact with their children may put the children at risk. Gay fathers need reassurance that the disease cannot be transmitted through any but the most intimate of sexual contacts. Moreover, it is advised that gay men avoid biological parenting or sperm donation unless they and their partner have been monogamous for at least five to seven years. This time period is recommended because of the long incubation period between exposure to the AIDS virus and the diagnosis of symptoms (Schulenburg, 1985).

QUALITY OF GAY FATHERS' PARENTING

Scallen (1981) assessed the relationship between sexual orientation and fathers' childrearing attitudes and behaviors. He also explored fathers' self-assessment of their performance of the paternal role. Data were obtained from response to the Eversoll Father Role Opinionnaire, the Kinsey Scale, the Father/Son/Daughter Practice Report, and a demographic questionnaire. The findings suggest that there *is* a relationship between sexual orientation and espoused paternal attitudes. Gay fathers were more endorsing of paternal nurturance, less endorsing of economic providing, and somewhat less traditional in their overall paternal attitudes than were nongay (heterosexual) fathers. In addition, gay fathers demonstrated a significantly more positive self-assessment of their performance in the paternal role than did the nongay fathers. Also, both gay and nongay fathers endorsed an active, caretaking stance regarding the paternal role, which, according to Scallen, tends to substantiate the trend toward increasing paternal role expectations.

In the study by Turner, Scadden, & Harris (1985) it was found that about half of the fathers did not encourage sex-typed toys for their children, and that most of the fathers made efforts to provide an opposite sex role model for them. These researchers conclude that (1) most gay fathers have positive relationships with their children; (2) the father's sexual orientation is of little importance in the overall parent/child relationship; and (3) gay fathers try harder to create stable home lives and positive relationships with their children than one would expect from traditional heterosexual parents. In the study by Harris & Turner (1986), in which gay and nongay and lesbian and nonlesbian parents were compared, they found no significant differences in the relationship of the parents with their children except that nongay parents tended to make a greater effort to provide an opposite sex role model for their children. The authors sum by stating that being gay is compatible with effective parenting, and that the parents' sexual orientation is not the major issue in their relationships with their children. It also appears that fathering by gay men who remain married and do not disclose their homosexuality to their children is of lesser quality than that of fathers who do. Often, married gay fathers spend less time with their children because their free time is frequently spent seeking out sexual partners. Father-child relationships are hurried and filled with tension; these men also tend to be workaholics, which also keeps them away from home (Miller, 1978, 1979a,b). Furthermore, gay fathers who are honest and open with their children regarding their homosexuality frequently live in a stable domestic relationship, often with a permanent partner; they are dependable, and they tend to spend quality time with their children. Generally, these are not descriptors of married gay fathers (Miller, 1979a). Hence, based on the available research evidence, it seems that an openly gay father is preferable to one who keeps his homosexuality hidden from his children (Bozett, 1984).

IMPLICATIONS FOR PROFESSIONALS

There are multiple implications for professionals in many disciplines. Several of the most salient are mentioned here.

Importance of Self-Examination

Regardless of the person's role or work setting, it is essential for all professionals who work with gay fathers and their children (or with any client for whom homosexuality may be an issue or concern) to engage in self-examination regarding their feelings about their own sexuality, and their attitudes and feelings about homosexuality and gay fathering. This self-examination is important because one's views on such basic matters cannot be homonegative or greatly counter to those of the client if the relationship is to be therapeutic (Bozett, 1984).

Reducing Homophobia

Individuals who are uncomfortable working with gay clients can take specific measures to reduce their feelings of discomfort. Many people have never questioned their values and beliefs about homosexuality, but, once questioned, if they are negative it appears that they can be altered (Morin & Nungesser, 1981). Education through courses in sexuality is valuable (but only if content on homosexuality is included, and is taught from a positive perspective). Reading about homosexuality, gay lifestyles, and gay fathers is one of the easiest ways to acquire knowledge (Robinson & Barret, 1986). Exposure to only one article on homosexuality has been reported to significantly change a person's attitude toward homosexuality (Morin & Nungesser, 1981). Visiting gay social settings such as churches, bars, and gay political meetings in which direct interaction with gays in their natural environment can take place seems to be especially beneficial in altering both attitudes and behavior.

Education for Sexuality

Dulaney and Kelly (1982) remark that the subject of homosexuality is neglected in the training of human service personnel. They point out that there are entire courses devoted to the elderly and to blacks, each of whom comprise between 11 and 12 percent of the population, but rarely are their courses on homosexuality, even though 10 percent of the population is gay. It behooves educators who prepare individuals in service professions to require didactic content in human sexuality including content on homosexuality that is presented from a positive viewpoint. Students in education, social work, nursing, medicine, psychology, law, and other human service disciplines should have practical experience in the area of sexuality directed by expert faculty so that when they are full-fledged practitioners they are better qualified to manage problems or situations that have a sexuality component. The wide variability in family forms, including the advantages and potential problems of each, also needs to be part of professional curricula. This is crucial for two reasons: problems are rarely individual; they almost always have a family component, and more than half of all marriages end in divorce (Spainer, 1986). The so-called "traditional" family, comprised of both biological parents and children is no longer the norm. Hence, professional workers need depth knowledge of the functioning of multiple other family forms.

Advocating for the Client

Robinson and Barret (1986) stress that it is important to employ the advocate model (Berger, 1977) when working with gay fathers and their families. The advocate model treats homosexuality as a normal variation in sexuality and lifestyle as contrasted with the traditional model that approaches it from a deviant, pathological perspective. As advocates, professionals would use the term "gay" rather than "homosexual" since the latter term has a negative connotation, and female homosexuals would be referred to as "lesbian" rather than "gay." Moreover, they would have some understanding of what their gay father clients have experienced such as the difficulties of coming out, or the feelings of guilt surrounding their extrasexual liaisons, so that the client would not need to spend time explaining background data that is rudimentary. It is also essential that human service personnel have information about local and national gay resources, such as the Gay and Lesbian Parents Coalition International. Professionals may also be of assistance to the wives and children of gay men whereby application of the advocate model is equally appropriate.

CONCLUSIONS

Research findings on gay fathers have been presented. Gay men marry for a variety of reasons. At the time of marriage, many, if not most, of them are either unaware of their homosexuality, or unsuspecting of its significance. From dating and marriage these men proceed through a relatively predictable life course referred to as the gay father career. Miller (1986) points out that the sexual resocialization that occurs in the lives of these men entails an orderly and identifiable sequence of status passage. However, identity foreclosure can occur at any point along the career trajectory. It is likely that most gay fathers foreclose early while yet married, disallowing the satisfaction gained by removing their masks and presenting themselves to others as the gay fathers they know themselves to be. On the other hand, it is probable that there are some gay fathers for whom living behind the screen of "heterosexual" marriage is the best course, but it is doubtful that it is a truly satisfying lifestyle for most of these men. Gay *identity* may be chosen but homosexual *orientation* is not. In the moral career continuum proposed by Miller (1986), he stresses that the continuum should not be construed as reifying transient states into types. The number of stages is not finite, and not every father passes through every step. Consequently, Miller believes it is more accurate to talk about career paths or sets of careers, rather than a single path. The greatest fear of gay fathers is that their children will reject them. Although others including their children may not understand, and acceptance may not be immediately forthcoming, rejections are rare. Moreover, gay fathers who come out to their children appear to be closer to them, to be "better" fathers, and to have a higher quality father-child relationship as compared to gay fathers who keep their homosexuality concealed.

Through the process of disclosure and sanction along with participation in both worlds the gay father gradually develops acceptance of himself as both gay and as a gay father. Thus integration occurs, in which there is an internalized converging of the gay and father identities with a commingling of the father's gay and nongay significant others with him in both his gay and nongay worlds. There is congruence between feelings and lifestyle concurrent with the integrity to express both identities in both worlds.

> Now it is over and we are divorced after three years filled mostly with bitter wrangling. We've all come to accept what has happened in one way or another. Do I think it was all worth it? Oh, yes. My only regret is that I did not have the courage to tell my wife earlier and to deal honestly with her about that secret and innermost essential part of me. Would she have understood me? I don't know, but that course — had I taken it — would have been far better than waiting as I did until I made that final slip on my precarious climb down into hell. It is always better to jump than to be pushed. . . . I wish the world had let me make that choice much earlier or that I had had the courage to make it in spite of the world's ways (Gay Fathers, 1981, pp. 17–18).

RECOMMENDATIONS FOR FUTURE RESEARCH

The need for additional study of gay fathers and gay father families in its many forms is intense since the number of studies to date is sorely limited. However, since the author has suggested elsewhere in some detail additional studies (Bozett, 1985), only several priority items will be mentioned here.

All studies to date have been comprised primarily of men who are white, divorced, middle to upper class, well educated, urban, and who are relatively open about their homosexuality, and are similarly accepting of it. Men who do not fit this description need to be studied to achieve a more complete understanding of the gay father phenomenon.

One of the greatest needs is for entire gay father family units to be investigated. If children are the psychological barometers of families as indicated by Spainer (1986), then the effects of this family form in its multiple variations on children's growth and development need serious investigation. Also, it seems that almost all gay fathers studied to date are more or less exemplary in the father role. It is necessary to study less exemplary gay fathers if our understanding of gay fathers and gay-father families is to be complete. Multiple designs using various methodologies are recommended; however, it seems to this researcher that the most pressing need is longitudinal study in which multiple research methods are employed.

NOTES

1.   It is important to note, however, that with the dramatic increase in AIDS, the incidence of casual sex among gay men appears to be on the decline concurrent with an increase in the number of committed monogamous relationships.

2.   This chapter is based upon research conducted by the author and others, as well as upon the author's four-year participation in a gay father support group and his association with gay fathers over a ten-year period. Unless otherwise noted all quotations of gay fathers in this chapter are derived from depth interviews conducted by the author. The interviews are housed at the Henry A. Murray Research Center at Radcliffe College.

3.   The term "come out" refers to acknowledgement of the self as gay. There are various levels of coming out. One can come out only to the self, one can come out to others by verbally informing them, and one can come out behaviorally or publicly by participating, for example, in gay social/political events. Because homosexuality is not outwardly discernible, coming out is a process that occurs repeatedly over the gay person's lifetime.

4.   Although the reported research on gay fathers does indicate that the primary mode of adjustment to homosexuality of the husband/father is separation and ultimately divorce, this may be an artifact due to bias of men who participate in research surveys. It is likely that most gay fathers do remain married. Married gay men are generally unwilling to participate in gay related research since they fear their gay identity or homosexual activities might be uncovered.

5.   M. W. Ross (1983) also makes the point that being married and gay does not necessarily create problems, and that many married gay men by compartmentalizing their lives or by having an open or understanding relationship with their wives manage as well or better than many conventionally married nongay couples.

REFERENCES

A. v. A., 514 P. 2nd 358 (Oregon, 1973). (Cited in Walters, L. H., & Elam, A. W. (1985). The father and the law. American Behavioral Scientist, 29, 78–111.)

Ablon, J. (1981). Dwarfism and social identity: Self-help group participation. *Social Science and Medicine, 15B*, 25–30.

Bell, A. P., & Weinberg, M. S. (1978). *Homosexualities: A study of diversity among men and women.* New York: Simon and Schuster.

Berger, R. M. (1977). An advocate model for intervention with homosexuals. *Social Work, 22*, 280–283.

Berzon, B. (1978). Sharing your lesbian identity with your children. In G. Vida (Ed.), *Our right to love: A lesbian resource book.* Englewood Cliffs, NJ: Prentice-Hall.

Bozett, F. W. (1979). The convergence of a dichotomized identity through integrative sanctioning. *Dissertation Abstracts International, 40*, 2608B-2609B. (University Microfilms No. 79–26, 643.)

____. (1980). Gay fathers: How and why they disclose their homosexuality to their children. *Family Relations: Journal of Applied Family and Child Studies, 29*, 173–179.

_____. (1981a). Gay fathers: Evolution of the gay-father identity. *American Journal of Orthopsychiatry, 51*, 522–559.

_____. (1981b). Gay fathers: Identity conflict resolution through integrative sanctioning. *Alternative Lifestyles, 4*, 90–107.

_____. (1982). Heterogeneous couples in heterosexual marriages: Gay men and straight women. *Journal of Marital and Family Therapy, 8*, 81–89.

_____. (1984). Parenting concerns of gay fathers. *Topics in Clinical Nursing, 6*, 60–71.

_____. (1985). Gay men as fathers. In S. M. H. Hanson & F. W. Bozett (Eds.), *Dimensions of fatherhood.* Beverly Hills, CA: Sage.

_____. (1986, April). *Identity management: Social control of identity by children of gay fathers when they know their father is a homosexual.* Paper presented at the Seventh Biennial Eastern Nursing Research Conference, New Haven, CT.

_____. (in press). Gay fatherhood. In P. Bronstein & C. P. Cowan (Eds.), *Fatherhood today: Men's changing role in the family.* New York: Wiley.

Churchill, W. (1971). *Homosexual behavior among males: A cross-cultural and cross species investigation.* Englewood Cliffs, NJ: Prentice-Hall.

Clark, D. (1977). *Loving someone gay.* Millbrae, CA: Celestial Arts.

Cory, D. W. (1951). *The homosexual in America.* New York: Greenberg.

Dulaney, D. D., & Kelly, J. (1982). Improving services to gay and lesbian clients. *Social Work, 27*, 178–183.

Fadiman, A. (1983, May). The double closet. *Life*, pp. 76–78, 82–84, 86, 92, 100.

Festinger, L. (1957). *Theory of cognitive dissonance.* Palo Alto, CA: Stanford University Press.

Gay Fathers of Toronto (1981). *Gay fathers: Some of their stories, experience, and advice.* Toronto, Canada: Author.

Giveans, D., & Robinson, M. (1985). Fathers and the pre-school age child. In S. M. H. Hanson & F. W. Bozett (Eds.), *Dimensions of fatherhood.* Beverly Hills, CA: Sage.

Hanson, S. M. H. (1985). Single fathers with custody: A synthesis of the literature. *The one-parent family in the 1980's.* Toronto: University of Toronto Press.

Harris, M. B., & Turner, P. H. (1985/86). Gay and lesbian parents. *Journal of Homosexuality, 12*, 101–113.

Harry, J. (1983). Gay male and lesbian relationships. In E. D. Macklin and R. H. Rubin (Eds.), *Contemporary families and alternative lifestyles.* Beverly Hills, CA: Sage.

Hunt, M., & Hunt, B. (1977). *The divorce experience.* New York: McGraw-Hill.

Jay, K., & Young, A. (1979). *The gay report.* New York: Summit.

Kingdon, M. A. (1979). Lesbians. *The Counseling Psychologist, 8*, 44-45.

Kinsey, A., Pomeroy, W., & Martin, C. (1948). *Sexual behavior in the human male.* Philadelphia: W. B. Saunders.

Lindesmith, A. R., Strauss, A. L., & Denzin, N. K. (1977). *Social Psychology.* New York: Holt, Rinehart, & Winston.

Maddox, B. (1982). *Married and gay.* New York: Harcourt Brace Jovanovich.

Mager, D. (1975). Faggot father. In K. Jay & A. Young (Eds.), *After you're out.* New York: Links.

Marciano, T. D. (1985). Homosexual marriage and parenthood should not be allowed. In H. Feldman & M. Feldman (Eds.), *Current controversies in marriage and family*. Beverly Hills, CA: Sage.

McCall, C. J., & Simmons, J. L. (1966). *Identities and interactions*. New York: Free Press.

Miller, B. (1978). Adult sexual resocialization: Adjustments toward a stigmatized identity. *Alternative Lifestyles, 1*, 207–234.

_____. (1979a). Gay fathers and their children. *The Family Coordinator, 28*, 544–552.

_____. (1979b). Unpromised paternity: The lifestyles of gay fathers. In M. P. Levine (Ed.), *Gay men*. New York: Harper and Row.

_____. (1986). Identity resocialization in moral careers of gay husbands and fathers. In A. Davis (Ed.), *Papers in honor of Gordon Hirabayashi*. Edmonton, Canada: University of Alberta Press.

Morin, S. F., & Nungesser, L. (1981). Can homophobia be cured? In R. A. Lewis (Ed.), *Men in difficult times*. Englewood Cliffs, NJ: Prentice-Hall.

Moses, A. E., & Hawkins, R. O. (1982). *Counseling lesbian women and gay men: A life issues approach*. St. Louis: C. V. Mosby.

Peterson, N. (1984, April 30). Coming to terms with gay parents. *USA Today*, p. 30.

Pies, C. (1985). *Considering parenthood: A workbook for lesbians*. San Francisco, CA: Spinsters Ink.

Robinson, B. E., & Barret, R. L. (1986). Gay fathers. In Robinson, B. E. & Barret, R. L. *The developing father*. New York: Guilford.

Rosenblum, K. E. (1986). Leaving as a wife, leaving as a mother. *Journal of Family Issues, 7*, 197–213.

Ross, H. L. (1972). Odd couples: Homosexuals in heterosexual marriages. *Sexual Behavior, 2*, 42–49.

_____. (1978). Modes of adjustment of married homosexuals. *Social Problems, 18*, 385–393.

Ross, M. W. (1983). *The married homosexual man*. London: Routledge & Kegan Paul.

Scallen, R. M. (1981). An investigation of paternal attitudes and behaviors in homosexual and heterosexual fathers (Doctoral dissertation, California School of Professional Psychology, Los Angeles). *Dissertation Abstracts International, 42* (9), 3809-B.

Schulenburg, J. (1985). *Gay parenting*. New York: Doubleday.

Spada, J. (1979). *The Spada report*. New York: New American Library.

Spanier, G. B. (1986). The changing American family: Demographic trends and prospects. In P. W. Dail and R. H. Jewson (Eds.), *In praise of fifty years: The Groves conference on the conservation of marriage and the family*. Lake Mills, IA: Graphic.

Turner, P. H., Scadden, L., & Harris, M. B. (1985, March). *Parenting in Gay and Lesbian Families*. Paper presented at the first meeting of the Future of Parenting symposium, Chicago, IL.

Weiss, R. S. (1975). The erosion of love and the persistence of attachment. In R. S. Weiss, *Marital separation*. New York: Basic Books.

Wyers, N. L. (1984). *Lesbian and gay spouses and parents: Homosexuality in the family*. Portland: School of Social Work, Portland State University.

2

AGAINST ALL ODDS: LESBIAN MOTHER FAMILY DYNAMICS

Barbara M. McCandlish

Lesbian mothers raise their families in a larger society that is hostile and uncomprehending and that fails to provide role models and adequate legal protection. Lesbian mother families in which two women couple, conceive using artificial insemination, and raise one or more children are especially appropriate for the study of lesbian family formation. These families pass through all the major stages of family development. Little exists in the current literature on family formation and psychotherapy for lesbian families in general or for these families in particular. The family dynamics and developmental changes within these families and the implications for the psychotherapeutic treatment of lesbian mother families are the subject of this chapter.

The family formation process is itself influenced by the larger social system. Lesbian and gay parents currently face enormous obstacles in custody battles (Davies, 1979; Harris, 1977; Hunter & Pollikoff, 1976; Payne, 1977/78; Reese, 1975). Custody outcomes clearly reflect the homophobia of the judicial system and the larger society, which is slow to change. Lesbian mothers now win 15 percent of custody battles compared to less than 1 percent in 1970 (Goldstein, 1986, p. 21). With only women as head of the household, lesbian mother families also suffer from less earning power and lower social status than families with an adult male.

Lesbian couples who use artificial insemination to conceive children face additional legal problems. The legality of artificial insemination is uncertain, especially if a physician does not perform the procedure (Elias & Annas, 1986; Sutton, 1980). Furthermore, the nonbiological mother may not legally adopt the child while the biological mother has custody. The effect of these legal precedents is that these family units have no legal existence, and further that the biological mother and nonbiological parent have unequal legal status as parents. The children bear the mother's name and are primarily in her custody with no biological father. The resulting family is the opposite of the prevailing norm where biological fathers have custody and where the children bear the father's name.

Available research continues to demonstrate that in spite of social and legal difficulties lesbian and gay parents provide effective parenting for their children (Golombok, Spencer & Rutter, 1983; Harris & Turner, 1985/86; Hoeffer, 1981; Kweskin & Cook, 1982; B. Miller, 1979; Mucklow & Phelan, 1979; Pagelow, 1980; Rees, 1980). The children of gay and lesbian parents have no more frequent psychiatric problems and gender dysfunction than do the children of heterosexual parents (Golombok, Spencer & Rutter, 1983; Goodman, 1973; Green, 1978; Hoeffer, 1981; Hotvedt & Mandel, 1982; Kirkpatrick, Smith & Roy, 1981; Miller, Mucklow, Jacobsen, & Bigner, 1980; Pagelow, 1980; Riddle, 1978; Weeks, Derdeyen, & Langman, 1975). This research deals almost exclusively with lesbian and gay parent stepfamilies whereas the health of children raised from birth in lesbian families has yet to be studied.

Hall (1978), Loulan (1984), and Pies (1985) emphasize the impact of social and legal censure on the lesbian family, and Hall (1978) especially underlines the importance of the psychotherapist being informed about these issues. Agbayewa (1984) and Osman (1972) fail to understand the impact of homophobia on the family and deal only with the family systems issues, thus reducing the effectiveness of the therapy. In my article on lesbian couples (McCandlish, 1981/82), I emphasize the strengths of two-women relationships in their capacity for communication and closeness and the difficulties of separation within the relationship, suggesting that these difficulties often result in limited sexual intimacy. Lindenbaum (1985) describes lesbian couple dynamics in a more precise manner. She observes the loss of separate selves and emphasizes the importance of differentiation and competition in the growth of the couple. However, she describes the deeper process as one in which the couple re-creates or has the capacity to re-create primal intimacy, which gives rise to excruciating terror of primal loss. In order to meet intimacy needs, the couple then relies on what she calls "undifferentiated merging" where sex is sacrificed entirely and where "felt difference" is unacceptable. Lindenbaum goes on to discuss the implications of these dynamics for envy and competition in the relationship.

When treating problems of sexual intimacy in lesbian couples, a useful therapeutic strategy is to give the partners the opportunity to face their deepest fears of merger through self-examination and active imagination. The cessation of sexual intimacy is then seen as an appropriate response to fear. What is needed is to rebuild a deeper level of trust which can provide the context for a deeper intimacy. The couple is aided in rebuilding trust through facing their differentness and individuality rather than relying on the illusion of being identical.

Mahler, Pine, and Bergman (1975) outline heterosexual nuclear family relational patterns from an object-relations perspective. Initially, the mother-infant relationship is symbiotic and exclusive in nature. Beginning in the fifth month the child begins to differentiate from mother and explore the world. A major developmental shift occurs at 15 to 22 months when the child develops a major relationship with another known adult in her move away from mother. This is an extremely important shift that can be crucial in the child's continuing differentiation. Major shifts during the first five years require the presence of at least one other adult or child with whom the child has a significant relationship. Thus a healthy family system is the necessary context for these developmental changes. As the child matures into latency and puberty, she comes in contact with an ever widening circle of adults and peers outside the family, thus continuing to move away from the mother-child relationship. There is some evidence that this process is different for males than females. A family member may develop psychological symptoms when this normal developmental process is hindered.

Agbayewa (1984) presents the case of a six-year-old boy and Osman (1972) the case of a fifteen-year-old boy, each in a lesbian mother stepfamily and each with behavioral problems. These problems result when an age-appropriate move away from mother is blocked in the family. In the first case, Agbayewa recognizes the developmental importance of the six-year-old calling his mother's partner "daddy" and developing strong connections with her. Thus the child is relying on the most appropriate adult within the family to make an age-appropriate move away from mother. The main difficulty is the mother's jealousy and attempts to block this move, which become the subject of the therapy. In the second case, Osman perceives a similar dynamic involving the mother's overdependence on her fifteen-year-old son. Here the son is blocked in his move toward stronger peer relationships, an important step in leaving home. The son fights with his mother's partner and expresses anger about his mother's lesbianism. Osman seems to have little understanding of the boy's genuine discomfort with his new social position and attributes his anger entirely to the family system. This therapy focused primarily on couple power imbalances.

The above theoretical considerations, research, and clinical observations demonstrate the effect of social and legal realities on the lesbian mother family. In spite of these difficulties, these families evidence effective parenting and no difference in pathology in the children when compared to heterosexual families. Limited clinical case material suggests that the children attempt and usually achieve the necessary developmental shifts. In order to further explore these relational patterns from a family development perspective, a preliminary study of five lesbian mother families was carried out. In each family a couple relationship existed prior to the birth of the first child. Unlike lesbian mother stepfamilies, artificial insemination lesbian families provide the opportunity to observe changes in the couple relationship and family system that accompany the birth of the first child.

METHOD

Subjects

Five lesbian mother families were contacted by word of mouth and all families contacted agreed to participate. The families were Caucasian middle class two-parent families with both adults employed and four families owning their homes. In these same four families the parents had acquired graduate degrees and training and were employed as professionals. In the remaining one family, the parents were employed in a particular specialized field. The couples had been in a committed cohabitating relationship for three to seven years prior to the birth of the first child. The parents ranged from 30 to 53 years in age. The children ranged from 18 months to 7 years, with 5 males and 2 females. Each family had at least one child five years old or younger. All the children were conceived using artificial insemination, with the donor known in one case, willing to be contacted in one case, and anonymous in five cases. The families were intact with the couple relationships ranging from 7.5 to 13 years in duration. In three families, the nonbiological parent expected to have no children of her own. In one family, each partner had one child. In the remaining family, the nonbiological mother expected to have a child of her own and was currently attempting insemination.

Procedures

Families were asked to participate in a study of lesbian mother families and were promised strict confidentiality. Each family was given a two-hour structured interview that included open-ended questions in the major areas of family formation, parent-child relationships, extrafamilial relationships, and the couple relationship. Families were interviewed in their homes by the primary investigator and all family members were present in four cases, and only one parent and the child in one case. Family interactions were noted, and developmental appropriateness and gender development of the children were observed. These data were later analyzed for common themes.

RESULTS

These five families had each completed the early stages of family formation, including couple formation, the decision to conceive, pregnancy, birth, and the first eighteen months to five years of childrearing. Four of the couples reported having achieved a satisfying sexually intimate relationship prior to the decision to have a child. The fifth couple was ambivalent about their prior sexual satisfaction. This couple had been together for three years prior to conception and was also reporting the greatest difficulties at the time of the interview. The couples had all made a commitment to be together prior to conception. The decision to have a child was different among the families. In the two families in which both parents were or planned to be mothers, the commitment to couple was made with the explicit expectation that both would bear children. In the remaining three families, the couple was formed first and then the decision was made that one partner would bear a child. Under these circumstances, the nonbiological parent had reservations about becoming a parent and considerable discussion was required to make this decision. The nonbiological parent had never expected to bear children herself and considered her lesbian identity incompatible with parenthood. Often the decision was made out of consideration and caring for the partner who wished parenthood, rather than a clear desire to become a nonbiological parent. In all cases, the biological mother had consciously sought motherhood.

Prior to conception, all the parents-to-be were lesbian identified, were out to their friends and had a functioning support system. They had also given some thought to their legal position and worked out a method of donor insemination with which they were comfortable. Two of the couples had wills and arranged guardianship for the nonbiological parent should the biological mother die. None of the couples had written agreements as to custody arrangements should the couple separate, although each couple verbalized basic agreement about what they would probably do, which ranged from full custody to the biological mother with extensive visitation rights for the nonbiological parent to joint custody. In two families, the nonbiological parent expressed discomfort with her lack of parental rights and expressed the desire to be able to legally adopt her partner's biological child.

In each family, some thought was given prior to conception as to the role of the nonbiological parent and how to explain the family to the child in an age-appropriate way. Both partners were clearly parents and labeled the living unit a family to the child. The biological mother was called mother and the nonbiological parent was called by her first name. The child always bore the last name of the biological mother, although often the middle name came from the other parent. All parents either had given or expected to give the child age-appropriate information about the insemination and the donor status when the child asked. Only one family described themselves as lesbians to the child.

During the pregnancy, the partners had dramatically different experiences. The biological mother entered the world of motherhood during this time in the eyes of her friends, coworkers, and extended family. Often the mother had not had satisfying contact with her family of origin, but with the pregnancy and birth she experienced becoming a family member. The nonbiological parent reported feeling entirely excluded during the pregnancy. Her extended family was relatively absent in four cases and warmed up slowly in one case after the birth. Her extended family did not consider the child "her child" or a member of the family.

All the parents were present at the birth. In every case, the nonbiological parent described an unexpected and immediate attachment to the infant. This was true regardless of this parent's interest in parenting prior to the birth. Two of the births were difficult ones involving some risk to the mother, who reported somewhat delayed bonding to the child due to exhaustion and necessary separation at birth. In these cases, the nonbiological parent held and nurtured the child in the first twenty-four hours. The biological mothers reported bonding, but without any affect of surprise.

From pregnancy on the partners reported being aware of the threat of censure from society. Explanations of some kind were often required, whether in the doctor's office, at childcare, or in the schools. Families were usually caught off guard with sudden questions from outsiders about the whereabouts of the father. The children themselves were free and truthful as only children under five can be. One child attempted to call the nonbiological parent "daddy" and when he was told this was inaccurate, he would explain to telephone callers who asked for his father that the nonbiological parent was like a father and was the person with whom to speak. Several children called the other parent "mom" in spite of adverse responses from the parents. Two of the families kept a low profile with all but close friends, family and coworkers and attempted to give the impression that they were two women living together, one of whom was a mother. The stress of possible censure was never completely absent from these families' lives and minds. Loss of employment, especially in a new job, was definitely considered a possible consequence of being completely out about their family arrangement. Open discussion and support within the family and giving the children clear explanations were considered important coping mechanisms. Additional coping mechanisms were to concentrate attention on matters at hand and to develop as much genuine support as possible in the workplace. The welfare of the child was a major concern in these matters.

During the early symbiotic period, the biological mother and child were a close unit. All the biological mothers nursed. At the time of birth, each took two to three months off from work, and when they returned it was less than full-time. The partners took at most two weeks off and tended to work full-time. Although the nonbiological parent was clearly bonded to the child and performed from 40 to 50 percent of the early childcare, she also experienced intense anxiety about whether the child had bonded in return. She reported searching for cues that the child responded to her quieting and presence. Without any defined legal and social role, the partner was wholly dependent on the child's response and the biological mother's expectations to give them a place in the family. As the child emerged from the symbiosis and spent less time nursing, the nonbiological parent was relieved that the child had clearly bonded to her. By the time the child was eighteen months, all parents reported strong connections among family members. In the interview, both parents engaged in age-appropriate warm and comfortable contact with the child or children. In all cases, both parents reported setting limits with the child and this was consistent with observed behavior in the interview. When asked how they felt about parenthood, every parent expressed appreciation for the experience, even while recognizing the tremendous changes and new responsibility. None expressed regret for their decision.

At the time of rapproachement, around fourteen to eighteen months, all families noted changes in the parent-child interactions. The child made a clear move away from the biological mother toward the nonbiological mother. These mothers welcomed more time for themselves and reported that the nonbiological parent did 60 percent of the childcare. This pattern of more frequent play and contact between the child and the nonbiological parent was also observed in the interview. In two other families, the biological mothers reported discomfort with the child's move away. In both cases, the children called the nonbiological parent mom or attempted to call the parent dad. The mother in one of these families immediately cut back on her work so as to spend more time with the child and to reinstate her position as the primary parent. The mother in the other family was openly uncomfortable, especially with the nonbiological parent being called mom. In the fifth family, each parent had a biological child who called both parents mom. These mothers reported that each child had made a healthy attachment to the other parent at an earlier age, and these attachments were easily observed in the interview.

At the time of the interview, all children who were talking evidenced healthy gender identity and knowledge of gender differences. No behavioral problems were reported by the parents or noted in the interview. Parents reported a number of instances where the children age four and older would ask about their father. Children would ask someone to be their daddy, ask where their father was, or express the wish to have a father. They would make up their own answers such as their father was dead or someone was in fact their father. The parents would answer all questions as honestly as possible and emphasize that families are different, name the people in the child's family, and talk about the love and caring that characterize a family. Since the birth of the first child, each family had actively added men and nongay families to their support system, partly to meet their new childcare needs and needs for support from other parents.

Each family reported changes in the couple relationship with the birth of the first child. Primarily, they reported increased hostility due to new unmet needs and the significant reduction or cessation of sexual intimacy. Partners reported feeling stressed in ways that increased their need for support from their partners. Partners differed in their expressed concern about the loss of intimacy. In four families, the biological mother was more concerned about the absence of sexual intimacy. At the time of the study, none of the couples had returned to a prepregnancy frequency of sexual intimacy, although two couples had plans to spend a weekend together without the children. For one couple, spending special time together had not resulted in the expected intimacy.

The couples reported new problems that had surfaced with the birth of a child. Primarily, they found themselves in new roles of biological mother and nonbiological parent. These role differences led to different needs and experiences, which had not existed prior to becoming parents. Some partners expressed envy at another partner's freedom or greater closeness with the child. These differences were a source of discomfort, had resulted in some open hostility, and had required considerable adjustment on the part of each parent. Four of the couples reported growth in themselves and in the relationship as they resolved and faced the differences, although they in no way reported an end to these problems. Two of these families had sought couple or individual therapy in order to resolve these differences. One family was in the process of considering separation and had sought couple therapy.

In summary, these five lesbian mother families evidence the effect of the current legal and social system on family functioning and the coping strategies with which the families face these difficulties. Significant changes occurred within the couple which became primarily a parenting unit, lost prior sexual intimacy, and struggled to deal with new role differences and conflicts. Warm and strong attachments developed between the parents and children, although the nonbiological parent and child tended to become more strongly attached after early infancy. Children who were under five showed normal psychological development.

DISCUSSION

The purpose of this investigation was primarily to develop a theoretical model of normal lesbian mother family structure, which would lead to more appropriate clinical services to these families and future research. Caution must be exercised in generalizing these preliminary findings. The sample is small and subjects were found through networking. The families are a special group in that a conscious decision to have children may contribute to greater satisfaction with parenting.

Also, all the children were age seven and under. Further longitudinal study of lesbian mother families, both stepfamilies and artificial insemination families with children of all ages, compared to nongay families would be needed to determine whether the relational patterns and coping mechanisms observed in the five families are typical of lesbian mother families.

The challenges and stresses of raising a family in the face of social and legal censure is evident in the daily life of these families. The families were able to develop coping mechanisms without prior role models. A major coping mechanism is the parents' ongoing communication about the family boundaries and identity to the children and to selected others.

Little literature exists about the early stages of lesbian mother family formation. Based on the family interviews, it seems that changes occur in the family when the child is born. Strong attachments are formed between parents and children. The children then are able to make the normal developmental shift from a primary mother-child attachment to an equal attachment to both lesbian parents. The children demonstrated no observable problems in gender identity or behavior. This is consistent with the current literature about the health of children in lesbian mother families. The couple relationship undergoes significant changes when a child is born. Sexual intimacy decreases or ceases completely and is not resumed during the first five years. Role differences and increased individual needs further stress the couple. Both Loulan (1984) and Pies (1985) also find that the parenting functions overshadow the couple relationship in lesbian mother stepfamilies. Based on Lindenbaum's (1985) formulation of lesbian couple dynamics, one explanation for the couple's failure to resume an intimate relationship is that as the partners become more open in bonding to the child, fears of primal merger increase.

IMPLICATIONS FOR CLINICAL INTERVENTION

Based on these findings and the current literature, three major areas of clinical intervention for lesbian mother families may be delineated: interventions that enhance the competence of lesbian mother families in dealing with social and legal censure and developing functional support systems; interventions that address family development and systems issues; and interventions that enhance mature couple relationships.

Although lesbian mother families seldom give homophobia as a presenting complaint, it is important that psychotherapists be sufficiently informed to understand the importance of these issues. The legal and social vulnerability of these families is a problem that is best dealt with directly. The first step is to clarify the actual external stresses on these families with the couple or family. The family may need information about the health of children in lesbian and gay families and clear support for their legitimacy as parents. The second step is to aid the family in defining their particular family and including the children in an age-appropriate way in this discussion. The third step is to encourage the development of a support system and appropriate and safe coming out by both parents and children. A fourth step may be to consider appropriate legal arrangements for the protection of the family. To accomplish each of these steps, lesbian and gay parenting literature, support groups, and friends may be of value.

The second area of intervention utilizes a family systems developmental model applied to lesbian mother families. As the study shows, appropriate developmental shifts can occur, regardless of the gender of the adults, as long as the child is able to attach to adults in addition to the biological or designated mother. In this study, all the children had access to males outside the family, which may be a factor in their healthy gender identity.

The third area of intervention focuses on the couple dynamics. The birth of a child seems to cause a crack in the couple's fantasy of sameness. Individual and group psychotherapy prior to and following the birth can aid couples in achieving a maximally satisfying adjustment. Psychotherapy can provide partners with the opportunity to examine their differences and unmet needs, including sexual ones, thus increasing their ego strength and trust. This process can lead to a more mature intimate relationship.

SUMMARY

In summary, the existing literature and the current study suggest a model of lesbian mother family development with implications for three major areas of psychotherapeutic systems and object relations theory. The model takes into account the particular relational patterns of lesbian women within the larger social system.

SUGGESTIONS FOR FURTHER RESEARCH

Further research on lesbian and gay parent families is needed in three major areas: the psychological health of the children; the relational patterns in the family; and the coping strategies and strengths of the families. The psychological health of the children in lesbian mother families compared to nongay families has been largely established. Both the health of the children and the parenting strategies of the parents need to be evaluated. Based on current research, these families are raising healthy children and deserve increased legal protection in terms of custody rights, and the legalization of adoption by the nonbiological parent in lesbian and gay parent families. Continued education of the larger society, increased support and education to the families, and the education of professionals serving these families are also much needed.

Future research might address the observations about lesbian mother families made in this chapter. Particularly, the early developmental shift in the child's relational patterns, the changes in the couple relationship, and the early bonding patterns in the family could be examined further. More rigorous research methods, such as a larger sample, a comparison group, and repeated observations, would be required in order to generalize these findings to the universe of lesbian mother families.

Continued research is needed to fully understand the effects of legal and social censure on gay and lesbian parent family structure. While some of these effects are certainly negative, it is also clear that these families develop healthy coping strategies that affect the lives of their children and may contribute to increased ego strength and social tolerance in all family members.

REFERENCES

Agbayewa, M. B. & Oluwafemi, M. (1984). Fathers in the newer family forms: male or female? *Canadian Journal of Psychiatry, 29*, 402–405.

Davis, R. (1979). Representing the lesbian mother. *Family Advocate, 1*, 21–24.

Elias, S. & Annas, G. J. (1986). Social policy considerations in non-coital reproduction. *Journal of the American Medical Association, 255* (1), 62–68.

Goldstein, R. (1986). The gay family. *Voice, 11*, (27), 19–29.

Golombok, S., Spencer, A. & Rutter, M. (1983). Children in lesbian and single parent households: psycho-sexual and psychiatric appraisal. *Journal of Child Psychology and Psychiatry, 24*, (4), 551–572.

Goodman, B. (1973). The lesbian mother. *American Journal of Orthopsychiatry, 43*, 283–284.

Green, R. (1978). Sexual identity of 37 children raised by homosexual or transsexual parents. *American Journal of Psychiatry, 135*, (6), 692–697.

Hall, M. (1978). Lesbian families: cultural and clinical issues. *Social Work, 23*, 380–385.

Harris, B. S. (1977). Lesbian mother child custody: legal and psychiatric aspects. 5 *Bulletin Am. Acad. of Psych. and Law*, 75.

Harris, M. B., & Turner, P. H. (1985/86). Gay and lesbian parents. *Journal of Homosexuality, 12* (2), 101–113.

Hoeffer, B. (1981). Children's acquisition of sex-role behavior in lesbian-mother families. *American Journal of Orthopsychiatry, 51* (31), 536–543.

Hotvedt, M., & Mandel, J. (1982). Children of lesbian mothers. In W. Paul, J. Weinrich, J. Gonsiorek, & M. Hotvedt (Eds.), *Homosexuality: social, psychological, and biological issues* (pp. 275–285). Beverly Hills: Sage.

Hunter, N., & Pollikoff, N. (1976). Custody rights of lesbian mothers: legal theory and litigation strategy. *Buffalo Law Review, 25*, 691–736.

Kirkpatrick, M., Smith, C., & Roy, R. (1981). Lesbian mothers and their children: a comparative study. *American Journal of Orthopsychiatry, 51*, (3) 545–551.

Kweskin, S. L., & Cook, A. S. (1982). Heterosexual and homosexual mothers' self-described sex-role behavior and ideal sex-role behavior in children. *Sex Roles, 8* (9), 967–975.

Lewin, E., & Lyons, T. A. (1982). Everything in its place: the coexistence of lesbianism and motherhood. In W. Paul, J. Weinrich, J. Gonsiorek, & M. Hotvedt (Eds.), *Homosexuality: social, psychological, and biological issues* (pp. 249–273). Beverly Hills: Sage.

Lindenbaum, J. P. (1985). The shattering of an illusion: the problem of competition in lesbian relationships. *Feminist Studies, 11* (1), 85–103.

Loulan, J. *Lesbian Sex*. (1984). San Francisco: Spinsters Ink.

Mahler, M. S., Pine, F., & Bergman, A. (1975). *The psychological birth of the human infant*. New York: Basic Books.

McCandlish, B. M. (1981/82). Therapeutic issues with lesbian couples. *Journal of Homosexuality, 7* (2/3), 71–78.

Miller, B. (1979). Gay fathers and their children. *The Family Coordinator, 28*, 544–552.

Miller, J. A., Mucklow, B. M., Jacobsen, R. B., & Bigner, J. J. (1980). Comparison of family relationships: homosexual versus heterosexual women. *Psychological Reports, 46*, 1127–1132.

Mucklow, B. M., & Phelan, G. K. (1979). Lesbian and traditional mothers' responses to adult response to child behavior and self-concept. *Psychological Reports, 44*, 880–882.

Osman, S. (1972). My stepfather is a she. *Family Process, 11*, 209–218.

Pagelow, M. (1980). Heterosexual and lesbian single mothers: a comparison of problems, coping and solutions. *Journal of Homosexuality, 5*, 189–205.

Payne, A. T. (1977/78). The law and the problem parent: custody and parental rights of homosexual, mentally retarded, mentally ill, and incarcerated parents. *Journal of Family Law, 16,* 797.

Pies, C. (1985). *Considering parenthood: a workbook for lesbians.* San Francisco: Spinsters Ink.

Rees, R. A. (1980). A comparison of children of lesbian and single heterosexual mothers on three measures of socialization (Doctoral dissertation, California School of Professional Psychology, Berkeley, 1979). *Dissertation Abstracts International, 40,* 3418–3419B.

Reese, S. E. (1975). The forgotten sex: lesbians, liberation and the law. *Williamette L. J., 11,* 354.

Riddle, D. (1978). Relating to children: gays as role models. *Journal of Social Issues, 34* (3), 38–58.

Sutton, S. (1980). The lesbian family: rights in conflict under the uniform parentage act. *Golden Gate Law Review, 10,* 1007.

Weeks, R. B., Derdeyn, A., & Langman, M. (1975). Two cases of children of homosexuals. *Child Psychology and Human Development, 6,* 26–32.

II

THE CHILDREN OF GAY AND LESBIAN PARENTS

3

CHILDREN OF GAY FATHERS
Frederick W. Bozett

The scientific literature devoted solely to the topic of children of gay fathers is limited to one report, whereas research on the children of lesbian mothers is more extensive (see Chapters 4 and 5). The reason for this discrepancy is most probably due to the fact that lesbian mothers, like nonlesbian single mothers, are much more likely than fathers, gay or nongay, to have child custody. Lesbian mother custody cases have received considerable publicity (see Julian, 1985), sparking researchers' interest in studying the potential effect of the mothers' sexual orientation and lifestyle on their children. Custodial gay fathers are less common. Because of their relative invisibility, gay fathers and their children have been less accessible for study. Although it has been thought that the numbers of gay fathers (and hence the numbers of their children) were not sufficiently substantial to warrant study, it is now known that this assumption is erroneous. There are at least 1 to 3 million gay men who are natural fathers (see Chapter 1). Also, this figure is conservative since it does not take into consideration gay men who adopt children, who are foster or stepfathers, or who achieve fatherhood by other less traditional means (for example, sperm donation). Likewise, it is difficult to estimate the number of children of gay fathers. However, Schulenburg (1985) estimates the combined number of children of lesbian mothers and gay fathers to approximate 6 million, whereas, according to Peterson (1984), there are 14 million. Hence, the number of both gay fathers and their children is sufficient to warrant serious study.

In addition, the American family has been undergoing radical change within the past twenty years. No longer can the term "family" be used to refer to a characteristic or typical family form. The so-called "traditional" nuclear family, which consisted of two biological parents of opposite sex with the father as breadwinner, the mother as homemaker, and one or more children is now less than one-third of all families with children (Hayes, 1980, in Bloom-Feshbach, 1981). Moreover, gay father (and lesbian mother) families appear to be increasing in number. Whether or not the number is real or is an artifact of more homosexually-oriented parents letting their sexual orientation be known is unknown. Nevertheless, as Hunt and Hunt (1977) point out, hundreds of thousands of formerly married individuals, many of whom are parents, are leaving their "heterosexual" marriages and are entering the gay world. Thus, it behooves professionals in many disciplines to have an understanding of this particular family form.

The purpose of this chapter is to present what is known about the children of gay fathers. It is based upon the author's research (Bozett, 1986), the research of Miller (1979), panel presentations by such children at professional meetings attended by the author, and upon informal personal discussions with several of these children. The chapter begins with a discussion of the children's reactions to their fathers' disclosure of his homosexuality. How gay fathers manage their homosexuality and their gay lifestyle vis-à-vis their children is addressed next, and is followed by a discussion of the children's development of their sexual identity. Following this, the advantages and disadvantages of having a gay father are identified. Recommendations for educators and counselors are presented, and the chapter concludes with suggestions for further research.

CHILDREN'S REACTIONS TO HAVING A GAY FATHER

Research by the author in which 19 children of gay fathers were interviewed, (6 male and 13 female, ages 14 to 35), found that the overriding concern of these children was their fear that others would think that they, too, were gay if their fathers' homosexuality became known. This fear can be explained on the basis of several theoretical premises. Lindesmith, Strauss, and Denzin (1977) comment that one's "self" cannot be separated from one's social environment, that "self" implies others." In addition, Goffman (1963) remarks about the informing nature of the "with" relationship. For example, it is assumed that if an individual is seen with others who have a particular trait, that person, too, has that trait. The presumption is that one is what the others are. In addition, homophobia in the United States is especially acute (Altman, 1982). Thus, fear of identity contamination by the children of gay fathers is understandable.

To manage their public image it was found that children use social control strategies, which are specific behaviors children of gay fathers employ vis-à-vis their father so that they are perceived by others as they want to be perceived — gay or nongay. Acting as agents of control can be thought of as the "identity work" of the children of gay fathers. Heterosexual children use these strategies primarily to assure that others will not think that they are gay. Gay children may or may not use the strategies, depending upon their acceptance of their own homosexuality. It is logical to assume that gay or lesbian children who are unaccepting of their own homosexuality, and thus do not want it known, would behave similarly to nongay children in the use of the strategies. Thus, the father's expression of his homosexuality would be kept in check to prevent others from possibly correctly identifying them as gay (the "with" relationship). However, this is not borne out in the research reported here since all of the gay respondents were accepting of their homosexuality.

Social Control Strategies

The first social control strategy is referred to as *boundary control*, which has three facets. The first of these is control by the child of the *father's* behavior (behavioral or verbal) in order to control expression of his homosexuality. For example, one subject refused to allow her father to bring his lover to her Christmas party although she hoped her father would come alone. Another respondent asked her father to keep his hands off his boyfriend's thigh during a party at her home. The second boundary control strategy is control by the child of their *own* behavior in relation to the father. For example, one child would not invite his father and his father's lover to visit his place of employment because the son was afraid that his fellow workers would correctly identify them as being gay. Another subject did not invite her father to a celebration at her home because "I didn't want people talking about me behind my back or pointing at me going 'Oh, her dad's a fag.' I don't want the shame of it." Another subject refuses to be seen in public with her father since she is certain that his homosexuality is readily evident.

The third boundary control strategy is controlling *others* vis-à-vis the father. An example of this is the child who will not bring certain friends home to keep them from encountering both the father and his lover. The function of boundary control strategies is to keep the boundary of the father's expression of his homosexuality within the limits set by the child. By controlling the father, the self, and others in relation to the father, the child controls others' perceptions of him or herself as being nongay. Moreover, the use of these strategies helps children avoid the embarrassment they feel because of their father's "shameful differentness" (Goffman, 1963, p. 140). In addition, the first two strategies help to inform the gay father of where the boundary of acceptable behavior is drawn (Higgins & Butler, 1982) by their children.

A second major social control strategy is *nondisclosure*. Unless children are certain it is safe to do so, children avoid telling others that their father is gay in order to avoid soiling their own identity. One young respondent stated: "I don't tell anyone else because I'm afraid they won't like me . . . [I'm] afraid they'll think I'm gay." An adult son who lives with his father rarely tells anyone since he thinks others might think he is also gay. He said, "I [do] not want to be perceived as a person who's gay because I certainly am not!" Nondisclosure may take other forms, such as referring to the father's lover as an "uncle" or a "housemate," or hiding artifacts such as gay newspapers when friends visit (Bozett, 1980). The children believe that not telling others prevents identity contamination, that it helps to maintain relationships, and that it keeps them from becoming social pariahs.

The last social control mechanism is the opposite of the one just discussed, *disclosure*. It was found that the most common reason for disclosing was that others are potential discreditors, that they are homophobic, that they will be derogatory about *them* (the child), if they discover the father is homosexual, and thus others need to be "prepared" before meeting the father. It seems that many of these children attribute exceptional decoding capacity to others; they assume that upon first meeting the father others are able to discern that he is gay. In addition, telling others is highly selective because closure of information channels is usually impossible. For example, one male respondent explained that it was very important to choose who to tell very carefully because "you have to be sure they won't tell somebody else. I was worried [about] people knowing [because] I was afraid of what they'd think of me; maybe it would be embarrassing." A gay informant *does* disclose his father's homosexuality to friends because he talks a lot about his family, and his father's homosexuality is "just one part of my family. It's significant." This may appear to be a contradictory finding but it is not.

Gay children who are accepting of their own and their fathers' homosexuality may use the strategy of disclosing their fathers' homosexuality, thus, through the "with" relationship, allowing their own gay identity to be known, or at least assumed without necessarily disclosing it directly.

Influencing Factors

From the foregoing it is possible for the reader to have the impression that children of gay fathers are concerned in the extreme about their fathers' homosexuality, and that they are excessively embarrassed by it. This is *not* necessarily the case. Although social control strategies are used in order to negotiate a public persona, in the research being reported here it was also discovered that there are *influencing factors* that determine the extent to which the children utilize the strategies just described. *The influencing factors are as important to understanding the reactions of these children as are the social control strategies.*

The first influencing factor is *mutuality.* Mutuality refers to identification by the child with the father. When the child identifies or links him or herself in some way with also being different, or the child feels that he or she varies in some way from societal norms in terms of behavior, lifestyle, values, or beliefs or believes there are other mutual links with the father such as sharing similar tastes in music or movies, then the more accepting the child is of the father as gay, and the less the child uses social control strategies. In addition, for children who consider themselves to be nontraditional, the father's homosexuality seems to help legitimate their own feelings of variance. An example of mutuality is the overweight respondent who remarked, "There's a lot of hostility toward heavy people, too. I don't like being labeled, and I understand what labeling is like. I think it's easier for me to accept a difference in someone else." Another subject explained that both she and her father had a drinking problem that linked them together. An adolescent son stated:

> In some ways I'm kind of jealous of my dad being different because I don't want to be like everyone else; I want to be different. My dad is hip. He likes all the music I do, he like the movies and TV shows I see, and we just like to do the same things. I think I'm much more like my dad (than my mother) and I think that helps me.[1]

The second influencing factor is *obtrusiveness*, which refers to how discernable the child believes the father's homosexuality to be. What constitutes discernability is determined by each child, but generally it refers to the culturally determined stereotypical symbols and manifestations of gay behavior such as the presence of gay artifacts in the household, the father's use of effeminate gestures, or his wearing excessive jewelry. It also includes the father asking his children to participate with him in gay social settings such as dining in gay restaurants. Any external manifestation that "increases the difficulty of maintaining easeful inattention regarding the stigma" (Goffman, 1963, p. 103) may be considered by the child to be obtrusive. One young son explained that he walks twenty feet behind his dad when his father walks arm and arm with another man, whereas another adolescent subject stated: "I feel at ease when I'm in public with my dad. My dad does not act homosexual. He does not! And Joe [the father's lover] does not act like that."

The third influencing factor is *age* of the children. If they are young they have less control over their own, their fathers', and others' actions, whereas the older the children are the more control they can exercise. For example, younger children may use the strategy of nondisclosure by referring to the father's lover as an uncle, whereas an adult child could avoid that situation entirely if the child so chose. Another facet of age as an influencing factor is the age of the child when he is told his father is gay. The older the child is, the more time the child has to take in society's homonegative attitudes and beliefs (Moses & Hawkins, 1982). However, if the child is told when he is young and grows up in association with gays, then it is more likely that the child will be comfortable with them and be relatively immune to the prejudice of others. This reasoning is supported by Turner, Scadden, & Harris (1985) who found that the fathers in their study related that children who were told at an earlier age were reported to have had fewer difficulties than those who found out when they were older.

The fourth and last influencing factor is *living arrangements*, which is often directly related to age. Living arrangements frequently dictate which controlling strategies are used and the extent of their use. For example, if children live with their father and the father's lover, they may have little control over interactions between themselves and their father, but they do exert control over their friends' contacts with their father. Thus, they may be highly selective regarding which friends they bring home. On the other hand, if children live with their mother or live independent of their parents they will probably have less need to use controlling strategies.

These four influencing factors are the ones that were extracted from the interview data. However, the odds are that this is not an exhaustive list. For example, another probable influencing factor is the degree of acceptance by the father of his own homosexuality. It is likely that the more accepting and matter-of-fact fathers are regarding their homosexuality, the easier it is for children to accept.

FATHERS' REACTIONS

Protective Strategies

It should be noted that characteristically gay fathers seem to be highly sensitive to their children's needs. They often attempt to avoid undue overt expression of their sexual orientation and gay lifestyle. It is also common for fathers to advise their children to refer to the father's lover as "uncle" or as "housemate." Also, if the children's friends are present the father and his lover often avoid even simple displays of affection, and the father may also put away gay artifacts such as newspapers or magazines. Another strategy is for custodial gay fathers to place their children in a school outside of their own school district. This provides the children with both school friends and neighborhood friends. If the father's gay identity is discovered by one group who then harasses the children, they still have another set of friends (Bozett, 1980). These are only several of the many means that gay fathers use to keep their homosexuality from public notice in order to protect their children from the torment of others.

However, a father's behavior may inadvertently be indiscrete. An example of the negative consequences of such behavior was related to the author by a fourteen-year-old son of a friend who explained that his father had visited the boy's school several times with "all his jewelry on. The teachers knew he was gay, and all the kids saw him and figured it out. It was obvious. They started calling me names like 'homoson.' It was awful. I couldn't stand it. I hate him for it. I really do" (Bozett, 1980, p. 178).

Role Modeling

Although gay fathers attempt to protect their children from the hostility of others, many gay fathers also want their children to understand that although the wider society disapproves of homosexuality and homosexual parenting, homosexuality is not a negative attribute, and the father is as moral and virtuous as other men. A Jewish gay father explained it this way:

> Any parent wants to show their kids good role models. As a gay parent you'd want to show your kids good gay role models to reinforce to your child that what you're doing is okay. And not only is it okay for you, but that there are also other gay family units out there that it's okay with. Because as a gay parent, I do have to think in my mind that my child is seeing something that is not the ordinary. And I want to have the obligation for her to at least see that this not ordinary thing is okay. And not only okay with me, but with enough people so she knows that although it may not be ordinary, it's out there, it's happening. And to see that, to make it easier, for whatever the future holds in store for her (Bozett, 1980, p. 176).

This father ended his comments by saying:

> I guess all you can do is give your kids the strongest feeling that what's going on is okay, so at least they'll be able to fight back. It's like being Jewish or being black. That kind of discrimination.
> And the kid is going to have to fight back as best he can and get the best support from home that he can get. This is just one of the realities (Bozett, 1980, p. 178).

There is yet another important facet of role modeling. If the gay father has a child who is gay or lesbian, then he has the responsibility to be a positive gay role model just as nongay fathers serve as role models for their heterosexual children. It is regrettable that most gay or lesbian children have no homosexual adult role models during their formative years. As a consequence, self-acceptance and adaptation to the gay world is often much more difficult than it would be otherwise. It is assumed that gay children who have an adult gay role model would experience a much smoother transition into adulthood than gays without such models. Research is needed, however, to bear this out.

CHILDREN'S DEVELOPMENT OF SEXUAL IDENTITY

Studies of the children of lesbian mothers (Golombok, Spencer, & Rutter, 1983; Green, 1978; Hoeffer, 1978, 1981; Hotvedt & Mandel, 1982; Kirkpatrick, Smith, & Roy, 1981; Weeks, Derdeyn, & Langman,

1975) have found no areas directly related to parental homosexuality. The findings of this research can be summed by the statement of Green (1978): "Children being raised by transsexual or homosexual parents do not differ appreciably from children raised in more conventional family settings on macroscopic measures of sexual identity" (pp. 696–697). (Also see Chapter 5.) Although there are no reported studies on the development of sexual identity of children of gay fathers, there is no reason to assume that the findings would differ appreciably from those reported for the children of lesbian mothers. Even so, this is a much needed area of research.

In the study by Miller (1979), among the 27 daughters and 21 sons whose sexual orientation could be assessed, the fathers reported that one son and three daughters were gay. Among the 25 children in the author's study of gay fathers (Bozett, 1981a,b), no father reported having a gay or lesbian child, although not all of the children were old enough for their sexual orientation to be determined. In the author's study of 19 children of gay fathers (Bozett, 1986), two sons reported being gay, and one daughter considered herself bisexual. The remaining 17 claimed to be heterosexual. Thus, as Miller (1979) points out, the link between parental and children's sexual orientation appears weak. Thus, the myth that gay parents will raise gay children and that gay parents attempt to convince their children to be gay has no support from research data. Likewise, another issue brought up regarding gay fathers is that they may seduce or molest their children. There is no evidence that gay fathers are more likely than nongay fathers to seduce their children or to allow them to be seduced. Child molesters are primarily heterosexual, and the victims are usually female.

In addition, there is some evidence that gay fathers attempt to develop traditional gender identity and sex-role behaviors in their children. Harris and Turner (1986) found that the fathers in their study tended to encourage their children to play with sex-typed toys, whereas half of the gay fathers in the Turner, Scadden, and Harris study (1985) did so. Also, it was not uncommon for fathers of both sons and daughters in the author's gay father research (Bozett, 1981a,b) to express concern regarding the absence of a feminine influence in the household. Most of the fathers in the study by Turner, Scadden, and Harris (1985) are reported to have made an effort to provide an opposite sex-role model for their children. These researchers also state that most of their subjects reported that their children appeared to be developing traditional sex-role identification, and that they considered their children's behaviors to be no different from other children of the same age and sex.

Children may, however, worry about their own sexual orientation; they may believe that because their father is gay they will be too (Moses & Hawkins, 1982). This concern may be especially acute for the adolescent who has had a homosexual experience. These children need assurance that homosexual experimentation is not unusual among young people (Woodman & Lenna, 1980). Moreover, children need to understand that they have options. Riddle (1978) points out that children's exposure to cultural and individual diversity can be positive, and that "an increased comfort with diversity could result in a greater ability to make personal choices independent of societal pressures to conform" (p. 53). She continues by stating that

> children do not model specific sexual behaviors unquestioningly; rather, they experiment. After early childhood, peers and significant adults (not necessarily parents) serve as primary role models. Persons are selected as models because of perceived valued traits, and then those particular traits are adopted. What gays have to offer children is a non-traditional, multi-option adult lifestyle model, independent of sexual preference choices (p. 53).

HOMONEGATIVE REACTIONS OF CHILDREN

On the basis of current research, it appears that most children are accepting of their fathers as gay. According to Harris and Turner (1986), and Turner, Scadden, and Harris (1985), *initial* responses of children to learning that their fathers are homosexual as reported by their fathers were closeness, confusion, not understanding, worrying, knowing all along, shame, disbelief, anger, shock, and guilt. Wyers (1984), reporting on the initial impact on children, states that 40 percent of the fathers reported a positive impact, 35 percent were uncertain of the initial impact, and 25 percent indicated the impact was negative. The children's *current* feelings as perceived by the fathers in the first two studies mentioned above were indifferent, supportive, proud, confused, angry, hostile, and ashamed. Wyers writes that 50 percent of the fathers reported the current impact was positive, 45 percent were uncertain of the current impact, and 5 percent indicated that the current impact was negative. In all of these studies the number of children who remained negative toward their fathers as gay was small.

Hence, although most children are accepting of their fathers as gay, some are not. It also seems that almost all children who reject their father as gay continue to accept him in the role of father. Although rare, it is likely that there are children who react by severing ties altogether. In the author's research (Bozett, 1986) two grown daughters were found to be intensely homophobic. They both exhibited some characteristics of the authoritarian personality type: rigid conformity to middle-class values, little tolerance for ambiguity, generalized hostility, and punitive attitudes regarding sexual "goings on" (Babad, Birnbaum, & Benne, 1983). According to Herek (1984), "Heterosexuals who express hostile attitudes toward homosexual persons tend to endorse traditional ideologies of family, sexuality and sex roles, and often are prejudiced against other minorities as well" (p. 12). The quotations that follow are characteristic of the individual described by Herek. They exemplify the attitudes and feelings of these children toward gay persons and homosexuality in general, and toward their fathers in particular.

> I don't hate gays, I just hate the way they act. I don't like people acting weird which is not to say that I don't want people to be different to be proper. I want them to be polite. I mean my dad's fine as long as he's not acting like a fag. Sure I'd prefer for my dad to still be in the closet. There's no conflict [that way] (Bozett, 1983, p. 10–11).

Another example is the following:

> I'm embarrassed that my father's gay. A lot of times I would just like him to go away. I almost wish he would die because then I can lie about what he was like to the future hypothetical children I'm going to have. It's not normal. Normal people don't go around doing things like that (Bozett, 1984, p. 64).

Note that these statements provide support for the contention of Altman (1982) that "What affronts others is the blatant *sexuality* of homosexuals, not merely their transgression of sex roles" (p. 68).

Although these two children are undoubtedly the exception to the rule, these examples are provided in order to demonstrate some of the range of children's reactions to homosexuality and to having a gay father. This is not to say, however, that these children do not have a *cognitive* understanding of their father. For example, one of the children quoted above explained that on one occasion her father took her to a gay restaurant:

> Fortunately we got a table back in the corner. I remember him sort of making eyes at the waiter. That really pissed me off! It's not intentional. What I think he's trying to do is say, "Look. Accept me. This is the world I've chosen." I know he loves me. He wants to be accepted. And it's really hard for me to do

that. It's all right for him to live his life whatever way he's going to, but I'm separate from it and I don't want him to try to pull me into it (Bozett, 1983, p. 11).

Although this daughter understands that her father's attempt to integrate her into his gay world is because he values both her and his gay identity and lifestyle and wants her to share in his pleasure, she rejects his efforts because such participation is in conflict with her value system. In addition, since research has demonstrated significant correlations between the attitudes of parents and those of their children (Ehrlick, 1973), these examples point to the value of gay fathers inculcating in their children as they develop an acceptance and appreciation for an extensive diversity of human behavior.

ADVANTAGES AND DISADVANTAGES OF HAVING A GAY FATHER

Based upon the research literature, it appears that the advantages of having a gay father outweigh the disadvantages. One common advantage is that it seems that many fathers who have disclosed their homosexuality to their children are more open in their communication with them, which seems to evoke a reciprocal response in their children, creating a closer father-child relationship. One daughter explained that before her father came out to her she had only a father, but now she has both a father and a friend. One son remarked that since his father had come out to him communication "has been much better. Since then I've felt much more comfortable talking about anything. When I first moved in with him, on weekends we would sit and just talk from the time we got up in the morning around 8 o'clock until almost or 9 or 10 o'clock at night."

In his recent autobiographical account Robert Bauman (1986), the ultraconservative congressman from Maryland whose highly successful career was destroyed when his homosexuality was made public, writes about his four children and former wife knowing that he is gay. "At least we are able to talk without shame, seeking the truth and debating our differences. 'We would have never known who you are,' my daughter, Vicky, said in her youthful wisdom. And I would have never known my children fully, or myself" (p. 272). That disclosure generally fosters a close relationship is supported by the research on disclosure (Chelune 1979) and by Woodman and Lenna (1980, p. 102) who write that one of the effects of delaying disclosure is to postpone opportunities for a closer relationship with one's children. Another advantage children identify is that they learn to be more tolerant of persons different from themselves.

There appear to be few disadvantages. Two daughters commented that their fathers attempted to become too close, that they were *too* open and revealing about themselves. In this regard, Colman and Colman (1981) remark that children measure their parents against the simple images of parents in the culture and the media, and thus, even though fathers may want to be closer to their children, their children may allow them only more traditional limit-setting roles. The most common disadvantage in the author's research (Bozett, 1986) was that the children may have considered the father's homosexuality to be responsible for the breakup of the family. This topic was discussed by several subjects with considerable emotion. For example, one 33-year-old daughter poignantly stated:

> There's been so much that got taken away by my parents' divorce. I enjoyed the times I spent with my parents. It took that away. We don't have the house any more that we grew up in, and it was really a special house. It took away a lot of innocence, I quess. The world just looked different. You couldn't trust it so much any more. Things weren't as they seemed. It took away a family. It broke up a unit of people, and over the years I'm learning that that's a really valuable thing to have (Bozett, in press).

It is worth noting, however, that children who feel close to their father and express feelings of love and admiration for him do not necessarily approve of his homosexuality. These children seem to be able to separate their fathers' *gay* identity from his *father* identity. For example, one son who spontaneously discussed his love for his father also said, "I perceive his lifestyle as wrong. I don't want to perceive what he's doing as wrong, really, but I just never have been able to change that perception." Likewise, a daughter who said that her father might "burn in hell" because of his homosexuality also explained that "If he wasn't gay I'd say he was sent from heaven. That's how impressed I am with him. He's smart, he's successful, and he's also a very caring man." Even though these children may not approve of their fathers' homosexuality, their homonegative attitudes and beliefs do not appear to interfere with the father-child relationship. Turner, Scadden, and Harris (1985) generalized from the reports of the fathers in their study that a parent's homosexuality seems to create few long-term problems for children who seem to accept it better than parents anticipate. Note, however, the significance of the word "few"; it is reasonable to assume that some long-term problems may occasionally occur under certain circumstances as a result of parental homosexuality. Turner et al. also write that most of their subjects reported a positive relationship with their children, and that the parents' sexual orientation was of little importance in the overall parent-child relationship. These findings are corroborated in the present study. Furthermore, Turner, Scadden, and Harris (1985) remark that gay parents try harder than traditional heterosexual parents to create stable home lives and positive relationships with their children. Although the original research reported here involved data from children only, it does seem from the children's reports that, in general, they felt their fathers had put forth considerable effort to parent well. Lastly, Harris and Turner (1986) sum their study of gay parents by stating that being gay is compatible with effective parenting, and that the parents' sexual orientation is not the major issue in these parents' relationships with their children. Most certainly, the study reported here supports both of these findings. Yet again a caveat must be introduced in that surely it is possible that for some children the father's homosexuality could be a major issue. For the two homophobic daughters reported on earlier, their fathers' homosexuality was often a major issue in their relationship with him. Whether the fathers perceived it to be an issue in their relationship with their daughters is unknown. In short, it seems that the findings of the research on the children of gay fathers are in general agreement with the research reported on gay fathers.

IMPLICATIONS FOR PROFESSIONALS

The reader is referred to the "Implications for Professionals" section of Chapter 1, "Gay Fathers." Many of the author's comments in that chapter are equally applicable to professionals who work with the children of gay fathers. Several more specific comments will be made here. If it is known that a child's father is gay, it is important that the professional worker focus on the salient aspects of the child's circumstances, and not on the gay relationships in the child's household unless they are clearly relevant. It is an easy pitfall to attribute a child's problems to the fact that the father is gay (Bozett, 1984). This notion is supported by research findings suggesting that nonsexual psychological problems may be attributed to persons whose sexual orientation is unconventional (Davidson & Griedman, 1981).

Although there are exceptions, it is this author's belief that it is best for school officials to know about the father's homosexuality, especially if the father has child custody. Knowing about the family can alert school personal to problems which may have the home situation as their genesis. Likewise, if the father is known about by school officials, both the father and his lover may participate in school affairs, attend school functions, or the lover may pick the child up at school, all without the parents or the child having to make elaborate explanations. Whether or not to tell depends on many factors, not the least of which is the political climate of the particular geographical area. It may be too great a risk in more conservative segments of the country, or in small towns or rural areas. Even so, in such locations there may be at least one teacher who is trustworthy. It is a relief for both the father and the child to know there is one person at school with whom one can be open and forthright.

Children may have many and varied counseling needs. For example, depending upon the children's ages, the need to keep the father's homosexuality secret may be an issue (Lewis, 1980). This need for secrecy is not unique, however. It is not unlike other family circumstances in which the parent's identity is potentially discreditable, such as with a parent's mental illness, or incarceration. Not uncommonly, recovering alcoholics will disclose their alcoholism to their children but explain that since many people hold pejorative attitudes toward people who have a drinking problem, keeping the secret will help avoid problems. The father needs to help his children understand the difference between private family business and general information about the family which may be made public (Woodman & Lenna, 1980). Confiding in children also communicates to them that the topic is an acceptable one for discussion with the father if they have questions. It also indicates that the father loves and respects the children sufficiently to trust them with the information.

Some of the stress these children feel may not be related to the parent's homosexuality, but to society's attitudes toward it. Concurrent with helping children to express their thoughts and feelings about the father's homosexuality, it may be necessary to help them recognize situations that are within their power to control, and those situations that are not. Thus, counseling needs to be geared toward assisting children to identify situations in which they can exert control, and then helping them to implement controlling strategies. For example, the author received a telephone call from an adult son of a gay father. The man was obviously distressed. Through his tears he stated: "Yes, my father's gay, and I don't know what to do about it." The help this man needs is dealing with his own feelings about homosexuality and his father's gay identity, since "doing something about" his father's homosexuality is not within his sphere of control. On the other hand, if a son is embarrassed because his father wears jewelry, then the boy can be helped to identify how he can approach his father on the subject, since this is an area in which influence may be exerted. For further discussion of counseling needs the reader is referred to Chapter 4 on the children of lesbian mothers in which much of the advice included there applies also to the children of gay fathers. Also, see Chapters 10 and 11 regarding mental health considerations of gay fathers and lesbian mothers.

SUMMARY

Because research is limited, relatively little is known about the children of gay fathers. It appears, however, that there is little change in the father-child relationship after the child is informed of the father's homosexuality. Moreover, what changes there are tend to be toward a more mutually intimate relationship. Although children may not understand why their fathers are gay, and some of them may strongly disapprove, the child-father bond is maintained. Even though children may be accepting, their fathers' homosexuality is often an embarrassment to them, and they may also fear that others will think they are gay. Thus, they control their own and others' interactions with the father through the use of social control strategies which serve to reduce embarrassment, and which also serve to project an acceptable public image of themselves. However, there are factors that influence the child's use of controlling strategies such as the extent to which the child identifies with the father's differentness, and whether or not the child believes the father's homosexuality is discernable by others.

Also, gay fathers seem to understand their children's need for the fathers to keep their homosexuality from public notice; they take discretionary measures to prevent homophobic harrassment of their children, and to keep their children from becoming social pariahs. The fathers' homosexuality does not seem to exert an influence on their children's sexual orientation, and the advantages of having a gay father outweigh the disadvantages for most children. It must be kept in mind that the content of this chapter is based upon limited research. A great deal of additional research is needed in order to acquire a more complete understanding of the multiple and varied effects of the gay father's homosexuality on the growth and development of his children.

RECOMMENDATIONS FOR FUTURE RESEARCH

As discussed in Chapter 1, one of the greatest needs is for entire gay father family units in their various forms to be studied in order to determine the effect gay fathers and gay father families have on the growth and development of children. Also, what are the differences for boys and girls reared in these households? What is the relationship, if any, between children's achievement of stage-specific developmental tasks and parenting by a gay father? Replication of studies similar to those conducted on the children of lesbian mothers would be of value to determine the fathers' effect on the development of their children's gender identity and sex role behavior. It is argued that gay children (particularly adolescents) would benefit by having a gay parent to serve as a positive gay role model (Morin & Schultz, 1978). Research is needed to determine if, in fact, fathers who are gay do serve as role models for gay sons (or lesbian daughters — natural, adoptive, or foster). If they do, do they ease their sons' acceptance of his own gay identity? Do they act as agents of primary socialization into the gay community, and do they facilitate their sons' transition into the gay world? Also, what effects do they have on lesbian daughters? Correlational studies between children reared in gay and nongay households would be useful in order to objectively determine and describe the similarities, differences, strengths, and limitations of each for use by family educators and practitioners in various disciplines (Bozett, 1985). Other needed research is in the area of homophobia. To this author's knowledge there is no research on homophobia, or its treatment, in children. There is undoubtedly more research needed than the several suggestions mentioned here. But it is hoped that this list will provide the impetus for increased research, so that a better and more complete understanding of the children of gay fathers will eventually be achieved.

NOTES

1. Unless otherwise noted quotations in this chapter are derived from unpublished depth interviews conducted by the author. The interviews are housed at the Henry A. Murray Research Center at Radcliffe College.

REFERENCES

Altman, D. (1982). The homosexualization of America, the Americanization of the homosexual. New York: St. Martin's.

Babad, E. Y., Birnbaum, M., & Benne, K. D. (1983). *The social self: Group influences on personal identity.* Beverly Hills: Sage.

Bauman, R. (1986). *The gentleman from Maryland: The conscience of a gay conservative.* New York: Arbor House.

Bloom-Feshbach, J. (1981). Historical perspectives on the father's role. In M. E. Lamb (Ed.), *The role of the father in child development.* New York: Wiley.

Bozett, F. W. (1980). How and why gay fathers disclose their homosexuality to their children. *Family Relations, 29,* 173–179.

_____. (1981a). Gay fathers: Evolution of the gay-father identity. *American Journal of Orthopsychiatry, 51,* 552–559.

_____. (1981b). Gay fathers: Identity conflict resolution through integrative sanctioning. *Alternative Lifestyles, 4,* 90–107.

_____. (1983, October). *Gay father-child relationships.* Paper presented at the National Council on Family Relations, St. Paul, MN.

_____. (1984). Parenting concerns of gay fathers. *Topics in Clinical Nursing, 6,* 60–71.

_____. (1985). Gay men as fathers. In S. M. H. Hanson & F. W. Bozett (Eds.), *Dimensions of fatherhood.* Beverly Hills, CA: Sage.

_____. (1986, April). *Identity management: Social control of identity by children of gay fathers when they know their father is a homosexual.* Paper presented at the Seventh Biennial Eastern Nursing Research Conference, New Haven, CT.

_____. (in press). Gay fatherhood. In P. Bronstein & C. P. Cowan (Eds.), *Fatherhood today: Men's changing role in the family.* New York: Wiley.

Chelune, G. J. (1979). *Self-disclosure.* San Francisco: Jossey-Bass.

Colman, A., & Colman, L. (1981). *Earth father/sky father.* Englewood Cliffs, NJ: Prentice Hall.

Davidson, G., & Griedman, S. (1981). Sexual orientation stereotypy in the distortion of clinical judgment. *Journal of Homosexuality, 6,* 37–44.

Ehrlich, H. J. (1973). *The social psychology of prejudice.* New York: Wiley.

Goffman, I. (1963). *Stigma.* Englewood Cliffs NJ: Prentice Hall.

Golombok, S., Spencer, A., & Rutter, M. (1983). Children in lesbian and single-parent households: Psychosexual and psychiatric appraisal. *Journal of Child Psychology, 24,* 551–572.

Green, R. (1978). Sexual identity of 37 children raised by homosexual or transexual parents. *American Journal of Psychiatry, 135,* 692–697.

Harris, M. D., & Turner, P. H. (1986). Gay and lesbian parents. *Journal of Homosexuality, 12,* 101–113.

Hayes, C. D. (Ed.), *Work, family, and community: Summary proceedings of an ad hoc meeting.* Washington, D.C.: National Academy of Sciences.

Herek, G. M. (1984). Beyond "homophobia." A social psychological perspective on attitudes toward lesbians and gay men. *Journal of Homosexuality, 10,* 1–21.

Higgins, P. C., & Butler, R. R. (1982). *Understanding deviance.* New York: McGraw-Hill.

Hoeffer, B. (1981). Children's acquisition of sex role behavior in lesbian mother families. *American Journal of Orthopsychiatry, 51*, 536–544.

____. (1978). Single mothers and their children: Challenging traditional concepts of the American family. In P. Brandt, P. Chinn, V. Hunt, & M. Smith (Eds.), *Current Practice in Pediatric Nursing,* Vol. II. St. Louis: C. V. Mosby.

Hotvedt, M. E., & Mandel, J. B. (1982). Children of lesbian mothers. In W. Paul, J. D. Weinrich, J. C. Gonsiorek, & M. E. Hotvedt (Eds.), *Homosexuality: Social, psychological, and biological issues.* Beverly Hills, CA: Sage.

Hunt, M., & Hunt, B. (1977). *The divorce experience.* New York: McGraw-Hill.

Julian, J. (1985). *Long way home: The odessy of a lesbian mother and her children.* Pittsburg, PA: Cleis.

Kirkpatrick, M., Smith, C., & Roy, R. (1981). Lesbian mothers and their children: A comparative survey. *American Journal of Orthopsychiatry, 51*, 545–551.

Lewis, K. S. (1980). Children of lesbians: Their point of view. *Social Work, 25*, 198–203.

Lindesmith, A. R., Strauss, A. L., & Denzin, N. K. (1977). *Social psychology.* New York: Holt, Rinehart, and Winston.

Miller, B. (1979). Gay fathers and their children. *Family Coordinator, 28*, 544–552.

Morin, S. F., & Schultz, S. J. (1978). The gay movement and the rights of children. *Journal of Social Issues, 34*, 137–148.

Moses, A. E., & Hawkins, R. O. (1982). *Counseling lesbian women and gay men: A life-issues approach.* St. Louis: C. V. Mosby.

Peterson, N. (1984, April 30). Coming to terms with gay parents. *USA Today*, p. 30.

Riddle, D. I. (1978). Relating to children: Gays as role models. *Journal of Social Issues, 34*, 38–58.

Schulenburg, J. (1985). *Gay parenting.* New York: Anchor Press/Doubleday.

Turner, P. H., Scadden, L., & Harris, M. B. (1985, March). *Parenting in gay and lesbian families.* Paper presented at the first meeting of the Future of Parenting symposium, Chicago, Il.

Weeks, R. B., Derdeyn, A. P., & Langman, M. (1975). Two cases of children of homosexuals. *Child Psychiatry and Human Development, 6*, 26–32.

Woodman, N. J., & Lenna, H. R. (1980). *Counseling with gay men and women .* San Francisco: Jossey-Bass.

Wyers, N. L. (1984). *Lesbian and gay spouses and parents: Homosexuality in the family.* Portland: School of Social Work, Portland State University.

4

CHILDREN OF LESBIAN MOTHERS

Saralie Bisnovich Pennington

Members of the mental health, medical, legal, and education professions frequently voice concern about the well-being of children in lesbian mother families. Some of this concern is associated with the rapidly evolving American family of the past decade into new and viable forms that deviate from and challenge the once normative extended nuclear family. It is estimated that there are 400,000 to 3 million lesbian mothers that are part of this trend (Hoeffer, 1978; Martin & Lyon, 1972). Also, the number of lesbians who are electing to have children through artificial insemination is increasing dramatically (Pies, 1985).

In such questions as these, one can detect hostility or homophobia: "Can the children grow up to be normal adults?" "Are those mothers capable of caring for their children?" "Is it fair to the children; wouldn't they be better off with their fathers or with anyone else, for that matter?" and "Won't it make them gay to have two gay parents (in the situation where the lesbian mother has a lover who is a coparent)?"

These and other questions have generated a body of research that supports the normalcy of these children (Cramer, 1986; Green, 1978; Hoeffer, 1981; Hotvedt & Mandel, 1982; Kirkpatrick, Smith, & Roy, 1981; Lewin & Lyons, 1982; Pagelow, 1980; and Steckel, 1985). According to Cramer (1986), children from lesbian mother households do not differ from their counterparts raised by nongay parents in relation to sex-role socialization, gender identity, accomplishment of developmental tasks, intelligence, reaction to father absence, parental separation and divorce, and general adjustment and development. What appears to be most crucial for the emergence of normal healthy growth, development, and behavior is the *quality of mothering* rather than the mother's sexual orientation.

There is a meager body of published information pertaining to clinical work with children from lesbian mother families (Baptiste, 1987; Osman, 1972; Shernoff, 1974; and Weeks et al., 1975). Baptiste (1987) remarks that

> despite recent efforts by the two (the primary psychiatric and psychological associations) major mental health service providers to have homosexuality viewed less negatively and the persuasive research evidence that supports the belief that a gay lifestyle is neither deviant nor pathological, the sexual orientation and lifestyle of gay men and women are still viewed as indicators of maladjustment or psychopathology by many members of society. Consequently, even under the best of circumstances, children in gay step-families may experience difficulty since it is not easy for them to grow up in a family that is disapproved of by society and to be labeled as pathological or undesirable by association.

Fear of legal reprisals and the insensitivity or hostility of professionals have kept many lesbian parented families from seeking help through community clinics or private practitioners. Acknowledging family or individual problems could be tantamount to being declared unfit mothers. Fortunately, in recent years there has been an increasing number of gay-sensitive psychotherapists who are in a position to provide much needed services to these families.

The purpose of this chapter is to discuss the major issues confronted by children living in lesbian mother households. It is based on the author's ten-year clinical experience working with both individual members of these families and with the families as a whole. It is also based upon the limited literature available, which will be referred to throughout the chapter. (Also, refer to Chapter 5 on the psychosocial development of the children of lesbian mothers.)

CLINICAL SAMPLE

Demographic Data

The clinical sample referred to in this chapter includes 32 children from 28 lesbian mother families treated by the author since 1977. Thirty of the children were seen at Operation Concern, an outpatient psychotherapy clinic for gay men, lesbians, and their families in San Francisco, California. With the exception of three children who were seen solely in individual therapy, all participated in family therapy. Nineteen children were seen in both individual and family therapy. The typical length of therapy was six months to one year. The children included 22 females and 10 males, from ages 5 to 29; most were between 7 and 15. Twenty-two were Caucasians; of this group several also identified as Hispanic. Five of the children were black and five were biracial (black and Caucasian, including some with Hispanic backgrounds). The major U.S. religions and a wide range of socioeconomic backgrounds were represented.

Only one child seemed to have no awareness of the mother's lesbianism. Because of his age (seven years), the family's disorganization, and his individual pathology, his mother's sexual orientation was less of an immediate concern. Three other children (one aged five and two others aged seven) were struggling to understand what it meant for them to have a lesbian mother. These children, all of whose mothers had a female lover, were trying to work out their relationship to the mother's lover. Two additional teenage females had mothers who indirectly indicated a lesbian sexual orientation.

Marital/Parenting Status

Five of the mothers did not have a lover. How the mothers perceived their mothering role is as follows: fourteen identified primarily as single mothers; ten considered themselves to be in a coparenting relationship with their lover; and four thought of themselves as being in a stepfamily situation with their live-in lover as the stepparent. Children from four families saw their fathers on a regular basis; the majority had no contact with their fathers or none since parental separation. Two of the children had gay fathers as well as lesbian mothers. Neither parent in either of the couples was aware of their sexual orientation until after the children were born.

Referral Sources

All clients entered into the therapy situation on a voluntary basis. Mothers were either self-referred or referred by other individuals, social agencies, or gay/sensitive organizations. The mothers were aware of or informed that although their sexual orientation would be addressed, neither it nor the mother herself would be blamed for the child's or the family's dysfunction.

During this same time period I worked with approximately fifteen lesbian mothers in individual therapy focusing on child-related issues. In some of these families the mothers had not disclosed their sexual orientation to their children and were afraid to do so. In others, the children were under the age of five and thus were too young to participate in family therapy involving issues related to the mother's sexual orientation. In others the children expressed no concern regarding having a lesbian mother. In some families the children were grown and lived away from home. Lastly, in four instances the children had been kidnapped from the mothers by their fathers.

ISSUES AND PROBLEMS

It is essential for the reader to understand that there is no inherent pathology in lesbian mother families. The central focus is the profound impact of a homophobic culture. The children face the dual challenge of living in a different family form and of having a different kind of mother (Baptiste, 1987; Lewis, 1980).

Disclosure and Its Ramifications

A fourteen-year-old female client reported, "I do not want to think about what kids would say or do if they found out my parents (lesbian mother and her female lover) are gay. They would make fun of me or not trust me. I've wished sometimes they weren't lesbians, but it's their decision, as long as I don't get blamed for it." The same client explained an advantage of having two lesbian parents as, "I didn't feel as inhibited with all girls or women in my house when I got my period."

A thirteen-year-old female client stated, "When I was around five, my mom and Lois told me they were lesbians. I said good, and thought, I want to be just like my mom. Well, when I reached about the fifth grade . . . I heard kids calling someone a faggot as a swear word, and I thought, 'My God, they're talking about my mom.'"

Every lesbian mother, sooner or later, has to decide if, when, and how to disclose her sexual orientation to her children. When secrecy surrounds mothers' lesbianism, serious communication problems can result, and children in this situation (in my sample all were early teenage girls) were perceived by themselves and their mothers to be moody, depressed, and withdrawn. The mothers did not realize that the secrecy or silence surrounding their lesbian orientation was related to their daughters' psychological problems.

Children around seven years of age and younger tended to be more concerned with the parents' separation or divorce rather than with their mother being a lesbian. They expressed concern that they might be deprived of parental attention. It is also significant that younger children tended to respond with more anxiety than older ones to the separation or "divorce" of their mother from a female partner when the female partner had been a stable parenting figure in these children's lives. Older children would sometimes entertain the fantasy that such a breakup would mean that their mother was no longer a lesbian. Moreover, when having a lesbian mother was considered to be a problem by either the child or the mother, it was never the only issue that surfaced in treatment.

When the children of lesbian mothers are old enough to realize that same-sex relationships are not generally accepted, they commonly fear that other children will find out that their mother is a lesbian. This awareness frequently occurs after seven years of age and intensifies during pubescence and the early teenage years. It tends to subside as the child's sexual awakening gives way to a firmer sexual identity concurrent with gradual separation from the mother (Berzon, 1978; Cramer, 1986; Shernoff, 1974).

Children may fear being ostracized and isolated if their mothers' sexual orientation becomes known. They often are afraid of physical harassment by their peers (Lewin & Lyons, 1982). Girls, more than boys, commonly fear that they, too, will be gay or that people will think they are gay (Berzon, 1978; Lewis, 1980).

Interestingly, nowhere in the literature was I able to find that daughters have greater difficulties than sons regarding their mothers' lesbianism. It is my observation that, when told the truth regarding their mothers' sexual orientation, teenage daughters became more upset than teenage sons. Boys tended to think they could settle their feelings by overtly retaliating against any peer abuse by physically fighting to defend their mothers' honor. Specific consideration is given to the problems faced by boys with lesbian mothers by Hall (1978) and Lewis (1980).

Osman (1972) discusses the bruised self-esteem of the male children of lesbian mothers and Weeks et al. (1975) addresses feelings of male rejection by boys in lesbian mother households.

Typically, sons are able to put more distance between themselves and their mothers and thus not identify with them to the extent daughters do. However, regardless of whether they are boys or girls, the children will be sensitive to such pejorative terms as "faggot" and "dyke" (Lewin & Lyons, 1982). These children may join in or feel forced to join in hurtful name-calling to protect against being ridiculed themselves (Lewis, 1980).

Out of fear of discovery of their mothers' homosexuality, these children can become anxious, withdrawn, hypervigilant, or secretive, and may attempt to control their mothers' behavior. Some children, particularly as they approach their teens, shy away from friends and refuse to bring them home out of concern that someone will "find out." These reactions generally indicate that other issues in the family need professional attention (Osman, 1972; Shernoff, 1974). Quite possibly family communication is dysfunctional or the children's pain is denied by the mother.

Generally, the more open and relaxed the mother is regarding her sexual orientation, the more accepting will be the child of the idea in reality of having a lesbian mother. The more realistic and understanding the mother is of the issues and problems this presents for both herself and her children, the more successful will be the child's adjustment. One child in a family may react negatively while another is more accepting (Lewis, 1980; Shernoff, 1974). One child may be more rational and direct in his or her approach with the mother, requesting that she act in a certain way in front of friends so they won't think she is a lesbian. Another child in the same family may refuse to bring friends home altogether.

I have not found, as has Lewis (1980), that children *completely* deny their negative feelings regarding having a lesbian mother. I have found tremendous ambivalence about disclosure of mothers' lesbianism. Self-contradiction during therapy and minimization of the extent of their feelings are especially characteristic during early adolescence. I found that those children of mothers who had come out more recently, or had in the past denied the sexual nature of their relationship had greater difficulties with their mothers and experienced some problems with trust. Related to this lack of trust were reactions of withdrawal, depression, and anxiety.

Positive aspects of disclosure that the *children themselves state* are: "You really find out who your friends are"; "the family really sticks together"; and "I learned not to care as much about what other people think and that it is more important for me to feel good about who I am."

Relationship Issues

As stated before, girls worry more than boys about becoming homosexual as a result of having a lesbian mother. Girls who are dealing with their emerging sexuality may experience same-sex feelings and same-sex attractions. When this happens to a child with a lesbian mother, she may fear that this means that she too is a lesbian. Boys are able to maintain a greater distance from the impact of their mothers' sexual identification, are less identified with them, and generally less concerned with relationships than are girls.

Although I have seen a few angry and one enraged male child who attempted to beat up his mother's lover, boys generally do not react with the kind of intrusiveness and negativity that is more characteristic of girls. However, boys do occasionally feel left out and invalidated by their mother and her lover. This results in feeling less worthy of attention (Lewis, 1980; Weeks, 1975). These feelings often reflect the boys' inner process rather than actual denial and exclusion by the mother.

Once a lesbian mother realizes and acts on her identity in terms of finding a partner with whom to establish an intimate relationship, we have the potential for new problems to arise. Since women are generally conditioned to be nurturers and caretakers, women partners are often baffled and hurt by what they perceive to be rejection by the child. The child's reaction depends on the child's age and how carefully they have been prepared for this new person and the willingness of the adults to demonstrate flexibility (Lewis, 1980).

Daughters will compete more overtly than male children with a lover for the mother's attention. This is not unlike the competition found in heterosexual families (Lewis, 1980). It is often difficult for children to understand or acknowledge the nature of their mother's relationship with her lover. Since there is no validation for or guidelines from the larger culture for this family form, children have difficulty discerning clear limits and boundaries in their relationship with their mother's lover. It is often difficult for the adults, especially the nonbiological partner, to be clear regarding their role with the children. This is a problem lesbian mothers have in common with single mothers in general. Children however, often don't take the relationship that their mother has with the female partner as seriously as they would if the relationship were with a male partner.

Typically, there is a direct relationship between the extent to which the mother feels guilty about being a lesbian and the resulting overcompensating "super-mom" behavior (Goodwin, 1973). Factors such as guilt, internalized oppression, and protectiveness contribute to the mother possibly allowing the child more access to her, and more intrusion into the relationship with her lover than is characteristic in nongay families. All parties may collude to devalue the relationship between the two women (Hall, 1978).

On the positive side, because of the lack of societal prescriptions, there are neither preconceived notions of nor actual role models for how these families are supposed to function. Children have greater freedom to negotiate roles, and to have more flexible relationships with their mothers (Goodwin, 1973).

From my observations lesbian mothers will do anything to help their children deal with their differences in a homophobic world except "go back in the closet." For example, they will be extremely careful not to show affection to a partner in front of anyone except immediate family and friends. They will be careful not to exhibit any literature, art or home decoration that could be interpreted as lesbian-oriented. They may even encourage their children to refer to their lover as "aunt" in order to make it more comfortable for them to bring friends home. These measures often work to assuage the child's concerns and may be indicative of the mother's sensitivity and flexibility.

Because there are so few guidelines and role models, lesbian mother families have had the option to be more creative in their parental styles. In my experience, this parenting approach has provided children greater opportunities for decision making and problem solving. The reality for children of lesbian mothers may be a harsh one, just as it is for any child who is identified with an oppressed group. Both mother and children have to walk a fine line between self-effacing guilt, and health self-protection, which is not unlike any other member of a minority group who can pass as part of the majority culture.

I cannot emphasize enough that children fare best in homes where the mothers are secure in both their lesbian identity and their parental role, and where they have a strong support system that includes other lesbian mother families. This point of view is also supported by Lewin & Lyons (1982) and Goodwin (1973). Children and mothers have to establish a shared culture intentionally as it is not an experience that occurs automatically (Baptiste, 1987).

Children's reactions to mother "coming out" generally range from "please, can't you change, you're ruining my life!" to "I'm proud of my mom, and if other kids don't like it, then I don't want that kind of person to be my friend." It is also important to note that loving and close relationships may exist between mothers and their children without public disclosure of the mother's sexual orientation (Berzon, 1978). Many lesbian mothers are unable or unwilling to disclose, for many reasons such as job loss, disruption of friendship networks, loss of church affiliation, custody battles, and because of potential extended-family problems or rejection by family members (Lewin & Lyons, 1982; Shernoff, 1974).

Fear of disclosure tends to be more common among women who have come out later in life and who likely identify more with a segment of the heterosexual community such as their church group or extended family. Moreover, the lesbian mother who cannot disclose has the potential for empathy for and identity with her child who has parallel fears of the mother's sexual orientation being discovered.

The burden that the mother's lesbian orientation poses for both mother and child has positive ramifications as well, including the opportunity for the child to have female role models that can be strong, independent, and nurturing. They can see women as complete people who can "do everything." For a girl, in particular, this can be a positive experience. Children in these households develop an appreciation of differences and of different ways of living. They learn not to worry so much about what other people will think, and they have the potential for being more self-reliant and self-confident.

Custody

It is important to realize that nearly all children react to the breakup of the family unit as being the primary problem; they do not perceive the mother's sexual orientation as their foremost concern (Berzon, 1978; Cramer, 1986; Kirkpatrick, 1981). Having a lesbian mother is often not an issue until some time after the heterosexual breakup, since the mother herself may be unaware of her sexual orientation at the time. Younger children are generally more concerned with the ending of what is familiar and secure, while older children respond more to what they perceive as a major change in their mother. As time passes, children are generally more accepting of the parental separation. A chaotic, hostile heterosexual situation can be replaced with one that is loving and consistent and that includes the mother and maybe the mother's lover. I have also found it interesting that younger children tend to react with similar upset to the breakups between mothers and their female lovers. This is so because the breakup is a threat to their feelings of family stability and security.

Why is custody such an important issue for these children? Being a lesbian and being a mother has been, and still is, considered to be unnatural and antithetical to traditional family values (Lewin & Lyons, 1982). Therefore, lesbian parents always live with the fear that a bid for custody can be made by the child's father or any member of the extended family such as a grandparent. It is also common for grandparents, aunts, or uncles to be highly supportive of both the lesbian mother and her children. Fathers also frequently maintain positive relationships with their ex-wives — the mothers of their children. When positive intrafamily relationships occur, children's general adjustment and well-being are enhanced, and the children's acceptance of and ability to handle the differences in their family are facilitated. The tragedy is that there is so little support for lesbian mother families, in particular, and single mother families in general (Cramer, 1986; Goodwin, 1973; Lewin & Lyons, 1982; Lewis, 1980).

Much of the earlier research on children of lesbian mothers and their lifestyles was focused on attempting to demonstrate the acceptability and legitimacy of lesbian motherhood in court cases. The phrase, "in the best interests of the children" was the judicial consideration, and the concern of the courts was based on the following notions: fear of sexual molestation of the children by the parent or friends of the same sex; fear that the children were likely to become homosexual; and peer stigmatization. Research has demonstrated the first two fears to be unfounded, and it has been found that the third, when peer stigmatization occurs, can be positively handled (Cramer, 1986; Hall, 1978; Lewin & Lyons, 1982).

I have worked with mothers who lost custody of their children based solely on their sexual orientation and with others who have experienced custody battles or have been threatened with a custody suit based solely on their sexual orientation. Sometimes the reasons for litigation, actual or threatened, are overt, and sometimes they are more covertly implied. Although the mother's sexual orientation was not made public in some situations, the father used it as a trump card without which they would probably not have sued for custody in the first place.

For some children their mothers' sexuality does not become an issue for years after separation or divorce, since some mothers do not "come out" until years after separation. How the father, if he remains involved, and the extended family handle their feelings and conduct themselves regarding the mother's homosexuality, and how appropriately open the mother is regarding her sexual orientation are crucial factors in the child's adjustment (Berzon, 1978; Cramer, 1986; Hall, 1978).

Children who are torn between parents because of custody battles are more prone to adjustment problems. They share this difficulty with children from nongay families who are litigating custody. However, a critical difference between children in gay and nongay families is the ever present threat of possible changes in custody arrangements (Cramer, 1986; Lewin & Lyons, 1982). Both the children and the mother often fear public disclosure and all of the potential negative ramifications that can accompany a custody case. In these situations there is a tremendous amount of anxiety generated in both the mother and children regarding the possibility of loss of custody and maternal caretaking and societal homophobia. Coping with this anxiety is the extra burden of homosexual parents.

Societal Attitudes in General

There is no support for the lesbian mother family on many levels. There is little or no visible recognition that this is a viable family form, either within or outside of the gay/lesbian community. There are no ritual ceremonies of official recognition for these families. Marriage is not allowed, and the larger community is most often hostile and rejecting (Baptiste, 1987; Berzon, 1978; Goodwin, 1973; Lewin & Lyons, 1982). Often children may obtain support from others who express sympathy for their apparent plight. Children may pick up on this sympathy and attempt to use it to their "benefit" (Osman, 1972; Shernoff, 1974). For example, I had a young client who tried to use her mother's lesbianism to get sympathy from a teacher for not doing her homework. Furthermore, having a lesbian mother could be sufficient reason for the child, parent, or both to be referred to a school counselor (Berzon, 1978; Osman, 1972).

The parent is often put in the position of seeking reassurance and approval from her children regarding her sexual orientation, and, most important, the mother may want reassurance that the children do not feel different or ostracized. In the therapy situation we look together at this problem, particularly at the meaning of differences for each family member and how they impact upon each other. Having a parent that is different in any way is especially difficult for adolescents. Children do not have to accept the parent's sexual orientation; however, it is important for the parents to expect that their way of life would be respected. At this time the child is often coping with either resentment or guilt for having love/hate feelings for the parent. This situation requires extreme patience and understanding from the parent, who can be struggling with issues of self-respect and self-esteem.

IMPLICATIONS FOR PROFESSIONALS

Implications for Therapists

The first point to be made is that it is important not to assume all your clients are heterosexual. It is estimated that approximately 18 percent of the lesbian population in the United States are mothers (Cramer, 1986). You must expect that some of your clients who are mothers are also lesbians, and that some of your younger clients have mothers who are lesbian.

It is also essential for practitioners to assess their own attitudes toward homosexuality and about working with gay/lesbian clients. If one is unable to resolve his or her own homophobia, the practitioner should not serve this population. For therapists who work with these children and families, the following guidelines are useful. Do not assume that individual or family pathology is related to the mother's sexual orientation. Do not assume that the children in these families are suffering and need sympathy because they have a lesbian mother. I recently had the experience of working with a woman who considered herself to be a lesbian, but had begun to date a man. Her eight-year-old daughter was dismayed by this and told her mother that she preferred her to have a "girlfriend." This child was responding to the disruption of her equilibrium, and it was more important to her that the mother be consistent rather than heterosexual. This points out that clinicians should not jump to the conclusion that children will automatically prefer a nongay home situation.

Do look at the quality of mothering and, as in any therapy situation, assume a psychosocial focus and consider individual and family issues from both the mother's and the child's perspectives. It is important to recognize the stress on all family members that attends such issues as disclosure, custody, possibly ambiguously defined family relationships, sexuality and dysfunctional societal attitudes. It is also paramount to be aware of the mother's own internalized homophobia, and in particular its manifestations in the form of guilt and overcompensation. Lesbian mothers are often defensive about being judged as mothers. They are also in a position of needing reassurance; they want to show the therapist that their children are not suffering because they have a lesbian mother. Therapists need to recognize that teenagers' reactions to having a mother who is different are not dissimilar to children reacting to other maternal differences. What is unique is that children of lesbian mothers may have the understanding and support of individuals and institutions that are generally more supportive of the parental perspective.

It is important that all family members be allowed to air their concerns in therapy. Likewise, it is also essential that the mother be given clear support for the expression of her sexual orientation. Children do not have the right to dictate parental behavior. Clinicians also need to be aware of resources other than therapy that are available for both children and parents. Workshops, training, lectures, and literature that focus on gay family issues and information are invaluable aids to the therapist's professional growth. Communicate this knowledge to your colleagues and your clients. Also, as M. Hall (1978) concurs, get to know some lesbian mothers and their children who are not in therapy and who are not besieged by problems so that you will have "normal" lesbian families against which your client's situation can be gauged.

Children's feelings vary a great deal about therapy. Lewis (1980) found that few children felt therapy was helpful because the mother's sexual orientation was not revealed or it was ignored. If the therapist was gay or lesbian, the children felt unsupported in that they felt the mother had a coconspirator. The therapist needs to establish impartiality and integrity. Lewis (1980) recommends peer support groups for children. In my own work I have found that children reject such involvement in spite of their parents' desires. This attitude on the part of children is associated with their general resistance to therapy, and their specific concern about formally associating with children of other gay or lesbian parents. An informal drop-in group might be more acceptable to both children and teenagers who otherwise are often averse to counseling. In general, children rarely request therapy. Teenagers, although perhaps more self-motivated, have rejected participation in groups for teens of lesbian mothers. This is not to suggest that groups should not be offered and encouraged. Rather, I am emphasizing, in addition to the above, the resistance related to the children's own internalized homophobia, which is one of the reasons groups need to be encouraged by therapists.

I have found, as has Lewis (1980), tremendous ambivalence on the part of the children in their attitudes toward their mothers as lesbians. Of particular relevance to therapists are the verbal self-contradictions that occur in therapy, particularly children's feelings about others finding out that the mother is a lesbian. Older children also have a tendency to threaten the mother with wanting to live with the other parent. Although I know instances in which two daughters and a son moved in with their fathers, these changes took place without a formal change of the custody arrangements. In all three cases the mother's lesbianism was not the primary reason for the change.

In summary, I recommend that clinicians first become aware of their own attitudes and then educate themselves as is necessary in order to provide therapy that is in no way grounded in homophobic biases. Also, become aware of resources for the children and the mothers in these families. It is important to treat your lesbian mothers and their children as you would any client population while, at the same time, having an awareness of their special needs. Furthermore, don't make heterosexual assumptions. It is also essential for you to do all you can to enhance your client's family experience. Lastly, it may be necessary to serve as an advocate for these clients, not only within the field of mental health, but also in the judicial and education arenas.

Implications for Other Professionals

To other professionals who come in contact with these children and their families I advise the following. First, I suggest that you also examine your feelings about lesbians to discern any homophobia; this applies to gay and lesbian professionals as well as to nongays. Be alert for the sometimes subtle and covert feeling that it is better to be heterosexual than gay. This bias is often a stumbling block for people who are otherwise extremely supportive of lesbian and gay rights.

Administrators and educators need to include positive information on gay and lesbian people and their varied lifestyles in public school family life and human sexuality classes. However, this alone is not enough. Educators must speak out for the rights of both gay teachers and students, and they must be exquisitely sensitive to the fact that there are gay and lesbian students in their school, regardless of how well they may hide themselves.

Teachers and counselors must be aware that the gay teenager's internal struggle can be reflected in academic problems, social withdrawal, truancy, and a serious decline in overall functioning. Schools whose teachers are more accepting of gay students and who are aware of their special vulnerability can facilitate the children of lesbian mothers to be more open about themselves and their family situation to teachers and other school officials. The school is also an ideal source of support because of its central importance in the lives of children. As in the case of therapists, counselors need to inform themselves about gay/lesbian member households and to be available to students, parents, and teachers for support and guidance. Teachers should not allow subtle or overt homophobic remarks to be made in the classroom, on the playing fields, or in the locker rooms. Family life classes, social sciences, the humanities, the sciences, and physical education classes all present opportunities to heighten awareness in a supportive, instructive and both direct and indirect manner by the teacher involved. He or she can set a personal example and lend status to those students who might otherwise be the object of harassment.

CONCLUSION

In conclusion, in lesbian mother families the children's problems and family psychopathology are not necessarily correlated with the mother's sexual orientation. What is most important is the quality of mothering, and the quality of the relationships in the household. The primary problem is not the mother's sexuality and lifestyle but, rather, societal homophobia. It is also important to recognize that the children in these families have the right to have problems, as do all children.

With the tremendous concern that is being generated about the disintegration of the family, the more supportive the society and its subcommunities are toward alternative family forms, the stronger and more productive will these families and their individual members be.

They, in turn, will add to the strength of the fabric of our communities, our society, and our world.

SUGGESTIONS FOR RESEARCH

Lesbian mothers are a heterogeneous group in which individual women differ in their styles of parenting and lifestyles in general. The small body of research to date strongly implies that children of lesbian mothers do not differ with respect to emotional problems from those raised by heterosexual counterparts. Larger, ethnically representative studies, with control groups, may be of help in identifying specific areas for attention that relate more clearly to the needs of this population. The following concerns related to direct clinical practice need to be explored:

therapists' attitudes toward children of lesbian mothers and to the mothers themselves in order to ascertain how these attitudes influence therapy outcome;
the impact of the sex and sexual orientation of the therapist on the child based on the child's age, gender, and stage of development;
under what conditions is it more effective to do individual or family therapy; and
internalized homophobia in children and its treatment possibilities.

Exploratory comparative studies would be useful to:

investigate any differences that might emerge in children from one-parent and two-parent lesbian mother households;
assess the variety of effects, if any, that having a lesbian mother presents for male and female children; and
assess if lesbian divorce changes children's expectations of mother's sexual orientation and if children experience changes in self-esteem related to changes in those expectations.

REFERENCES

Baptiste, D. (1987). Psychotherapy with gay/lesbian couples and their children in "Stepfamilies": A challenge for marriage and family therapists. *Journal of Homosexuality, 14* (1/2), 217–232.

Berzon, B. (1978). Sharing your lesbian identity with your children: A case for openness. In G. Vida (Ed.), *Our right to love*. Englewood Cliffs, NJ: Prentice-Hall.

Cramer, D. (1986). Gay parents and their children: A review of research and practical implications. *Journal of Counseling and Development, 64*, 504–507.

Goodwin, B. (1973). The lesbian mother. *American Journal of Orthopsychiatry, 43*, 283–284.

Green R. (1978). Sexual identity of 37 children raised by homosexual or transexual parents. *American Journal of Psychiatry, 135*, 692–697.

Hall, M. (1978). Lesbian families: cultural and clinical issues. *Social Work, 23*, 380–386.

Hoeffer, B. (1978). Single mothers and their children: Challenging traditional concepts of the American family. In P. Brandt, P. Chinn, V. Hunt, & M. Smith (Eds.), *Current practice in pediatric nursing*, Vol. II. St. Louis: C. V. Mosby.

_____. (1981). Children's acquisition of sex-role behavior in lesbian-mother families. *American Journal of Orthopsychiatry, 51*, 536–544.

Hotvedt, M. E., & Mandell, J. B. (1982). Children of lesbian mothers. In W. Paul, J. D. Weinrich, J. C. Gonsiorek, & M. E. Hotvedt (Eds.), *Homosexuality: Social, psychological, and biological issues* (pp. 275–285). Beverly Hills, CA: Sage.

Kirkpatrick, M., Smith, K., & Roy, D. (1981). Lesbian mothers and their children: A comparative survey. *The American Journal of Orthopsychiatry, 51*, 545–551.

Lewin, E., & Lyons, T. (1982). Everything in its place: The coexistence of lesbianism and motherhood. In W. Paul, J. D. Weinrich, J. C. Gonsiorek, & M. E. Hotvedt (Eds.), *Homosexuality: Social, psychological, and biological issues* (pp. 249–273). Beverly Hills, CA: Sage.

Lewis, K. G. (1980). Children of lesbian parents: Their point of view. *Social Work, 25*, 198–203.

Mandel, J. B., & Hotvedt, M. E. (1980). Lesbians as parents. *Huisants and Praktijk, 4*, 31–34.

Martin, D., & Lyon, P. (1972). *Lesbian/Woman*. San Francisco: Glide.

Osman, S. (1972). My step-father is a she. *Family Process, 11*, 209–218.

Pagelow, M. (1980). Heterosexual and lesbian single mothers: A comparison of problems, coping and solutions. *Journal of Homosexuality, 5*, 189–204.

Pies, C. (1985). *Considering parenthood*. San Francisco: Spinster's Ink.

Shernoff, M. (1974). Family therapy for lesbian and gay clients. *Social Work, 19*, 393–396.

Steckel, A. (1985). *Separation-individuation in children of lesbian and heterosexual couples*. Unpublished doctoral dissertation, Wright Institute, Berkeley.

Weeks, R., Derdeyn, A., & Langman, M. (1975). Two cases of children of homosexuals. *Child Psychiatry and Human Development, 6*, 26–32.

Wyers, N. (1984). *Lesbian and gay spouses and parents: Homosexuality in the family*. Unpublished manuscript, Portland State University, School of Social Work.

5

PSYCHOSOCIAL DEVELOP-
MENT OF CHILDREN OF
LESBIAN MOTHERS

Ailsa Steckel

Most of the literature on child development is based on children raised in traditional heterosexual nuclear families. Alternatives to the traditional family unit have been considered deviant, and harmful to the healthy development of a sense of self (Abelin, 1971; Biller, 1972; Hetherington & Deur, 1971; Johnson, 1977; Mead and Rekers, 1979; Stendler, 1954). Increasingly, however, children in our society grow up in single-parent (usually single-mother) families, extended families, black matrifocal families, communal living arrangements, lesbian or gay families, or other alternatives to the traditional heterosexual nuclear family unit. These alternatives present rich material for research on ego development, differentiation, and the growth of the self.

After providing definitions of terms, this chapter reviews the research to date on children of lesbians. This research has been undertaken as a response to society's fear that children raised by lesbians will be confused in their sexual identity and/or that they, too, will become lesbian/gay (Mandel & Hotvedt, 1980; Solomon, 1982). The primary question regarding these children is how the mother's sexual orientation affects the sexual identity, sex roles, and sexual orientation of the children. Following this review, implications for professionals in various disciplines are briefly addressed. The chapter concludes with suggestions for further research.

TERMS DEFINED

Sexual identity is defined as the subjective sense that one is male or female. *Sex roles* consist of behaviors that are culturally ascribed to either females or males. Recent research (Bem, 1974) suggests that flexibility, rather than rigid adherence to either "masculine" or "feminine" roles, is correlated with healthier adjustment. *Sexual orientation* refers to sexual partner preference, usually homosexual, heterosexual, or bisexual.

REVIEW OF RESEARCH

The initial research on lesbian mothers and their children was designed for use in post divorce custody cases. The predominant concerns in custody cases are:

> that the mother's sexual orientation will influence the child's sexual choices, that the child will have an unclear or improper sexual identity, that the child will suffer from a sexual stigma in peer group relationships and that the child's general welfare would be neglected because the mother will be too involved in her own lifestyle (Mandel & Hotvedt, 1980, p. 32).

Almost all the lesbian mothers studied are women who had children before they identified themselves as lesbians. The children in most of the samples ranged from six to twelve years of age.

Several studies have focused on the children of lesbians and how they may be affected by the lesbianism of their mothers (Green, 1978; Hoeffer, 1981; Kirkpatrick, Smith & Roy, 1981; Lewis, 1980; Mandel & Hotvedt, 1980; Mucklow & Phelan, 1979; Nungesser, 1980; Puryear, 1983; Steckel, 1985; Weeks, Derdeyn & Langman, 1975). None of the comparative studies found major differences in adjustment and development between children of lesbian and heterosexual single mothers.

Green (1978) examined 37 children ranging in age from 3 to 20 years (mean = 9.3) raised by lesbian or transsexual parents to determine whether or not their sexual identity differed from that of children raised in heterosexual settings. Sexual identity of the younger children was measured by toy and game preference, peer group (which is typically same-sex in latency age children), clothing preference, roles played in fantasy games (which are typically of the same sex as the player), vocational aspiration, and the Draw-A-Person test (the gender of the first person drawn is usually considered to reflect sexual identity). The sexual identity of adolescents was assessed on the basis of information about romantic crushes, erotic fantasies and interpersonal sexual behavior. Thirty-six of the children reported or recalled games, toys, clothing, peer group preferences, and vocational aspirations that were sex- and age-appropriate with respect to cultural stereotypes. Only one child appeared to have an atypical sex-role orientation. While the author states the need for longitudinal research on these questions, he suggests that children raised by lesbian (or transsexual) parents do not differ appreciably from children raised in more traditional families on measures of sexual identity and psychosexual development.

Mandel and Hotvedt (1980) reported on the psychosocial development of prepubescent children living with their lesbian or heterosexual single mothers. Data from 50 women identified as lesbians and their children aged 3 to 11 were compared with responses from 35 heterosexual single mothers and their children. Mothers were interviewed and completed questionnaires about such subjects as parenting experiences, upbringing, relationship patterns, and attitudes toward sex roles, education and discipline. Children were interviewed about play preferences, friendships, television habits, and thoughts about growing up. They were also tested using the WPPSI (Wechsler Preschool and Primary Scale of Intelligence) or WISC-R (Wechsler Intelligence Scale for Children — Revised), several tests for sex-role behavior and gender identity, and the Bene-Anthony Family Relations Test. Mandel and Hotvedt found no significant differences in peer group relationships, sexual identity, or relationships with fathers and other males, suggesting that the parenting of single lesbian mothers was as effective as the parenting of single heterosexual mothers.

Children's acquisition of sex-role behavior in lesbian mother families was examined by Hoeffer (1981). She studied the only or oldest children, ages 6 through 9, of 20 lesbian and 20 heterosexual single mothers. Children's sex-role behavior was measured by a version of Block's Toy Preference Test. This test consists of pictures of sex-typed masculine, feminine, and neutral toys. The child divides them into three groups the child most, somewhat, or least prefers. The child then shows and explains eight of her/his favorite toys or activities to the researcher. Since a child's play is a means of practicing and preparing for adult roles, a child's preferences for sex-typed masculine, feminine, or neutral toys and activities suggests the development of future sex-role behaviors. No significant differences were found between the two groups as a function of the sexual orientation of the mothers. Significant differences did occur between sex-typed toy preferences of boys and girls, irrespective of the sexual orientation of the mothers, suggesting the importance of outside influences.

In a theoretical paper, Nungesser (1980) discussed the theoretical bases for research on the acquisition of sex-roles, specifically for children of lesbian mothers. He reviewed several descriptive studies of lesbian mothers that suggest that lesbians tend to be more androgynous and exhibit more behaviors considered "masculine" on the Bem Sex Role Inventory. Using the argument that a model's ability to induce imitative behavior is increased if the model is perceived as similar to the subject, the author hypothesized that female children brought up by lesbians would be more androgynous than female children brought up in heterosexual families. Steckel's (1985) study on children of lesbian couples, in contrast to those on children of single mothers, attempted to bear out Nungesser's application of modelling theory. She found that preschool-age girl children of lesbian couples were not significantly more "androgynous" or displaying more "masculine" behaviors than girl children of heterosexual couples. However, boys of heterosexual couples did appear slightly more aggressive than their counterparts from lesbian couples. Modelling theory is presumed to be only one factor in this distinction. Steckel's work will be discussed in greater detail later in this chapter.

Kirkpatrick, Smith and Roy (1981) did a comparative study of emotional health and psychopathology in 10 boys and 10 girls between the ages of 5 and 12, who were living with their single lesbian mothers, and a comparison group of children of single heterosexual mothers. Each child was given the WISC, Holtzman Inkblot Technique and Human Figure Drawing, and was seen for a 45 minute semi-structured playroom interview which included questions about early memories, dreams, future plans and gender-related interests. Although more than half the sample were evaluated as having at least moderate emotional problems, this was seen as resulting from the distress of longstanding marital discord that preceded the parents' divorce. Neither the type nor the frequency of pathology differed as a function of the mothers' subsequent choice of sexual partner.

Weeks, Derdeyn and Langman (1975) presented two cases of adolescents living with gay or lesbian parents in an attempt to understand the difficulties that children living with openly gay parents might experience. They, too, concluded that the children of lesbian or gay parents, having experienced the turmoil of their parents' marital discord and subsequent divorce, manifest the difficulties common to children of divorce.

Lewis (1980) interviewed 21 children, ranging in age from 9 to 26, whose mothers were lesbians. Unstructured interviews indicated that the children were often more upset over the divorce of their parents than about the disclosure of their mother's lesbianism. Younger children expressed the need for secrecy about their mothers' lesbianism, while older children struggled with concerns about the reactions of their peers and questions regarding their own sexual preferences.

Two studies (Mucklow and Phelan, 1979; Puryear, 1983) examined the effects of parental lesbianism on self-concept. Mucklow and Phelan (1979) wrote of two recurring themes in research on parents and children: a positive correlation between a mother's and a child's self-concept; and the view that childrearing is a product of maternal attitudes, values, and personality characteristics. These two points have been elaborated by object relations theory and the widely held idea that children respond to the unconscious of the parent. To determine whether or not significant differences existed in lesbian mothers that might adversely affect their children, Mucklow and Phelan compared self-concepts and maternal attitudes of 34 lesbian and 47 heterosexual mothers. Both groups were administered the Adult Response to Child Behavior test, slides of children's behavior to which the subjects give responses which are categorized as adult-, child-, or task-centered. Each subject also rated herself on a 300 adjective checklist which was examined in terms of self-confidence, dominance, and nurturance. Chi-square tests indicated no significant differences in mean scores of the two groups of mothers, and suggested that lesbian and heterosexual mothers are more similar than different in maternal attitudes and self-concept, as measured by this study, and that parental lesbianism is not in and of itself damaging to the developing child.

Puryear (1983) examined latency-age children's concepts of themselves and their families. She compared 15 children between the ages of 6 and 12 of lesbian and 15 children of heterosexual single mothers. Self-concept was measured by the Piers-Harris Children's Self-Concept Scale and the children's views of their families was assessed from kinetic family drawings. No major differences in self-concept and family view were found between the two groups of children. The primary finding was that children in both groups were more affected by the availability of the father than by the sexual orientation of the mother.

All of the above mentioned research studied children of lesbians who had previously been in heterosexual relationships. Increasingly, however, lesbians are choosing to have children outside the context of heterosexual relationships, either as single mothers or in the context of lesbian relationships. This social phenomenon raises questions about normal developmental processes in these children. How does it affect a child's sense of self to not have a father available? To not have a father be known (as in the case of alternative conception through anonymous insemination)? To have a female other-than-mother parent?

Steckel (1985) addressed these issues in her exploratory study comparing separation-individuation in children of lesbian and heterosexual couples. She examined how the femaleness of a lesbian coparent, rather than a father, might facilitate or hinder a child's intrapsychic separation.

Separation-individuation refers to the psychological birth of the human infant, the hatching from the symbiotic mother-child unity into a separate and distinct individual. Separation and individuation are considered two complementary developments: "the one consisting of the child's emergence from a symbiotic fusion with the mother [cf. Mahler, 1952], and the other consisting of those achievements marking the child's assumption of his own individual characteristics" (Pine & Furer, 1963, p. 326).

Mahler and associates (1975, 1979) studied normal infants and toddlers during the first three years of life in relation to their mothers, observed the behavior of mothers and children together, and suggested a relationship between the unconscious conflicts of the mother and the development of the child's sense of self.

Mahler's theory has two major lacunae, particularly regarding normal separation-individuation for children of lesbians. First, the thirty-eight children studied were all from intact heterosexual families, and second, the child's intrapsychic separation was examined primarily in relation to the primary object, the mother; little attention was paid to the role of a second parent. Abelin (1971, 1975, 1980) and others have examined the role of the most immediate outside influence, the father. They proposed that the father's presence was critical for helping the developing infant to differentiate out of the symbiotic bond with the mother and resist the temptations of re-engulfment. Abelin suggests that it is the father's maleness, his visible differentness from the mother, that aids separation and individuation. This research, too, is limited to a sample of intact heterosexual families.

How do variations from the nuclear family, such as the lesbian family, affect separation-individuation? Steckel identified behavioral indicators of the developmental tasks of separation-individuation, focusing on independence, ego functions, and object relations. The successful completion of these tasks, culminating in the achievement of object constancy and a differentiated sense of self, normally occurs by the age of three. For this reason, subjects in the study were three and four years old. Eleven children were in each group. Independence, ego functions, and object relations were measured through use of a structured parent interview, a Q-Sort administered to parents and teachers, and a projective Structured Doll Technique interview with each child.

The major finding was that the children of lesbians and heterosexuals showed many more similarities than differences. Neither group revealed more psychopathology or difficulties in separation-individuation than the other group. Yet findings also demonstrated significantly different experiences of separation and individuation for lesbians' and heterosexuals' children. Children of heterosexuals had a more aggressively tinged separation process, seeing themselves as more aggressive and being seen by parents and teachers as more bossy and domineering, more active in asserting themselves, more negativistic, and more involved in power struggles. In contrast, children of lesbians demonstrated a more lovable self-image, expressed by more helplessness, and were seen by parents and teachers as more affectionate and responsive, more verbal and more protective toward younger children. The more aggressively tinged separation of children of heterosexuals was hypothesized to be due to three factors: the presence of a more aggressive role model; a more dyadic mother-child relationship in the heterosexual families (the fathers in this sample participated less in daily caregiving than the lesbian coparents) from which children have to separate more forcefully; and a more intense oedipal rivalry with fathers than with female coparents. The study concluded that the presence of a female coparent, rather than a father, does not adversely affect the child's progression through the separation-individuation process, but does establish a qualitatively different separation experience. The author stressed the need for broad-based longitudinal research to assess the ways in which the development in children of lesbian couples may be affected by this particular type of family structure.

IMPLICATIONS FOR PROFESSIONALS

Although many people in society continue to fear for the psychological health of children of lesbians, studies to date have consistently failed to find significant differences between children of lesbians and children of heterosexuals along the dimension of psychosocial development. Mental health professionals need to be aware of the complex issues facing children and parents in lesbian families. Although lesbians are a heterogeneous group of varying personality styles, lesbians and their children tend to share some common experiences of feeling "different." Clinical work with these families might involve exploring children's often conflicting feelings about their parents and themselves, helping children learn to deal with teasing from others, improving children's capacities to cope with conflict and potential loyalty issues raised by parental divorce, and working toward increasing self-esteem. It is critical that clinicians do not categorically pathologize either these children or their mothers, but rather examine the particular individuals and their unique ways of developing and coping.

Educators and legal professionals, too, must take care not to view these children as necessarily damaged by their home environments. Teachers might help lessen the sense of differentness of children of lesbians by presenting pictures of varying family constellations. They can be open to a lesbian coparent's participation and interest in her child's education and treat a lesbian (or lesbian couple) as a valid parenting unit. Legal professionals, particularly in custody cases, must avoid making custody decisions simply on the basis of a mother's lesbianism. Factors such as a mother's psychological health, her support network, and the quality of relationship with her children are vastly more important than her sexual orientation.

CONCLUSIONS

Although society has been concerned that children raised by lesbians (that is, without a father in the home) will be adversely affected and will be confused in their sexual identity, research to date suggests that children of lesbian mothers do not differ significantly from children in more traditional families in their fundamental sexual identity and choice of sex roles. Research is only beginning to address children borne and raised by single lesbians and lesbian couples. In contrast to much of the literature on the harmful affects of father absence, various theorists (Kellam, Ensminger, & Turner, 1977; Weiss, 1982) have suggested that any second adult who is committed to the child can be useful in facilitating the child's development. This could be a mother's lover (male or female), a friend, a grandparent, an older sibling, or a friend of the family. Mother aloneness, rather than father absence, was shown to predispose children to difficulties in development and adaptation. It would appear, then, that factors other than the mother's sexual orientation are critical in affecting the psychological well-being of a child. It is true that children of lesbians face issues particular to their family situation. Additional research will hopefully alleviate some of the fears and prejudices and help create an environment in which a healthy sense of self is facilitated in all children.

SUGGESTIONS FOR FURTHER RESEARCH

Although the studies reviewed above consistently demonstrated a lack of significant differences between the children of lesbians and heterosexuals, further research needs to be done. Longitudinal research will be most helpful in determining long-term effects of maternal lesbianism on children's development. More stratified (according to age) sample studies will provide data assessing differences according to age related developmental levels.

Since there are many variables which impact all children's lives, comparative studies might examine potentially significant variables in lesbian and heterosexual family constellations. Such variables might include family structure (single parents, couples, extended and stepfamilies), presence or absence of father, and children's psychological relationships with actual or fantasied fathers, particularly in cases of unknown donor insemination. Other relevant factors to be explored include the gender of the child, custody issues (mother or father as custodial parent), and whether the mother's lesbianism is explicit or hidden from the children. Further research will enable us to more fully assess the effects of parental lesbianism on child development.

REFERENCES

Abelin, E. (1971). The role of the father in the separation-individuation process. In J. B. McDevitt & C. F. Settlage (Eds.), *Separation-individuation* (pp. 229–252). New York: International Universities Press.

————. (1975). Some further observations and comments on the earliest role of the father. *International Journal of Psychoanalysis, 56*, 293–302.

————. (1980). Triangulation, the role of the father and the origins of core gender identity during the rapprochement subphase. In R. F. Lax, S. Bach & J. A. Burland (Eds.), *Rapprochement: The critical subphase of separation-individuation* (pp. 151–170). New York: Jason Aronson.

Bem, S. (1974). The measurement of psychological androgyny. *Journal of Consulting and Clinical Psychology, 42*, 155–162.

Biller, H. B. (1972). The mother-child relationship and the father-absent boy's personality development. In U. Bronfenbrenner & M. A. Mahoney (Eds.), *Influences in human development* (pp. 306–319). Hinsdale, Ill.: Dryden Press.

Green, R. (1978). Sexual identity of 37 children raised by homosexual or transsexual parents. *American Journal of Psychiatry 135 (6)*, 692–697.

Hetherington, E. M., & Deur, J. L. (1971). The effects of father absence on child development. *Young Children, 26*, 233–248.

Hoeffer, B. (1981). Childrens' acquisition of sex-role behavior in lesbian mother families. *American Journal of Orthopsychiatry, 51* (3), 536–544.

Johnson, M. M. (1977). Fathers, mothers and sex-typing. In E. M. Hetherington & R. D. Parke (Eds.), *Contemporary readings in child psychology* (pp. 263–275). New York: McGraw-Hill.

Kellam, S. G., Ensminger, M. E., & Turner, R. J. (1977). Family Structure and the Mental Health of Children. *Archives of General Psychiatry, 34*, 1012–1022.

Kirkpatrick, M., Smith, C. & Roy, R. (1981). Lesbian mothers and their children: A comparative study. *American Journal of Orthopsychiatry, 51* (3), 545–551.

Lewis, K. G. (1980). Children of lesbians: their point of view. *Social Work, 25* (3), 198–203.

Mahler, M. S. (1979). *Selected Papers*, volumes I and II. New York: Jason Aronson.

Mahler, M. S., Pine, F., & Bergman, A. (1975). *The psychological birth of the human infant*. New York: Basic Books.

Mandel, J. B., & Hotvedt, M. E. (1980). Lesbians as parents. *Husiarts & Praktijk, 4*, 31–34.

Mead, S. L., & Rekers, G. A. (1979). Role of the father in normal psychosexual development. *Psychological Reports, 45*, 923–931.

Mucklow, B. M., & Phelan, G. K. (1979). Lesbian and traditional mothers' responses to adult response to child behavior and self-concept. *Psychological Reports, 44* (3), (pt. 1), 880–882.

Nungesser, L. G. (1980). Theoretical bases for research on the acquisition of sex-roles by children of lesbian mothers. *Journal of Homosexuality, 5* (3), 177–187.

Pine, F., & Furer, M. (1963). Studies of the separation-individuation phases. *Psychoanalytic Study of the Child, 18*, 325–342.

Puryear, D. (1983). *A comparison between the children of lesbian mothers and the children of heterosexual mothers.* Unpublished doctoral dissertation, California School of Professional Psychology, Berkeley, CA.

Solomon, K. (1982). The masculine gender role. In K. Solomon & N. B. Levy (Eds.), *Men in transition.* New York: Plenum.

Steckel, A. (1985). *Separation-individuation in children of lesbian and heterosexual couples.* Unpublished doctoral dissertation, Wright Institute, Berkeley, CA.

Stendler, C. B. (1954). Possible causes of overdependency in young children. *Child Development, 25,* 125–146.

Weeks, R. B., Derdeyn, A. P., & Langman, M. (1975). Two cases of children of homosexuals. *Psychiatric Spectator, 10* (8), 3–4.

Weiss, R. S. (1982). Attachment in adult life. In C. M. Parkers & J. Stevenson-Hinde (Eds.), *The place of attachment in human behavior* (pp. 171–184). New York: Basic Books.

III

ALTERNATIVE GAY AND LESBIAN FAMILIES

6

THE ADOPTIVE AND FOSTER GAY AND LESBIAN PARENT

Wendell Ricketts and Roberta Achtenberg

Lesbians and gay men, as many have noted, can be both benefited and disadvantaged by their ability — unique among minority groups — to conceal themselves. Indeed, one wit remarked that the gay rights movement would take a quantum leap forward if all homosexuals awoke one morning to discover themselves colored an attractive shade of lavender. Perhaps no revelation would be more surprising, should such an event come to pass, than the vast numbers of women and men who are not only homosexual, but also mothers and fathers. In the meantime, lesbian and gay parents, whether biological, custodial, de facto, adoptive, or foster parents, remain largely invisible to the general public.

Paradoxically, the invisibility that many gays and lesbians have allowed to exist may, at least in some cases, have served to increase their likelihood of adopting or of becoming foster parents. In most instances, lesbians and gay men seeking to become foster or adoptive parents do not actively misrepresent their sexual orientation, they simply make no mention of it. Caseworkers, courts, and administrative staff either look the other way or succumb to their presumption of applicants' heterosexuality. If anecdotal evidence can be of use — and, indeed, there is virtually no published information on gay and lesbian foster and adoptive parents — a large number of workers in state and private child welfare agencies routinely take one of those two approaches.

It is essential to note, however, that the invisibility of lesbian and gay foster and adoptive parents — whether promoted by gay people themselves or by the "make no waves" ethic in most placement programs and agencies — can ultimately only contribute to stereotypes of homosexuals as child molesters, sex criminals, and emotional neurotics. In virtually every case in which openly lesbian and gay parents confront the glare of media publicity or the scrutiny of judicial or administrative review, they must endure spoken and unspoken prejudgments about their unfitness as parents — judgments that arise out of stereotypes to which invisibility and silence offer no challenge.

Gay and lesbian people who can be open about themselves deserve much credit for advances and victories in foster and adoptive parenting by lesbians and gay men. But almost no one has had it easy. Fairly or not, lesbians and gay men often have the task of educating family court personnel, social workers, agency administrators, licensing programs, and home evaluators, among others, that gay and lesbian people are as able to be fit, loving, appropriate, and generous parents as anyone else. They must often be the "guinea pigs" for agencies trying to cope with the reality of new families. The goal of this chapter, then, is to provide as many resources as possible to gay men and lesbians who are, or who hope to become, foster or adoptive parents.

THE RECENT HISTORY OF GAY/LESBIAN FOSTER AND ADOPTIVE PARENTING

The limited information that has appeared on gay and lesbian foster and adoptive parenting is not to be found in the mainstream press or the professional literature. Our research revealed the following cases of interest, but a more detailed inspection of lesbian and gay periodicals would doubtless turn up many more.

1973: Chicago, IL. The Director of the Department of Children and Family Services revealed that children with "homosexual tendencies" were being placed in homes with gay foster parents. The *Advocate* considered it the first time that such placements had been made public. It reported, however, that for some time it had been aware that "[g]ay organizations in several cities have quietly arranged for such placements but have shunned publicity for fear an uproar would result which would wreck their work" ("Agency Reveals," 1973, p. 2).

1974: Washington State. The Secretary of the Department of Social and Health Services proposed new regulations that appeared to exclude gays and lesbians from consideration as foster parents, although the *Advocate* reported that a number of gays had already been licensed and were acting as foster parents in Washington ("New Rules," 1974). The section banning gay foster care was later deleted from the official version of the guidelines ("Ban on Gay," 1974).

1974: Philadelphia, PA. A family court judge approved the placement of a fifteen-year-old transvestite boy in the home of a lesbian couple, after several unsuccessful placements in "straight" foster homes ("Judge Places," 1974).

1974: New York City. An experimental program, sponsored by the National Gay Task Force, had placed about thirty homosexual teenagers in foster care with adult gay men or couples in the New York area (Franks, 1974).

1974: Oregon. The Department of Human Resources ordered the Children's Services Division not to allow any state supervised children to be placed in openly gay foster homes. The order came after a caseworker recommended to a circuit court judge that a fourteen-year-old "confirmed homosexual" be placed in a gay foster home ("Agency Backs Down," 1974).

1975: Vancouver, WA. A judge ordered a sixteen-year-old gay youth to be removed from his four-month foster placement with a male couple, despite a lengthy hearing in which caseworkers, administrators, and expert witnesses all testified in favor of the placement (Shilts, 1975).

1976: California. The Department of Social Services adopted a policy allowing gay people with "clean records" and without a "proclivity to sexually assault children" to be licensed as foster parents ("CA Gay Foster," 1976).

1977: Washington, D.C. A local child-placing agency notified the gay press that it was actively seeking single or coupled adult homosexuals to serve as foster parents for young gays ("Gay Foster," 1977).

1979: Trenton, NJ. The Division of Youth Services revealed that the state had established its first homosexual foster home in 1975, and had continued to place a few homosexual teenagers with gay couples on an "informal basis" ever since ("New Jersey," 1979).

1981: Minneapolis, MN. A lesbian couple, who were already caring for a fifteen-year-old boy, were granted a license to take other foster children into their home ("Short Takes," 1981).

With regard to adoptions, the recent record is less clear. Although The *Advocate* reported the adoption of a seven-year-old boy by an unmarried Atlanta, Georgia, man in 1974, it did not identify the man as homosexual (Fortune, 1974). That same year, two Minneapolis men applied to local adoption agencies, as a married couple, for consideration as adoptive parents. Their caseworker admitted that the likelihood of a placement was "remote," and two months later the men filed discrimination complaints against several area agencies for refusing to consider their application ("Married Males," 1974). The *Advocate* also noted the growing number of single-parent adoptions in California, a practice that seemed to present new opportunities for gay men and lesbians to become adoptive parents ("Families By," 1974).

As early as 1976, the Los Angeles County Department of Adoptions put out an appeal to single men to apply to adopt one of a "bumper crop" of young boys over nine years of age. The Department stated, rather cryptically: "We seek the single adoptive parent who is comfortable in his sexual role and accepting of the opposite role" ("Los Angeles," 1976).

It was not until March 1979 that the *Advocate* reported what it believed to have been the first adoption by an openly gay couple. The adoption of an infant child, which took place in Los Angeles, made parents of a Metropolitan Community Church pastor and his lover, a physician ("Gay Couple," 1979). In June of that year, an openly gay Catskill, New York, man won permanent custody of the thirteen-year-old boy who had lived with him and his male lover for a year (Vecsey, 1979).

A GROWING TREND

What newspaper accounts would not reveal, and what has been true for many years, is that hundreds of lesbians and gay men have, in fact, adopted children and been licensed as foster parents across the country. For a variety of reasons, however, the issue of their sexual orientation was never officially raised or made public. Either they did not fit state or agency officials' stereotypes of lesbians or gay men and they were therefore not suspected of being homosexual, or their sexual orientation was known to caseworkers and was overlooked. Such an "official" response is particularly likely if an applicant is well qualified in all other aspects.

Family lawyers have consistently advised their lesbian and gay clients not to volunteer information regarding their sexual orientation, but to tell the truth if asked directly. More recently, however, many lesbians and gays have expressed a desire to present themselves in a clearer light, and choose to reveal their sexual orientation to a social worker or evaluator at the outset. In this way, they hope to avoid problems that can arise from withholding information that may be discovered later, and to protect themselves and any children who might be placed with them. Moreover, couples seeking to become foster or adoptive families often do not want to pretend that they are merely roommates, when in fact they are life mates. As a result, a number of states have developed policies regarding the licensing of foster parents and the approval of adoptive homes as they relate to the homosexuality or bisexuality of the applicant.

Particularly with regard to foster care, there is evidence that a growing number of public and private agencies across the country are beginning to see lesbian and gay homes as appropriate placements for homosexually identified and other sexual minority youth. Welcome as such a trend may be, certain biases clearly lie beneath it. In most cases, agencies are reluctant to place adolescents with homosexuals — especially with those of the same sex as the child — for fear the lesbian or gay parent will "contaminate" the nascent sexuality of her or his charge (see Ricketts, in press). But gay men and lesbians may be allowed to take in older children, including adolescents, if caseworkers are convinced the youth are "confirmed" homosexuals.

Frequently, such children have experienced a number of unsuccessful placements with families or in group homes in which their homosexual feelings and behavior were discouraged, ridiculed, ignored, or punished. They may enter the foster care system through the juvenile courts or through runaway and street outreach programs. (Indeed, shelter workers in our informal survey estimated that from 30 to 70 percent of the juvenile prostitute, street, and runaway population are lesbian or gay youth.) Their experience on the street, their distrust of adults, and the trauma associated with multiple unsuccessful placements may combine with sexual identity issues to give these children complex, pressing needs. Prospective homosexual foster or adoptive parents may find that only such difficult-to-place children, including those who have been severely abused or neglected or who have serious emotional or mental health problems, are among those made available to them. In a number of large cities around the country, in addition, departments of social service are beginning to turn to the lesbian and gay community to care for the growing number of AIDS babies born to needle-drug addict or prostitute mothers.

But regardless of the motivation behind the availability of these children to lesbian and gay parents, there can be no question that they are in special need of the acceptance that a gay or lesbian home may provide. Whether homosexual would-be parents are denied access to more "desirable" children is a matter that civil libertarians and public policymakers should address and remedy. In the meantime, for lesbians and gay men with love and resources to give to a child, it may matter little what the special problems of such a child may be.

LEGAL BARRIERS TO ADOPTIVE/FOSTER PARENTING BY HOMOSEXUALS

Only two states explicitly regulate the ability of homosexuals to become foster or adoptive parents. As is discussed below, the Massachusetts DSS (Department of Social Services) promulgated regulations that virtually prohibit gays and lesbians from qualifying as foster parents. The state of Florida, in addition, statutorily prohibits lesbians and gays from adopting. To date, no court challenges to the constitutionality of Florida's statute have been initiated.

As Rivera points out in this volume (see Chapter 12) twenty-six states and the District of Columbia continue to have antisodomy laws on their books. Although these laws are rarely enforced, their existence has been a significant negative influence upon judicial decision making in the custody and visitation arena, and there is every reason to suspect a corollary effect with respect to adoption and foster parenting.

An interesting case-in-point arose in the Pima County, Arizona juvenile court.[1] In this instance, an openly bisexual applicant for preadoption certification was thoroughly investigated by the state and was recommended to the juvenile court as qualified for certification. Upon discovering that the department had recommended an admitted bisexual, the judge took the unusual step of appointing independent counsel to represent both the court and the class of children that could potentially be adopted by the applicant. The judge's action appeared to be premised on the threat to children which he believed was posed by the applicant because of his sexual orientation. During the hearing, the judge asked the applicant whether he would molest a child placed in his custody or would attempt to "convert" a child to homosexuality. The judge accused the agency worker, who had done the home study, of trying to hide the applicant's homosexuality in her report. He also asked her to find out if there were a test that could be given to the applicant to determine whether he would molest a child. This line of inquiry seemed to have been prompted solely by the judge's antipathy toward homosexuals as a group, by his obvious dislike of the applicant, and by his total ignorance of issues of sexual orientation as they relate to one's qualifications to be a parent (or, in this case, an adoptive parent). The judge denied the application on the ground that the "[p]etitioner is a bisexual individual who has had, and may in future have, sexual relationships with members of both sexes" (p. 4). In upholding the decision, the Arizona Court of Appeals reasoned that while the applicant's bisexuality, standing alone, would be an insufficient basis on which to deny him certification, his homosexual conduct, proscribed by Arizona law, was.[2] The court stated:

> It would be anomalous for the state on one hand to declare homosexual conduct unlawful and on the other hand create a parent after that proscribed model, in effect approving that standard, inimical to the natural family, as head of a state-created family. (p. 12)

Statements like these, and those found in custody and visitation decisions in states where sodomy laws are still on the books, make licensing of openly gay foster or adoptive parents less likely. The "sodomy standard" is not, of course, applied equally to heterosexual and homosexual "crimes against nature," since heterosexual applicants are not rejected on the basis of their potential to commit illegal sexual acts.[3]

States in which the appellate courts have treated the homosexuality of a parent as a per se disqualification in custody or visitation cases should also be considered places where it is unlikely that openly lesbian or gay applicants will be treated favorably in their attempts to become foster or adoptive parents. In states where there are neither sodomy laws nor per se rules regarding homosexuality and child custody, lesbians and gay men have been making the greatest progress in their efforts to become foster and adoptive parents.

In California, for example, the sodomy law was repealed over a decade ago and appellate case law requires that custody be determined without undue emphasis being placed on the sexual orientation of the parent, unless a direct relationship can be shown to exist between the sexual orientation of the parent and active harm to the child.[4] The State Department of Social Services takes the position that it is required by California law to refrain from discriminating solely on the basis of a foster care or adoption applicant's homosexuality.[5] Because the DSS is county administered in California (as it is in thirty-eight states), prospective adoptive or foster parents may find, however, that this policy of nondiscrimination is enforced inconsistently across the state. In the more conservative counties, for example, there remains a tendency to restrict gays from becoming adoptive or foster parents. In countries where there are larger gay populations, and where social service agencies and courts are more familiar with gay people as parents, the resistance to lesbians and gay foster and adoptive parents is breaking down.[6]

Nonetheless, even in San Francisco, where the oldest program exists for the licensing of gay and lesbian foster parents, homosexual applicants are scrutinized more carefully and are held to a higher standard than are their heterosexual counterparts.

A SPECIAL WORD ABOUT ADOPTION

Rules regarding qualification for adoption vary from state to state (see Achtenberg, 1985, Section 1.04[2]). Most states allow both agency and independent adoption. In the former, a private or public adoption agency evaluates the home and places the child with the prospective adoptive parents. The agency also makes a corresponding recommendation to the court, which has the ultimate discretion to grant or deny the adoption.

In an indepedent adoption the natural parent or parents choose for themselves the person or persons with whom they want the child placed. After the child is physically placed or, in the matter of an interstate adoption, after the placement has been chosen but before the child has been physically placed, a state or private agency evaluates the prospective home and makes some form of recommendation to the court.

For lesbians and gay men wishing to adopt, it is certainly preferable to seek independent adoption. Practically speaking, the would-be adoptive parent avoids having to wait in line at an agency that will invariably give first preference to married couples (either as required by policy or as manifested in practice) and will give unmarried and gay people access, if any, only to those children whom the agency considers "difficult to place." Even more importantly, however, once a child has been placed in an adoptive home by the natural parent, that placement is given some weight in any ultimate determination by the court as to whether that adoption would be in the child's best interests.

Common practice, at least in the case of independent adoptions, has been to inform the birth parent(s) of the sexual orientation of the prospective parent(s). Generally, this is done pursuant to a regulation or policy requirement of "full disclosure" regarding the adoptive parent before the birth parent signs a consent form. This disclosure "requirement" can be abused, however. In a recent northern California case,[7] a birth mother placed her child for adoption with a woman she knew to be a lesbian. The social worker called the birth mother and badgered her about what the worker believed to be the potential harm to the little boy of being raised in the home of a lesbian. The birth mother immediately contacted the social worker's supervisor and registered a complaint about the harassing phone calls, but not all birth parents respond in this way upon learning that a prospective adopting parent is homosexual. The disclosure "requirement" is something of which lesbians and gay men desiring to adopt should be mindful.

In both agency and private adoption an investigation of the prospective parent is conducted, and the investigator (usually a social worker) makes a recommendation to grant or deny the adoption. Invariably, when the applicant is lesbian or gay, the case is subjected to closer scrutiny. It is not unusual for the social worker's recommendation to be reviewed at the highest levels of the evaluating agency. Those conducting the investigation often know little or nothing about homosexuality or about the impact of a parent's homosexuality upon the psychological development of a child. It can be useful to offer to provide that information to the social worker and to his or her supervisor so that, even if the worker is intuitively inclined to approve the home, he or she can have the ammunition necessary to wage a war with a superior, particularly in places where lesbian or gay adoption is a new phenomenon. Even in places where such adoptions have occurred more frequently, it may be necessary to educate social service agency personnel about the issues. It is also during this period of investigation and evaluation that it may be necessary to retain a lawyer, if only to make it clear that the applicant expects the same fair and impartial evaluation to which all applicants are entitled.

JOINT AND SECOND-PARENT ADOPTIONS

Finally, even where openly homosexual men and women succeed in adopting, they are forced to do so as single individuals, even if they are in couples and even if their partners are actually co-parenting with them on an equal basis. All states allow adoption by unmarried persons and, until recently, all states required that the unmarried person adopt only as an individual (Achtenberg, 1985, Sect. 1.04[3]). In most jurisdictions, the adoption statutes do not state explicitly that unmarried individuals are prohibited from adopting the same child jointly. It has always been assumed, however, that no agency would recommend and that no judge would grant a joint adoption by an unmarried couple.

In 1986, in two northern California counties, lesbian couples jointly adopted, each with a positive recommendation by the state's social service department.[8] California's adoption statute does not explicitly prohibit such a result,[9] and the California courts have a long history of interpreting the adoption statute liberally in order to further the best interests of the child being adopted.[10] The DSS is now having second thoughts about having recommended these adoptions and is considering a policy to prevent joint and second-parent adoptions by unmarried couples.[11] Although the proposed policy applies to both unmarried heterosexual and homosexual couples, the policy will obviously have a vastly disproportionate impact on homosexual couples. It is also obvious that the motivation for the policy is antipathy toward lesbians and gay men, since a child clearly benefits from having two legal parents. Joint adoption is a recognition that both parents comprise a child's family. It is no accident that in the judge's chambers, after he had granted one of the joint adoptions mentioned earlier, he looked at the child, then at each of the parents, and stated, "I hereby declare you a family."

A final category of adoption involves a child's sole legal parent seeking to obtain legal recognition of the parental relationship that has arisen between the child and the child's nonbiological coparent — usually, but not always, the legal parent's lover. Particularly in situations in which lesbian couples have children by artificial insemination and where the birth mother is the child's sole legal parent, there has arisen a desire to validate in law the claims of both the child and the coparent to an ongoing parental relationship with one another, whatever may happen to the relationship between the adults. The first second-parent adoption by a lesbian couple occurred in Oregon in 1985.[12] It was followed by a comparable adoption in Alaska where, as a result of the adoption, the child had three legal parents.[13] Recently, in California, two heterosexual unmarried couples were granted second-parent adoption,[14] and a lesbian couple is now seeking to do the same for their four-year-old who has been coparented by them since her birth.[15] Similar cases are being planned throughout the country.

What is crucial about second-parent adoption is that, like joint adoption, it provides a child with two parents recognized in law upon whom the child can depend for emotional, financial, and moral support. Each parent has a right to make critical decisions for the child, should that become necessary. If anything happens to the birth parent, nothing can disrupt the relationship between the child and the nonbiological coparent. Legally guaranteed and enforceable rights of the second parent add stability and permanence to a child's life and contribute to the child's healthy sense of self (see, for example, Green, Mandel, Hotvedt, Gray, & Smith, 1986; and Steckel, 1985).

Despite the obvious benefits to a child of second-parent adoption, such adoptions will be a long time coming in most areas of the country. The symbolism and strength of gay family relationships recognized in law is not lost on those who make these decisions.

FOSTER PARENTING: A FOCUS ON
THE BOSTON FOSTER CARE CASE

In spring of 1985 two Boston men, David Jean and Donald Babets, applied to the Massachusetts Department of Social Services to be licensed as foster parents. In some ways, the two men were more stable, upstanding, and financially secure than many of those who apply for licensure in Massachusetts and across the country. Babets was a senior investigator for the Boston Fair Housing Commission and Jean was the business manager of a nursing home. Actively involved in church and community affairs and in local electoral politics, the men brought with them letters of recommendation from Mr. Babets' priest and Mr. Jean's minister.

What was unusual, however, was that the men, who have lived together for more than ten years, decided to submit their application as a gay couple. They felt that it was better to enter the situation candidly than to risk the possibility of having the nature of their relationship "discovered," to their detriment.

Slightly more than a year later, after an evaluation period at least twice as long as that for most potential foster parents and a particularly extensive round of interviews, home visits, and investigations of the men's reputations on the job and in the community, the Department of Social Services approved Babets and Jean's application and granted them a license. A short time later, two little boys — aged three and nearly two — were placed in the Babets and Jean home. Their mother had given written approval for the placement.

Less than two weeks after the children were placed with Babets and Jean, the *Boston Globe* broke the story of the placement in a May 8, 1985, article that took the front page of the *Globe's* "Metro" section (Cooper, 1985b).

The *Globe's* story created a flurry of activity within the DSS. On the morning of the day the story appeared, the Commissioner of Social Services assured Babets and Jean that the boys would not be taken from their home (K. Cathcart, personal communication, July 7, 1986). But by the afternoon, the DSS abruptly removed the children.

Although the *Globe's* original story did not identify Babets and Jean by name, there was no doubt that theirs was the foster placement in question. Kenneth Cooper, the reporter who prepared the story and who continued to write follow-up articles for several months, admitted that he had spoken to Don Babets about the initial story before it ran and that Babets "suggested to me that if I did the story the kids could be taken out of the home. I wasn't persuaded of that. He was" (K. Cooper, personal communication, July 29, 1986).

As the situation developed, the *Boston Globe* remained a powerful influence. The editors' opinion of foster placements with lesbians and gay men, which the May 8 story had demonstrated more covertly, became crystal clear in a series of editorials that appeared on its Op-Ed page. Said one:

> The state's foster-care program . . . should never be used, knowingly or unknowingly, as the means by which homosexuals who do not have children of their own . . . are enabled to acquire the trappings of traditional families. ("A Model Foster-Care Policy," 1985)

Another, published to mark the anniversary of the removal of the children from the Babets and Jean home, opined,

> One year ago, the Department of Social Services removed two young boys from the home of the two homosexual men who were serving as their foster parents. As difficult as it might have been to envision then, the incident has produced major benefits for foster children. ("Foster-Care Lessons," 1986)

The "benefits" envisioned by the *Globe's* editors included an emphasis on what it called "normal" families, in which the husband worked outside the home and the wife stayed home to care for the children. More hypothetical than tangible, however, such a "benefit" failed to provide relief for the significant numbers of children awaiting foster care in Massachusetts. A December 1985 report by the

Commonwealth's Legislative Subcommittee on Foster Care noted that 50 to 58 percent of state and private foster placement agencies maintained waiting lists. The report estimated that, at the time of its publication, as many as 750 children were awaiting foster care in inappropriate or emergency settings (Hildt, Kollios, Parente, & Buell, 1985).

If the *Globe* had intended to embarrass the DSS and the governor because of the absence of a separate policy governing lesbian and gay foster placements, it succeeded. Like most states, it was true, Massachusetts's foster care policy made no specific mention of gay or lesbian applicants. But Governor Dukakis and the Massachusetts DSS blindly accepted the *Globe's* premise that not having a specific policy was evidence of negligence or indifference on their parts. As Babets and Jean's attorney, Kevin Cathcart, noted,

> The DSS looked foolish because they didn't seem to have a policy to cover gay people. Instead of saying, "Yes, we have a policy and Jean and Babets fit!" they set out to write a new and separate policy. (personal communication, July 7, 1986)

The Dukakis administration's lack of courage is even more apparent when it is understood that the foster placements that had all along been taking place with lesbian and gay people were no secret, no matter of inadvertence. In 1976, Governor Dukakis received a report on foster care from a Department of Public Welfare Study that he had commissioned. The Summary of the Project's final report stated, in part:

> [T]he results of the review in this category do not indicate that alleged or professed homosexuality, per se, is evidence of unsuitability as a foster parent. Rather, greater cause for concern was found in the issue of supporting and assisting workers in dealing with cases that may involve single (male) parents and/or homosexuality. (Warden, 1976, p. 3)

The report, which was made public, was the subject of an *Advocate* article in which the author, Assistant Welfare Commissioner Beth Warden, discussed the cooperation of the Boston Gay Community in the preparation of the report ("No Evidence," 1976). At the time the Babets and Jean story broke, however, Dukakis stated that he was unaware the state was making gay foster placements (Cooper, 1985a).

On May 24, 1985, a new foster care policy was announced that divided prospective parents into four categories, in order of priority: (1) relatives of the child or married couples with parenting experience; (2) married couples without parenting experience; (3) unmarried couples or single parents; and (4) gay and lesbian couples or singles. The new regulations required the department to place children with foster parents in the first two categories before even considering the latter two, and made placements in the third and fourth categories impossible without the express written approval of the commissioner of Social Services. At the press conference announcing the new policy, Secretary of Human Services Johnston admitted that future placements with gay and lesbian foster parents were "highly unlikely" (Cooper, 1985a).

Outcry against the new policy began almost immediately at public hearings and at a statewide professional conference of mental health and children/youth organizations. But despite a massive opposition effort by individuals, by state politicians, by the newly formed Gay and Lesbian Defense Committee, and by representatives of virtually every human service organization and agency in Massachusetts — including the National Association of Social Workers, the Massachusetts Human Services Coalition, the National Lawyers Guild, the Massachusetts Society for the Prevention of Cruelty to Children, the Civil Liberties Union of Massachusetts, and the Massachusetts Psychiatric Society, to name a few — the new regulations were approved.

In December 1985, the Massachusetts Committee for Children and Youth sponsored a "Speakout on Foster Care," a forum for legislators, policymakers, and child welfare workers to discuss problems in the Massachusetts foster care system. In its report on the Speakout, the committee noted that the new foster care policy,

> [which placed] priority on placement in traditional two parent foster families, discourage[d] placement with single parents and virtually eliminat[ed] gay foster parents from among placement possibilities, has exacerbated many of the problems listed [herein], particularly recruitment. It . . . excludes many competent, nurturing people from among the pool of foster parent resources. (Summary of Proceedings, p. 6)

The Litigation

In January 1986, after an Administrative Appeal process had failed, Babets and Jean joined a number of other plaintiffs and brought suit against Governor Dukakis and the DSS. They alleged that the new priority system established by the promulgation of the policy (officially, CMR 7.101):

create[d] an arbitrary and irrational presumption that all unmarried couples and single persons, even those with parenting experience, are always less suitable as foster parents than are married couples (even those without parenting experience).

In addition, the Complaint challenged the new requirement that prospective foster parents divulge their sexual orientation on the DSS screening form. One of the plaintiffs, the Reverend Kathryn Piccard, had been a foster parent for six years. During that time, seventeen children had been placed with her. She was removed from the list of licensed parents, however, when she refused to answer the sexual orientation question prior to being approved for an eighteenth placement.

Plaintiffs further charged that the intent of the state's new regulation was to create an "arbitrary, invidiously discriminatory, and unreasonable classification of foster parents" based on sexual orientation. The new regulation made state policy on the presumption that unmarried or homosexual individuals were per se unfit to be foster parents, the plaintiffs argued. The DSS, however, was prohibited by law from rejecting foster parents on the basis of such an arbitrary classification, particularly in the absence of any rational basis for the presumption (for example, scientific evidence) and without a demonstration that the distinction served or protected an important purpose of government. Almost immediately, the state moved to have the lawsuit dismissed, alleging that none of the plaintiffs' legal claims was valid.

In September 1986, Judge Thomas R. Morse, Jr., ruled on the defendants' Motion to Dismiss, upholding what were perhaps the most important of plaintiffs' allegations. Judge Morse's ruling, however, was essentially only an opinion on the validity — as a matter of law, not as a matter of fact — of the plaintiffs' complaint. That is, he determined whether or not the plaintiffs had a valid legal complaint, assuming they could prove all the facts they alleged. The issues of fact — for instance, whether or not it was actually true that the state intended to discriminate against single people and homosexuals — are still to be decided after all the evidence is presented at a trial.

First, Judge Morse upheld the claim that the creation of an arbitrary classification, on the basis of which some individuals were prevented from becoming foster parents, violated the plaintiffs' rights to equal protection under both the Massachusetts and U.S. Constitutions. The guarantee of equal protection of the laws "is essentially a direction that all persons similarly situated should be treated alike" (p. 10). The court noted: "If the best interests of the child are to govern all out of home foster placements . . . then any distinction between married couples and single persons is wholly arbitrary and capricious and adverse to the needs of children" (p. 13).

As Judge Morse noted in his Order, and as plaintiffs will emphasize at trial, the Babets and Jean home had been carefully and systematically examined by the DSS before the men were licensed as foster parents and children were placed with them. In the two weeks between the placement and the removal of the children, the couple did nothing to warrant the revocation of the placement, and the DSS discovered no new information which showed that parenting by homosexuals was detrimental to children. In light of that, the state's reliance on no new facts to support the termination of a placement they had already approved reveals the new foster care policy as arbitrary on its face. Judge Morse concluded:

> Any exclusion of homosexuals from consideration as foster parents, all things being equal, is blatantly irrational. . . . Plaintiffs are entitled to prove that discrimination based on sexual preference stems from the defendants' "bare desire to harm a politically unpopular group," and that it is not a legitimate state interest. (pp. 15–16)

General Principles from the Boston Foster Care Case

The Babets and Jean case is ongoing,[16] and it will be many months before there is a final legal decision on the factual allegations raised in the suit. The experience of Babets and Jean, however, has some important implications for lesbian and gay foster care applicants in other states:

1. Lesbians and gay men who apply to become foster parents are commonly investigated more extensively than most other people. In some circumstances, this is a self-education process for the child-placing agency and also a way for them to make sure they know all the facts about the placement in the event it is ever challenged.
2. Just as Babets and Jean brought rather exceptional resources to their situation, many of the gay men and lesbians who are able to traverse the system bring with them special skills, training, resources, and stability. Frequently, those gay people who do make it to licensure have, in addition to other special resources and abilities, a knowledge

of how to work within bureaucracies that serves them well in social service delivery systems.

3. Perhaps the most important lesson of the Babets/Jean case is a demonstration of the way in which media attention thwarts the construction of a rational policy. Once a particular placement has become a media issue, agencies and politicians tend to respond in reactive, defensive ways. The thoughtful, affirmative strategies of groups working beforehand to construct policies that benefit lesbian and gay people would, in ideal cases, always be preferable. Media attention may simply make such efforts too difficult.

4. Finally, the mobilization of the lesbian/gay community and its dissemination of alternative information is the only effective counter to media distortions and sensationalism. The harnessing of the entire apparatus of the gay and lesbian community is both a means of protecting those who attempt to make advances and a way to ensure that the political clout and outrage of the community are assessed.

ADDITIONAL RESOURCES FOR PROSPECTIVE PARENTS AND THEIR ATTORNEYS

The following groups and agencies are able, to a greater or lesser extent, to assist lesbians and gay men who want to become foster (or, in some cases, adoptive) parents. They range in practice and approach from projects such as The Triangle Project (Los Angeles, CA), which actively recruits lesbian and gay foster parents with the cooperation of the state DSS, to the Philadelphia Mayor's Committee on Sexual Minorities, whose function is primarily to provide referrals and advocacy. In almost every instance, however, contact people are aware of supportive networks that can help lesbian and gay people achieve the goal of becoming foster or adoptive parents.

The Triangle Project
1299 N. Fairfax Avenue, West Hollywood, CA 90046
(213) 656-5005

Institute for the Protection of Lesbian and Gay Youth
110 E. 23rd Street, 10th Floor, New York, NY 10010
(212) 473-1113

Lutheran Social Services
1202 Payne Avenue, St. Paul, MN 55101
(612) 879-0668

Child and Family Services
1600 Albany Avenue, Hartford, CT 06112
(203) 236-4511

Sexual Minority Youth Assistance League (SMILE)
1638 R Street NW, Washington, D.C. 20009
(202) 232-7506

The Shelter
1020 Virginia Street, Seattle, WA 98101
(206) 622-3187

Mayor's Committee on Sexual Minorities
143 City Hall, Philadelphia, PA 19107
(215) 686-2191

Other resources include written materials available from the Lesbian Rights Project, including sample legal briefs, copies of published studies on the psychological health of children of lesbian and gay parents, and bibliographies.

CONCLUSIONS

Despite the conservative political climate, lesbians and gay men continue to make progress in their efforts to become adoptive and foster parents. Sometimes, it is true, success seems far away. Indeed, as Stephanie Ronek described her and her partner, Celia's experience in pursuing the adoption of a boy, five, and a girl, six,

> [t]here were many steps along the way when we could have felt we weren't wanted. And I think lots of people just walk away (from an agency) believing that they're not going to be allowed to do it. But at least some of the hassles have more to do with bureaucracies than with homophobia. It's important to just keep going with it. . . . Sometimes I think back to the beginning and wonder what ever made us presume that we could do this! But we wanted it badly enough and we thought we had to try.

For the children, Stephanie says, "it's an ongoing process of understanding that we are who we are, that we're both women and that we're girlfriends." But it appears that one of the major benefits of lesbian and gay families — an appreciation of diversity — is beginning to take hold. Stephanie reported, "One day when I was talking to Marie about the ways in which we're different from some of her friends' parents she said, 'You mean, sometimes a Princess could be waiting for another *Princess* to come?'" Clearly, this family is an example of what so many gay men and lesbians are fighting for.

AREAS OF CONCERN/SUGGESTIONS
FOR FUTURE STUDY

There is a great need for human service workers to be educated about lesbian and gay families. The American Psychiatric Association, the American Psychological Association, and the National Association of Social Workers all have adopted official nondiscrimination statements (see, for example, the recent action of the American Psychiatric Association on foster parenting, "Position Statement," 1986), but practice varies greatly. Lesbian/gay counsels within those professional assemblies need to make a priority of educating their colleagues about issues relating to lesbian and gay parenting. Education is essential, too, for attorneys, judges, and family court personnel.

Because courts and agencies are, generally out of ignorance, concerned about the potential psychological harm to children who have lesbian or gay parents, there is a need for further research to show that such children are not adversely affected — particularly longitudinal studies and those that deal specifically with adoptive or foster children. Although the extant literature is somewhat scattered, it is no longer scarce (see, for example, Kirkpatrick & Hitchens, 1985; Kleber, Howell, & Tibbits-Kleber, 1986).

For reasons that are perhaps understandable, the gay community has been reluctant to address the needs of lesbian and gay youth, particularly those who are runaways or very young adolescents. But such reluctance must end. Lesbian and gay youth comprise a large proportion of the juvenile prostitute and street populations, and existing resources and shelters are inadequate to their needs. The time may be appropriate for the gay and lesbian community to reassess its obligation to these children.

Agencies and groups that work with foster children must modernize their understanding of the children whom they serve. In two recent publications on the problems of homeless and "multiple placement youth" (National Network of Runaway and Youth Services, 1985; Pardeck, 1985), the authors ignore the importance of sexual identity issues in understanding why some children experience unstable foster placements, are removed from foster homes, or fail to be served by the system.

NOTES

1. *Pima County Juvenile Action*, #B–10489, (Ariz. Sup. Ct., Pima County, August 30, 1985); *In the Matter of the Appeal in Pima County Juvenile Court*, Action #B–10489, CA-Civ. #5548 (Arizona Court of Appeals, Division 2, August 11, 1986).

2. The Arizona sodomy statute is Ariz. Rev. Stat. Ann. Section 13–1411 (1978): "A person who knowingly and without force commits the infamous crime against nature is guilty of a class 3 misdemeanor. . . ."

3. The judge dissenting from the majority opinion in the Pima County case felt that the existence of the sodomy law put the state under no compulsion to deny adoption applications from homosexuals or bisexuals. He responded that, were such the case, every applicant's past, present, and future sexual conduct would have to be scrutinized by the court in order to ascertain the absence of other activity forbidden by Arizona law (for example, adultery, cohabitation, and the heterosexual sex acts outlawed by the sodomy statute). He believed that the state should not involve itself in inquiries of that nature.

4. In *Nadler v. Superior Court*, 63 Cal. Rptr. 352 (1967), the Court of Appeal held that, in the case of a parent who is known to be homosexual, a custody decision cannot be made solely on the basis of that fact. The court must weigh all the evidence pertaining to the child's situation before making a custody determination.

5. In *Gay Law Students Assoc. v. Pacific Telephone and Telegraph Co.*, 24 Cal. 3d 458, 136 Cal. Rptr. 14, 595 P.Wd 592 (1979), the California Supreme Court held that arbitrary discrimination against an individual by a state or government entity due to homosexuality is impermissible and is a violation of the Equal Protection Clause of the California Constitution.

Accordingly, the state DSS cannot discriminate against a homosexual petitioner for adoption by denying his or her petition solely on the basis of homosexuality without violating the Constitution's Equal Protection Clause and the *Nadler* holding, that is, that homosexuality per se is not a sufficient basis upon which to consider custody by a homosexual parent contrary to a child's best interests.

6. The Lesbian Rights Project (LRP) has been contacted by people in San Francisco, Alameda, San Diego, Los Angeles, and Sacramento counties regarding successful attempts to become either licensed foster parents or to be approved as adoptive parents. At the same time, complaints continue to emerge from Orange County, perhaps the most conservative county in the state, where agency personnel

consistently discourage homosexual applicants by telling them that their applications for adoption or foster care licensure will stand no chance of being approved. The LRP is contemplating a lawsuit in this regard. In the meantime, the LRP is making efforts to require uniform enforcement of the adoption laws through its Adoption and Foster Parenting Project.

7.   Additional information available from the Lesbian Rights Project, 1370 Mission Street, 4th Floor, San Francisco, CA 94103, (415) 621-0674.

8.   No. 17350 (California Superior Court, Alameda County, April 8, 1986); No. 17945 (California Superior Court, San Francisco County, February 24, 1986).

9.   The relevant sections of the California Civil Code state: "Any unmarried minor child may be adopted by any adult person" (Section 221); and "Any person desiring to adopt a child may for that purpose petition the Superior Court" (Section 226). Therefore, any child may be adopted by any adult provided that the other requirements of the statutory scheme are met.

10.   See *Department of Social Welfare v. Superior Court* (1960) 1 Cal. 3d 1, 6; 81 Cal. Rptr. 345, for example, in which the California Supreme Court declared that the "adoption statutes are to be liberally construed," and the holding in *Reeves v. Bailey* (1975) 53 Cal. App. 3d 1019 that the adoption statute should be interpreted to effectuate a child's best interests, the governing principle in any adoption proceeding.

11.   The term "second-parent adoption" was officially coined by Zuckerman (1986).

12.   In the Circuit Court of the State of Oregon for the County of Multonomah, Amended Decree of Adoption No. D8503-61930, September, 1985.

13.   No. 1JU–85–25 P/A (Alaska Superior Court, First Judicial District of Juneau, 1986).

14.   No. A-10169 (California Superior Court, Riverside County, 1985); No. A-28345 (California Superior Court, San Diego County, 1985).

15.   Additional information available from the Lesbian Rights Project, 1370 Mission Street, 4th Floor, San Francisco, CA 94103 (415) 621-0674.

16.   Additional information available from Gay & Lesbian Advocates and Defenders, P. O. Box 218, Boston, MA 02112, (617) 426-1350.

REFERENCES

A model foster-care policy. (1985, May 28). *The Boston Globe*, p. 14.

Achtenberg, R. A. (Ed.), (1985). *Sexual orientation and the law.* New York: Clark-Boardman.

Agency backs down on foster children. (1974, July 17). *The Advocate*, #142, p. 22.

Agency reveals kids placed with gay couples. (1973, August 15). *The Advocate* , #118, p. 2.

Ban on gay foster care scratched from guide. (1974, July 17). *The Advocate*, #142, p. 11.

CA gay foster homes approved. (1976, June 30). *The Advocate*, #193, p. 11.

Cooper, K. (1985, May 25). New policy on foster care: Parenting by gays all but ruled out. *The Boston Globe*, pp. 1, 24. (a)

Cooper, K. (1985, May 8). Some oppose foster placement with gay couple. *The Boston Globe*, pp. 21, 24. (b)

Families by adoption: A gay reality. (1974, August 28). *The Advocate*, #145, p. 1.

Fortune, R. (1974, January 30). A son: Bachelor adopts. *The Advocate*, #130, p. 16.

Foster-care lessons. (1986, May 11). *The Boston Globe*.

Franks, L. (1974, May 30). Teens who have gay 'parents.' *San Francisco Chronicle*, p. 22.

Gay couple granted adoption of child. (1979, March 8). *The Advocate*, #262, p. 12.

Gay foster parents sought. (1977, June). *The Blade*, #6, p. 7.

Green, R., Mandel, J. B., Hotvedt, M. E., Gray, J., & Smith, L. (1986). Lesbian mothers and their children: A comparison with solo parent heterosexual mothers and their children. *Archives of Sexual Behavior, 15*, (2), 167–184.

Hildt, B., Kollios, P., Parente, M., & Buell, C. (1985, December). *In the best interest of the children?* Boston, MA: Commonwealth of Massachusetts Joint Committee on Human Services and Elderly Affairs, Legislative Subcommittee on Foster Care.

Judge places gay teenage boy in lesbian foster parents' home. (1974, May 22). *The Advocate*, #138, p. 8.

Kirkpatrick, M., & Hitchens, D. J. (1985). Lesbian mothers/gay fathers. In P. Benedek & D. Shetky, Eds., *Emerging issues in child psychiatry and the law* (pp. 108–119). New York: Brunner/Mazel.

Kleber, D., Howell, R., & Tibbits-Kleber, A. (1986). The impact of parental homosexuality in child custody cases: A review of the literature. *Bulletin of the American Academy of Psychiatry and Law, 14* (1), 81–87.

Los Angeles County Department of Adoptions. (1976, July 14). *The Advocate*, #194, p. 10.

Married males apply for a child. (1974, July 3). *The Advocate*, #141, p. A-12.

Massachusetts Committee for Children and Youth. (1985, December 18). *Summary of proceedings of the speakout on foster care*. Boston, MA: Author.

Morse, Hon. Samuel J. (1986). Memorandum and order on defendants' motion to dismiss. Commonwealth of Massachusetts Superior Court Action No. 81083.

National Network of Runaway and Youth Services, Inc. (1985). *To whom do they belong? A profile of America's runaway and homeless youth and the programs that help them*. Washington, D.C.: Author.

New Jersey putting gay youths in homosexual foster homes. (1979, November 27). *Los Angeles Times*, Pt. I, p. 13.

New rules proposed: Seek to block gay foster homes. (1974, May 22). *The Advocate*, #138, p. 8.

No evidence gay parents unsuitable. (1976, April 21). *The Advocate*, #188, pp. 12–13.

Pardeck, J. T. (1985). A profile of the child likely to experience unstable foster care. *Adolescence, 20* (79), 689–696.

Position statement on discrimination in selection of foster parents. (1986, November). *American Journal of Psychiatry, 143*, (11), 1506.

Ricketts, W. (in press). Homosexuality in adolescence: The reification of sexual personalities. *Journal of Social Work and Human Sexuality*.

Shilts, R. (1975, December 17). Foster homes for gay children: Justice or prejudice? *The Advocate*, #179, p. 11.

Short takes: Minneapolis. (1981, February 19). *The Advocate*, #350, p. 22.

Steckel, E. (1985) *Separation/Individuation in children of lesbian and heterosexual couples*. Berkeley: University of California, Wright Institute.

Vecsey, G. (1979, June 21). Approval given for homosexual to adopt a boy. *New York Times*.

Warden, B. (1976, March 3). *Summary of report: Administrative case review of foster care placements*. Boston, MA: Commonwealth of Massachusetts, Department of Public Welfare.

Zuckerman, E. (1986). Second parent adoption for lesbian-parented families: Legal recognition of the other mother. *U. C. Davis Law Review, 19*, 729, 731.

7

THE GAY AND LESBIAN STEPPARENT FAMLY

David A. Baptiste, Jr.

> . . . we're very much like other families in that we live in chaos, our children eat hot dogs and put peanut butter in their hair. The obvious difference is that there's two women in the relationship. (Linda, a lesbian stepmother. In A Family to me: Portraits of Four American Families. A documentary videotape by Linda Harness, 1986)

In the past two decades many important changes have occurred in the American family. The most noted changes have been the tremendous increase in the divorce rate and a concomitant increase in stepfamilies (Glick, 1984) resulting from divorce or death of a spouse and the subsequent remarriage of spouses. Societal interest in and concern about stepfamilies has to date focused only on concerns and issues specific to heterosexual stepfamilies — parents and children (cf. Einstein, 1982; Maddox, 1975; Nobel & Nobel, 1977; Nobel, 1981; Sager et al., 1983; Visher & Visher, 1979). Concerns and issues specific to gay/lesbian stepfamilies, a unique subset of stepfamilies, have been ignored. Thus, gay/lesbian stepfamilies remain invisible and are unrecognized as a legitimate family form by the American public.

Reports of gay/lesbian biological parents rearing children as single parents or with a same-sex partner are cited in the professional and lay literature (cf. Bozett, 1985; Goodman, 1980; Green, 1982; Hall, 1978;

Maddox, 1982; Richardson, 1981; Schulenburg, 1985). In most cases, however, the gay/lesbian single parent family structure is emphasized (for example, Lewin & Lyons, 1982), and the stepparenting role of the partner as well as the stepfamily structure of the family is unrecognized and deemphasized even though the family's living arrangement is reported to include children and two same-sex adults in a committed stepfamily relationship (cf. Robinson & Barret, 1985: pp. 145–147).

This chapter describes and discusses the dynamics of the gay stepparent family and the particular issues faced by members of such families (parents and children), the relationship of these family members to the larger community, the relationship between the adult partners, and issues specific to children in such families. Also included will be implications for professionals. The chapter will conclude with recommendations for future research. Much of the information presented in this chapter is culled from the author's clinical experiences with gay and lesbian stepparent families.

DEFINITION OF TERMS

Family/Stepfamily. As used here, "family" and "stepfamily" are intended to denote a cohabitive living arrangement involving two same-sex adults and their children, biological, adopted, or conceived through artificial insemination, from previous heterosexual relationships, marital or common-law. The relationship is characterized by mutual commitment, property sharing, and sexual intimacies similar to that found among cohabiting heterosexual couples with children.

Stepchildren. Stepchildren describes children, biological and nonbiological, who maintain a stepchild relationship with a nonsanguine related adult (and sometimes children) while living in a household parented by two same-sex adults.

Stepparents. The term stepparent describes a gay/lesbian adult who maintains a "parent-like" relationship with a same-sex partner's children in a "stepfamily-like" living arrangement involving a partner and his/her children.

STRUCTURE AND DYNAMICS OF
GAY/LESBIAN STEPPARENT FAMILIES

All families parented by gay/lesbian couples are, by virtue of their structure, stepfamilies, and the adults in such families are, by virtue of their role and relationship to the partner's children, stepparents.

Gay/lesbian stepparent families share some dynamics and concerns in common with heterosexual stepfamilies. For example, prior to coupling either one or both partners may have ended a heterosexual relationship through divorce. Either one or both partners may be a custodial parent. Given the tendency of courts to award child custody to mothers, lesbian mothers are initially more likely than gay fathers to be custodial parents, until their lesbianism becomes an issue and their fitness to be parents is challenged in court. In the case of lesbian-headed stepparent families, the family may be living economically at or below poverty level. Additionally, like heterosexual stepfamilies, gay/lesbian stepparent families often confront affectional issues such as rejection of a stepparent by his/her stepchildren, stepparent-stepchildren competition for the affection of the parental partner, and general stepparent-stepchildren conflicts common to all reconstituting families (Baptiste, 1987).

Despite some similarity, however, gay/lesbian stepparent families' dynamics and concerns are unique to such families and are unknown to their heterosexual counterparts. As a result, family life for the adults and children in gay/lesbian stepparent families can be a challenging, demanding and oftentimes precarious undertaking. Stepfamily living severely stresses the dyadic relationship as well as biological/stepparent-children relationships.

LACK OF LEGITIMACY AS A
RECOGNIZED FAMILY UNIT

Many gay men and lesbians are parents, but their exact numbers are unknown. It is estimated conservatively that between 10 and 25 percent of gay men are fathers (Bell & Weinberg, 1978; Harry, 1983; Jay & Young, 1979; Skeen & Robinson, 1984, 1985) and between 2 and 3 million lesbians are mothers (Hoeffer, 1978; Martin & Lyon, 1972). Despite this fact, a significant portion of the American public continues to believe that it is inherently contradictory that a person can be both homosexual and a parent. Perhaps the contradiction arises because parenthood implies heterosexuality and previous heterosexual contact. Furthermore, many Americans erroneously assume that gays/lesbians do not become parents, or more significantly, parents do not become gays/lesbians (cf. Walters, in Voellers & Walters, 1978, p. 149).

The issue of gay/lesbian stepparenthood is significantly more inconceivable to many nongay Americans than that of gay/lesbian biological parenthood. Consequently, unlike heterosexual stepfamilies and stepparents, gay/lesbian stepfamilies and stepparents are neither perceived as a legitimate family parental form nor are supported by nor institutionalized in society. Many of these families and the stepparents in them experience difficulties because of the lack of any special ritual(s) confirming family membership as well as lack of role legitimacy. The case of Sara and Ellen illustrates one aspect of these issues. Sara and Ellen, and Ellen's two daughters, ages six and twelve, respectively, lived together as a lesbian stepfamily. They sought therapeutic assistance because of stepmother-stepdaughter problems involving Niki, the twelve-year-old. Ellen, a nurse, frequently worked the 3:00 to 11:00 p.m. shift. In her absence it was explicitly understood that Sara was in charge. Despite the rule, Niki openly disobeyed Sara and questioned Sara's right to discipline or otherwise control her in Ellen's absence. Because of the need for secrecy, Sara had been presented to the girls as Ellen's good friend who shared the home for financial reasons. Ellen and Sara had not, and were not planning, to disclose their lifestyle to the girls. Because Niki was beginning to influence the six-year-old to disobey Sara, the parents were eager to legitimize Sara's authority with the children, without disclosing their lesbian identity. The stepmother-stepdaughter difficulties were also beginning to negatively affect the adult dyadic relationship. Therapy focused on exploring and implementing alternative ways of legitimizing Sara's presence in the home, beyond being a good friend, and her authority to parent the children in Ellen's absence.

Contrary to prevailing beliefs about the legitimacy of gay/lesbian stepparent families, observations of such families have shown overwhelmingly that when controlled for the sexual preference of the adults, the behaviors of gay/lesbian stepparent families tend to be indistinguishable from that of heterosexual stepparent families (Hotvedt & Mandel, 1982). Indeed, regardless of sexual preference and lifestyle, gay/lesbian parents — biological and step — experience the same joys and sufferings of parenthood as do heterosexual parents. As either biological or stepparents experiencing difficulties with their children, gay/lesbian parents may have more in common with their heterosexual counterparts than with gay/lesbian nonparents.

Frequently, gay/lesbian parenthood is discouraged by society because such parents are viewed as personally inadequate, emotionally unstable, behaviorally incompetent and, morally degenerate. Thus, they automatically have been denied the right to parent their biological children, adopt children (even if the children are gay or lesbian), or serve as foster parents despite the absence of any empirical evidence to support these actions. Contrary to this practice, however, neither the character nor the morals of heterosexual parents — biological or step — are subjected to the same scrutiny and their suitability to be parents is rarely, if ever, questioned unless there are persuasive, compelling, and unequivocal reasons to do so. Similarly, despite societal discouragement of interracial stepparent families (cf. Cheers, 1983; *Palmore v. Sidoti*, 1982), the decision to award or deny custody of children to such families usually rests upon the narrow issue of the potential stigmatization of the children living in such circumstances rather than upon the character and morals of the parents (Baptiste, 1984). Indeed, while racial minority groups and women generally are protected to some extent from discrimination by law, the same is not true for homosexuals of either sex, and certainly not for women who are lesbians.

STIGMA, SECRECY, AND RELATIONSHIPS WITH THE LARGER COMMUNITY

Stigma

Despite a greater societal tolerance in recent years for sexual diversity, homosexuality is still strongly disapproved of and severely stigmatized.[1] Because of the social stigma associated with their lifestyles, the societal disapproval of them as parents, and the fear of discovery, most parents (especially stepparents) in gay/lesbian stepparent families conceal both their lifestyles and their relationship and try to "pass" (Goffman, 1963) and live "conventional lives" in order to maintain a sense of family and protect their parental rights in a nonsupportive culture.

Secrecy

All gay/lesbian parents who retain custody of their children risk losing that custody if their sexual preference and lifestyle become known. Thus, the need to maintain secrecy is central to the family's existence. For gay/lesbian parents living in a stepfamily relationship, the usual homosexual concerns about secrecy are further compounded because of the presence of children. While some members of society may be accepting of a gay/lesbian biological parent and his/her children living together, or two gay men or two lesbians living together without children, they tend to be less accepting of gay/lesbian couples and children living as a family (Baptiste, 1987). Such living arrangements are perceived by many Americans as unhealthy, and as posing both a social and psychological threat to the children.[2]

The gay/lesbian stepfamily's need for secrecy results from the fear of discovery which often leads to community disapproval as well as concomitant negative effects such as loss of child custody, eviction from residence, or even termination from employment. In such families, secrecy creates a self-imposed isolation for the adults and the children as well. Isolation tends to be experienced more intensely by the children than the adults (Baptiste, 1982). Secrets about the adults' lifestyle are primarily of two kinds: parent-child and family-community.

Parent-child secrecy.

Parents in gay/lesbian stepparent families frequently confront the decision of whether or not to reveal their homosexual identity to their children. Despite caring for and wanting to be honest with their children, many gay/lesbian parents are justifiably hesitant to reveal to children the nature of their relationship with their partners. Often the adults' relationship is kept a secret from the children because of parents' uncertainty about the children's reaction to the disclosure. In the author's experience, most gay/lesbian parents feel that it is important that their children first learn of their homosexual identity from them rather than to hear from someone else. Many parents believe that by age five children are old enough to understand what being gay/lesbian means. But, most parents often postpone disclosure until the children are older, approximately age twelve (Riddle & Arguelles, 1981).

Children's reactions to a parent's disclosure of his/her homosexuality are varied. Following the disclosure some children may experience little or no emotional difficulty. Others may experience much difficulty in accepting and adjusting to the disclosure. Such children may react with confusion, depression and even open rebellion when they feel unable to accept and cope with the disclosure of their parent's homosexuality and the secrecy necessary to live in a gay/lesbian stepparent family. Children may also experience dissonance in their wish to be loyal to the parent in spite of the disclosure.

Family-community secrecy.

In a majority of contemporary American communities, the acceptable standards for families and family living have not evolved to the point where a gay/lesbian lifestyle is acceptable for purposes of rearing children either as a single parent or as a couple. As a result, gay/lesbian couples living in stepfamily relationships with children need to maintain secrecy about their lifestyle in the community. Although many gay/lesbian stepfamilies pretend to lead "conventional lives" within their communities, their living arrangements and sexual orientation still tend to be suspected by many. This tends to be more true for gay men than for lesbians since in this society it is socially acceptable for two women, with or without children, to share residence, without arousing suspicion about their sexual orientation. In many cases both women may be divorcees with children and since most women with children tend to experience financial difficulties post divorce (Ross & Sawhill, 1975), sharing residence with another woman, with or without children, for financial or child care benefits, is societally sanctioned.

On the other hand, the sexual orientation of two unrelated males living together for an extended period is often viewed with much suspicion, which is increased by the presence of children in such households.

Children in gay/lesbian families also share the responsibility of maintaining secrecy about the adults' relationship in the community. Oftentimes children tend to experience the community's disapproval of the adults' relationship as disapproving of them also. Although children may be perceived by some persons as unwilling or unfortunate members of such families, it is not unusual for some children, especially adolescents, to experience harassment because of their membership in such families. Under such circumstances the parent-child relationships, biological and step, may be negatively affected because of the children's anger at having to live in a gay/lesbian family.

Relationships with the Larger Community

Gay/lesbian stepfamilies' relationships with the larger community are negatively affected by the disintegrating effects of their nonacceptance as a family. Such families tend to live a dual existence in relation to the larger community. On one hand most gay/lesbian families ostensibly behave like other families in the community, especially single-parent families. On the other hand because such families are composed of two same-sex partners, and because the adults' relationship is shrouded in secrecy, their relationships with the various subsystems of their community tend to be restricted and incomplete. Often, interactions with friends, relatives, coworkers or institutions (for example, schools) are guarded since family members must deny the reality that they are a family — a "unity of interacting personalities" (Burgess, 1972), and behave "as if" they are what they appear to be or, more significantly, what the community wishes them to be.

The community in which gay/lesbian stepfamilies live consists primarily of four subsystems: (1) neighbors and friends in the home community; (2) ex-spouses, families of origin, and other relatives; (3) institutions with whom the family must interact; and (4) the gay/lesbian community. The family's relationships with these subsystems are fraught with paradox and are indeed the proverbial "double-edged sword." That is, if the adults in the family are open about their relationship they risk ostracism by the heterosexual community. If, however, they live in secret and are marginally integrated into the community, their "isolation" is likely to cause some persons to be suspicious about them and even speculate about their sexual orientation. A closeted existence as well as the presence of children may also cause other gays/lesbians, especially nonparents, to shun such couples.

Neighbors

Paradoxically, gay/lesbian stepfamilies, as a family unit, are invisible to their neighbors. Such families are often perceived by neighbors as a single man or woman, with children, living together with another same-sex friend who may or may not have children. Often, one of the partners and his/her children may have lived in the community prior to coupling. During the period of single parent living the gay/lesbian parent and his/her children often received the affirmation and legitimization of the community as a heterosexual single-parent family and was accorded all the rights and protection pertaining thereto. Following the joining of the two families, neighbors often continue to behave toward the newly formed group in like manner.

Because of the secrecy surrounding the family's lifestyle and the family's de facto isolation from the heterosexual community, the boundary between the family and the community becomes highly permeable thereby allowing boundary violations. For example, because neighbors do not know of the couple's committed relationship, they frequently request favors or make demands of one partner's time and energies without regard for the other partner's feelings. Contrary to this practice, in dealing with either cohabiting heterosexual couples or stepfamilies, neighbors routinely are careful to maintain adequate boundaries and consider the feelings of each partner when asking for favors from either partner.

Like all families with children, much of the gay/lesbian stepfamily's interactions with the community revolve around the children. However, relationships involving the family's children and neighborhood children are especially difficult because of the unfounded heterosexual belief that homosexuals are innately paedophilics. Neighbors are often reluctant to have their children visit the family's home if they are suspicious about the adult's sexual orientation or if it is known that the adults are indeed homosexuals. Consequently, children's visits to neighbors' homes are often filled with anxiety because of the possibility of being asked prying questions about their families. Similarly, inviting neighborhood friends to the family's home (for example, sleep overs) is also anxiety producing for the children and the adults as well. A central fear for the children as well as adults is the fear of being discovered. Thus, children often complain of feeling isolated from their peers in the community.

EX-SPOUSES, FAMILIES OF ORIGIN, AND OTHER RELATIVES

Although many gays/lesbians may have publicly come out to friends and coworkers, they tend not to tell their ex-spouses, their families of origin, or other relatives (for example, ex-inlaws) about their sexual preference, or that they and the children may be living as a family with a same-sex partner.

Relationships with ex-spouses tend to be most difficult for gay/lesbian stepparent families because of the fear of losing custody of the children to the ex-spouse. However, in some cases, the family's relationship with either one or both partners' family of origin or ex-inlaws can be just as difficult although the issues involved in dealing with an ex-spouse are quite different from the issues involved in dealing with families of origin or ex-inlaws. These issues tend to be different for gay men and lesbians.

Ex-spouses

The quality of the gay/lesbian parent's relationship with his/her ex-spouse is affected by: the general societal attitude toward the parent's homosexuality; the reasons for the ending of the heterosexual relationship; and the presence or absence of any acrimonious residue stemming from the ending of the heterosexual relationship.

If the predivorced spousal relationship was characterized by high conflict the quality of the postdivorce relationship between gay/lesbian parents and their ex-spouses tends to be affected negatively. In this regard, Ahrons (1986) has reported that for as much as five years postdivorce many heterosexual ex-spouses often continue to experience negative affects resulting from the divorce. For the gay/lesbian ex-spouse the intensity as well as the duration of any negative residual affects resulting from the divorce is further intensified and complicated because of the spouse's sexual orientation, which becomes a central issue postdivorce. Many nonhomosexual ex-spouses often report feeling intensely hurt and even used (as a cover) when the other spouse's sexual orientation is discovered. When the "hurt" is coupled with moral outrage about the ex-spouse's sexual orientation, the relationship tends to be even more difficult.

Families of Origin and Other Relatives

The family's relationship with the partners' families of origin is affected by the quality of the parent-child relationship prior to the child's declaration of his/her homosexual identity; the gender of the child; and the gender of the children involved. Although society generally tends to be more accepting of lesbians than gay men, many families of origin tend to experience much difficulty in accepting the decision of a lesbian daughter, who is a custodial parent, to couple with another lesbian. Children visiting the home of noncustodial gay male parents appear to be more easily accepted by families of origin. In the author's experience families of origin characteristically tend to be less accepting of male children living as part of a homosexual stepfamily, whether gay or lesbian.

Although many gay/lesbian persons do obtain the approval and support of their families of origin subsequent to the declaration of their gay identity, some do not. Gays/lesbians who are rejected by their families of origin tend to experience much difficulty in maintaining minimum ties with such families. Often the situation is further complicated by the grandparents' demand for frequent contact with grandchildren who are perceived (by grandparents) as objects of pity and with whom the grandparents on occasion may even ally to express anger and resentment toward their adult children.

Much of the anger stems from parents' feeling that their moral codes as well as their expectations for their children have been violated. Typically, parents expect their children to follow the usual societal paths of heterosexual marriage and parenthood that assures the grandparents' immortality through the grandchildren. Although many gay/lesbian partners may have fulfilled both societal "mandates," their declaration of a homosexual identity nevertheless is perceived as violating the family of origin's moral code.

Maintenance of a meaningful relationship in such a familial atmosphere is at best a difficult task which requires many subterfugal maneuvers by the gay/lesbian family — parents and children — to avoid detection of their lifestyle. Whether or not the gay/lesbian family's lifestyle is known to the family of origin, interaction between the two groups presents difficulty especially in regard to the grandparents' interactions with and influence upon the grandchildren.

Grandparents' Interaction with and Influence upon Grandchildren

Continuing contact with grandchildren who are a part of a gay/lesbian stepfamily requires much rethinking by the grandparents. Grandparents who may ostracize their children because of their lifestyle risk emotional loss of their grandchildren as well. In the author's experience grandparents often experience conflict between their wish to ostracize their own child and an equally intense desire to maintain contact with their grandchildren. Many grandparents have resolved the conflict through compartmentalization of the situation. That is, they continue to ostracize their gay/lesbian child and to lavish attention on the grandchildren. Seeing the grandchildren is often the explicit reason offered for grandparents' visits to the gay/lesbian family.

Like their counterparts in heterosexual interracial stepfamilies (Baptiste, 1984), children in gay/lesbian stepfamilies may be negatively influenced by their grandparents. Grandparental objection about the family's living arrangements are often made directly to the children. Objections frequently express the grandparents' feeling that the adults' relationship is unhealthy and eventually will create difficulties for the children. On occasion, parents of the heterosexual noncustodial parent or of the custodial gay/lesbian parent, rather than the noncustodial parent, have petitioned the courts for custody of their minor grandchildren. Three such grandparents known to the author have petitioned and won custody of their noncustodial son's children because the childrens' mothers were lesbians.

RELATIONSHIPS WITH THE GAY/LESBIAN COMMUNITY

Gay/lesbian stepparent families' relationships with gay/lesbian communities is a double-edged sword which presents such families with difficulties in at least three areas: their role as parents, their role as a gay/lesbian stepfamily, and their role as gay/lesbian persons.

Perhaps the most worrisome of the three roles in which the adults in such families must relate with other gays/lesbians is that of parent. Although many gays/lesbians are parents, the gay/lesbian community is essentially a childless one, and many gay men and lesbians do not approve of parenthood. Consequently, not only are gay/lesbian parents disapproved of by the heterosexual community, they are also disapproved of and even rejected by the gay/lesbian community. In this regard, Bozett (1981) has observed that whereas having children is a status passage in the heterosexual world, in the homosexual world it is often a stigma, especially for gay men.

Despite their commitment to a homosexual lifestyle, gay/lesbian parenting responsibilities become superordinate to sexual orientation and lifestyle. As a result, gay/lesbian parents live a marginal existence and experience much difficulty in reconciling their seemingly incongruous identities — homosexual and parent.

Gay/lesbian parents in stepfamilies often complain of ostracism by their gay/lesbian peers and of the tremendous feeling of isolation which such ostracism engenders. Ostracism from the heterosexual community is expected by gays/lesbians, but ostracism from their homosexual peers is unexpected and is often experienced as hurt, resentment and, often, identity confusion.

Ostracism of the adults is often extended to the children in these families. On occasion, in order to be accepted by gay/lesbian peers, some gay/lesbian parents will conceal from other gays/lesbians the fact that they are parents, biological or step. As a result, some children in gay/lesbian stepfamilies tend to be shadowy figures in the family and are not as exposed to their parents' friends to the same extent as are children in most heterosexual stepfamilies.

The difficulties experienced by gay/lesbian parents in relating to the gay community significantly affects their sense of self as gay/lesbian persons. For many of these parents, identification as a parent is equally as important as identification as a gay man or a lesbian. However, like other minority groups striving for solidarity of its members, the gay/lesbian community often demands "political correctness" (that is, the proper and appropriate group approved expression of one's gay/lesbian identity) from its members. Parenthood is not perceived to be "politically correct" in the gay/lesbian community! Political activism as well as "openness" about being gay/lesbian are considered "politically correct." Because of gay/lesbian parents' need for secrecy about their lifestyle they are more often than not unable to exhibit the political correctness required to remain "in good standing" with their gay/lesbian peers. As a result, maintaining contact with the gay/lesbian community as well as maintaining an identity as a gay/lesbian becomes increasingly difficult for gay/lesbian parents.

Gay/lesbian parents tend to relate to the gay/lesbian community in different ways because of their different needs for membership in their respective community. In the author's experience most lesbians — whether parents or nonparents — tend to view the lesbian community as an extended family. Consequently, many of them, even those who continue to maintain satisfactory relationships with their families of origin after coming out, often turn to the lesbian community for support (thus, the intense feeling of hurt when they are ostracized) in much the same way that heterosexual women typically turn to their families of origin for support.

For many lesbian parents, especially those rejected by their own families of origin, the lesbian community becomes a family to which they can turn for support and assistance in good times as well as bad times, for example, celebration of holidays or emotional and financial support during a crisis. For lesbian partners in stepfamilies, such groups can also provide support with the various tasks of parenting (for example, childcare) since such parents can look only to heterosexual parents for models of parenting in the absence of any explicit models for gay parenting with which they can identify.

Characteristically, beyond the focus on sexual orientation, gay men tend to manifest less of a need for a supportive community similar to lesbians (Jay & Young, 1979). However, gay male parents — biological or step — in stepfamilies tend to support the idea and need for a sense of community especially with other gay male parents because of their need for support and assistance in their parenting roles. For these parents, the gay community functions in much the same manner and fills a similar void as that of the lesbian community.

RELATIONSHIP BETWEEN THE PARTNERS

Currently there are many myths and misconceptions about the relationships of gay/lesbian partners. For example, it is erroneously believed that in such relationships one partner always assumes the male role while the other assumes the female role. Contrary to these prevailing myths, however, observations of the relationships of gay/lesbian partners in stepfamilies reveal that such partners do not assume dominant and submissive (that is, butch-femme) sex roles similar to heterosexual couples in traditional relationships, marital or common-law. Such polarization of roles among gay/lesbian partners in committed relationships, especially when children are members of the household, tends to be rare. Partners tend to emulate the sex role patterns similar to egalitarian heterosexual couples in the society.

Although currently there are some models for gay/lesbian couples' relationships, there are very few visible models for the relationships of gay/lesbian couples living as stepfamilies. For example, unlike heterosexual couples, homosexual couples see neither other homosexual couples in relationships on TV nor public expressions of such relationships. When such relationships are shown on TV or in film, the portrayal is often negative. The dyadic relationship is also significantly affected in positive as well as negative ways by the presence of children and the responsibilities attendant to parenting children.

The presence of children in the family significantly alters the relationship between the partners and tends to increase the partners' investment in "passing" as heterosexual single parents to protect against society's negative sanctions. Under such circumstances, partners are closed rather than open in the presentation of their relationship to both the children and outsiders. That is, they never become socially or politically involved with the gay/lesbian communities and spend little time in situations and circumstances specific to gay/lesbian lifestyles. Instead they tend to spend more time with nongay persons because of the children and the need to be perceived as nonhomosexual.

Relationship Difficulties

Like all couples with children who live together in a marital or common-law relationship, but especially in stepfamilies, gay/lesbian partners in stepfamily relationships experience some degree of difficulty in their relationships. Much of the partners' relationship difficulties can be directly attributed to their unique life circumstances and the difficulties experienced in maintaining a sense of being a couple in a proheterosexual culture that neither recognizes nor supports the status and concept of gay/lesbian marriages or family (Bernstein, 1977).[3] Partners in such families are also confronted by issues related to: parent-child, especially stepparent-stepchildren conflicts; intimacy and sexuality in the relationship; and maintenance of the dyadic boundaries.

Parent-child Conflicts

Like their heterosexual counterparts, gay/lesbian partners in stepfamilies experience biological as well as stepparent-children conflicts specific to stepfamily living. For gay/lesbian partners, however, the usual parent-children conflicts attendant to living in a stepfamily become complicated because of the structure of the family and the fact that children — biological and step — may be unaware they are living in a stepfamily.

Three of the more common causes of parent-child conflicts in these families are: (1) rejection of the stepparent by the partner's children; (2) competition for the biological parent's time and affection; and (3) the loss of parental role function by the stepparent. Many gay/lesbian parents often enter into stepfamily living after living as a single parent for a while. During that period the biological parent and his/her children often evolve a routine for living and establish homeostasis and rules of functioning which are interrupted by the introduction of the stepparent into the family. Children who are accustomed to behaving in a particular manner in the family often become resentful of the stepparent's presence and soon rebel. Frequently, the stepparent-child conflict spreads to the dyadic relationship and creates new problems for the couple.

Stepparent-child competition for the biological parent's time and affection is also related to the introduction of the stepparent into the single-parent family. The stepparent represents an adult with whom the biological parent can share affection when previously the children were the primary source and/or recipient of the parents' affection. In such situations partners who are themselves parents tend to be more understanding of the stepchild's behavior and are more likely to work with the biological parent to reach an amicable solution than are nonparent partners. Nonparent partners often perceive the partner's children to be an interference in the dyadic relationship. Such partners often demand that the dyadic relationship be the primary relationship, and that they be first in the other partner's hierarchy of relationships (Baptiste, 1987). As a result, the relationship usually develops problems if the biological parent attempts to appease both the children and the partner rather than seek a meaningful solution.

Stepparent partners often experience loss of parental role function because of lack of legitimacy as a part of the family unit. Often such a partner is neither introduced as a stepparent to the children nor is perceived by the children to be functioning in a stepparent role similar to that of heterosexual stepparents they may know. Not unlike heterosexual stepfamilies, the situation is further complicated by the ill defined stepparent role and absence of appropriate language with which to describe both the role and its functions.

Intimacy and sexuality in the relationship.

Because of the unique circumstances of the partners, the secrecy needed to maintain the relationship and the presence of children in the household, significant constraints are placed on both the intimacy and sexuality of the partners. Thus, partners in gay/lesbian stepfamilies experience much stress in being intimate at home (for example, spending time alone apart from the children) as well as outside the home.

Intimacy in the home is likely to be very different for the partners especially if the children are unaware of the relationship. Because children are present in the home, partners are not free to be openly affectionate with each other. Furthermore, partners need to exercise extreme caution lest they be discovered in a compromising situation such as sharing a bed. Not surprisingly, then, the compromises needed to maintain the illusion of heterosexuality in the presence of the children places the entire family, but especially the adults, under tremendous pressure.

Outside the home the partners face additional obstacles to being intimate. When in public, partners are constrained from expressing openly their affection for each other in intimate ways such as holding hands, hugging, or kissing. These are behaviors that routinely are publicly exhibited by heterosexual couples, and that are negatively sanctioned only when there are compelling reasons to do so or when they are exhibited by homosexuals.

Partners in gay/lesbian stepfamilies must also deal with the issue of sexual exclusivity versus sexual openness. Often, partners in long term relationships may lapse into sexual boredom either because of lack of sexual variety or because of the partners' diminished sexual desire. Central to the issue of sexual exclusivity/sexual openness is the level of trust between partners, especially gay males. Gay males tend to be less sexually exclusive in their relationships than are lesbians (Jay & Young, 1979). Often because of one partner's fear of infidelity by the other partner, the fearful partner may demand such stringent expressions of fidelity that the other partner is unable to comply. Unless partners are able to overcome these problems, they may face a situation which is more conflict prone than is true for partners in heterosexual stepfamilies.

Maintenance of dyadic boundaries.

Like the general family relationship, the dyadic relationship of gay/lesbian partners is vulnerable to boundary violations (by the children and others), which frequently can lead to dissolution of the relationship and the family as well. Because of the secrecy needed to "pass" in the heterosexual world, gay/lesbian partners in stepfamily relationships often pretend that they are no more than friends who are living together with their children.

Because others are unaware of the commitment of the relationship they often make demands upon the couple's time and energy and often intrude upon the dyadic boundaries. However, had the couple been heterosexual, the relationship boundaries would have been respected whether or not it was known that they were in a committed relationship. For example, one lesbian partner in therapy reported that post divorce her partner's ex-husband had been spending much time at their home, on occasions uninvited. The partner maintained an amicable co-parent relationship with the spouse for the children's sake as well as to deflect any suspicion about her lifestyle. The ex-husband's presence inhibited the partner's intimacy. He ignored hints that their "space be respected." On one occasion, the ex-husband was present when another male came to the couple's house. The ex-husband hid because he believed that the man was romantically involved with his ex-wife. He later explained that he did not want to intrude, although he had continually done so with the lesbian couple.

When the boundaries of the dyadic relationship are constantly violated by the children or others, the partners may experience much difficulty in maintaining a high level of intimacy in the relationship. And although some couples' relationship may survive these violations, many do not and result in the break up of the dyadic relationship and the family.

CHILDREN IN GAY/LESBIAN STEPFAMILIES

Because of the erroneous belief that it is unhealthy for children to live in homes parented by two gay/lesbian persons, many heterosexuals, epitomized by the courts and social service agencies, believe that removal of children from gay/lesbian homes is in the best interests of the children.

The belief that a gay/lesbian home is unhealthy for children is predicated on at least four fears:

1. Fear, especially in the case of gay fathers, that children might be sexually molested by the biological parent or the parent's partner. This fear persists although paedophilia appears to be disproportionately a heterosexual behavior (Hill, 1978; Miller, 1978); gay/lesbian parents virtually never commit such acts (Richardson, 1981).
2. Fear that children of gay parents are more likely to become gay adults or develop variant sexual behaviors. Contrary to this belief, a number

of research findings refute the notion that gay/lesbian parents will produce gay/lesbian children in numbers greater than might be expected of nongay parents (Green, 1982; Hotvedt & Mandel, 1982; Kirkpatrick, Smith & Roy, 1981).

3. Fear that children will be harmed by the stigmatizing process that inevitably surrounds such lifestyles.

4. Fear that children living in a gay/lesbian household, but especially with gay men, are more at risk of being infected with Acquired Immune Deficiency Syndrome, since it is erroneously believed by many that AIDS is solely a gay man's disease. In this regard AIDS has become a vehicle by which homophobia is legitimized in the minds of some Americans who cling to traditional values.

Because of these prevailing attitudes, even under the best of circumstances, children in gay stepfamilies experience some difficulties that are different from their heterosexual counterparts since it is not easy to grow up in a family disapproved of by society and to be labeled as pathological or undesirable by association. Furthermore, the current national hysteria about AIDS in the homosexual community has intensified society's disapproval of gays/lesbians and their lifestyles and, by extension, the children living in such families.

Stepsibling Relationships

Difficulties in the stepsibling relationship where both partners are custodial parents are frequently a concern for children. In general many of the issues tend to be similar for gay/lesbian as for heterosexual stepfamilies, for example, altered ordinal position, competition, and sexuality. In heterosexual stepfamilies, nonsanguine sibs are stepsibs. However, in gay stepfamilies, because legal ties are absent and children are often not aware that they are in a steprelationship, the appellation "stepsib" is not only inappropriate but confusing. Much of the confusion results from the children's perception of the nature of their relationship with their parent's partner and his/her children since neither the partner's presence nor role is well defined. The partner's children are, by extension, perceived by the children in the same light as the partner. Frequently, parents (biological and step), in their desire for increased family cohesion, will request that their children behave toward their partner's children in a manner similar to that expected for stepsibs in heterosexual stepfamilies, for example, babysit for or escort to a social event outside the home.

Unfortunately, because children are uncommitted to a "stepsib relationship," parental requests for fraternal cooperation between the two sets of children are resented and often rejected by the children. Furthermore, because the relationship of the couple is often a secret in the community, publicly referring to the children of one's parent's partner as stepsibs removes the veil of secrecy and may expose the family to negative sanctions from the community. As a result of the ambiguity, children experience much difficulty in relating to the children of their parent's partner, even when they are aware that the adults are living in a gay relationship.

Children's Relationships with Age Mate Kin

Children in gay/lesbian stepfamilies often express feeling isolated from and even rejected by heterosexual peers and their age mate kin as well. Parents of their age mate kin often discourage or limit their children's interaction with children living in gay/lesbian stepfamilies because of the perceived stigma attendant to their living situation. Relatives are often afraid that by associating with such children their own children will be coerced to be gay/lesbian, be infected with AIDS if the partners are male, or that the parents themselves may be perceived to be condoning a gay/lesbian lifestyle and family.

IMPLICATIONS FOR PROFESSIONALS

The implications for professionals in a variety of disciplines are multiple and diverse. However, space limitations demand that only the most salient be considered briefly in this section.

Educators

Although there currently exists a vast literature about gays/lesbians, ignorance, suspicion, and general homophobia about such persons and their lifestyles still abound. For this reason, then, it is important that educators at all levels begin early in the educational process to provide factual information in order to dispel the pervasive myths and misconceptions about gays/lesbians and their lifestyles.

Perhaps the most damaging myths about gays/lesbians is that such persons do not become parents. It is felt that those who persist in doing so should not be allowed to raise children. Because of the tenacity of this myth, gays/lesbians who are parents and choose to raise their children either alone or with a partner are denied the same recognition accorded heterosexual parents, biological, step, or even a parent cohabiting in a common-law relationship.

In the best interests of the children and parents in gay/lesbian stepfamilies educators need to disseminate information about alternative family forms, especially gay/lesbian families. This can help dispel the many myths that are so damaging to these parents and the children who live with them.

For public school teachers in particular the need for factual information about gay/lesbian families is crucial since the teacher's attitude toward both the children and their parents is important in helping the children deal effectively with their "difference." Often a gay/lesbian partner who has successfully adjusted to the stepparenting role can be made to feel left out by school authorities when dealing with such authorities on behalf of either the children or the family.

Mental Health Professionals

Many of the difficulties that gay/lesbian stepfamilies encounter in dealing with educators are also encountered in dealing with mental health professionals. Although both the American Psychological Association and the American Psychiatric Association have removed homosexuality from their lists of illnesses, many mental health professionals still subscribe to psychological theories about homosexuality which are influenced by homonegative beliefs. Such beliefs hold that homosexuals are immature and homosexuality is unhealthy.

Like their heterosexual counterparts, some gay/lesbian parents and their children may seek therapy. However, it is important to remember that there are many more gay/lesbian parents who neither need nor seek therapy for themselves or their children. For those who seek therapy, it is important that they receive assistance from professionals who are knowledgeable about gays/lesbians and their lifestyles, are sensitive to their personal biases and prejudices with regard to gay men and lesbians in general and as parents, and are aware that such attitudes can intrude and negatively affect the therapeutic process and its outcome.

Since many gay/lesbian parents and children must deal with the rejection and ostracism attendant to their lifestyle, they often seek therapeutic help when they tend to be at the lowest ebb of their lives. Consequently, mental health professionals need to understand the implications of their interventions with these families. If the intervention is supportive and recognizes the different expressions of loss, the professional will go a long way in helping the gay/lesbian family. If, however, the professional's homonegative beliefs do not allow him/her to unconditionally accept the gay/lesbian person or a child living in such a household, he/she should not accept the client. To do so is fraudulent!

SUMMARY AND CONCLUSIONS

This chapter has described and discussed the dynamics of gay/lesbian stepparent families, the particular issues faced by them, their relationship with the larger community, issues specific to children in these families, and the relationship between the adult partners.

Both the adults and children in these families experience many difficulties in relating to external systems. Adult members experience the greatest difficulties in their roles as parents since both the heterosexual and much of the homosexual worlds tend to approve neither of gay/lesbian parenthood nor of children being raised in homes parented by two gay/lesbian parents.

Children growing up in gay/lesbian families also face special difficulties attendant to their membership in such families. Relationships with biological as well as stepparents and "stepsiblings," if any are present, can be difficult whether or not the children are aware that they are a part of a gay/lesbian stepfamily. Additionally, relationships, with heterosexual peers as well as age mate kin, grandparents, noncustodial parents, and school officials often constitute problems because of the "closeted" existence of the family and the de facto isolation experienced by such children.

The relationship between the adult partners is also negatively affected by the societal proscription against their lifestyles, their right to be parents, and to parent children.

Despite the difficulties attendant to living as a gay/lesbian couple and raising children in such a family, gay/lesbian stepfamilies are viable alternatives and are positive environments in which to raise children effectively. However, to be effective in their functioning such families, compared to most heterosexual families, need more effort by all members. The ability of gay/lesbian parents to effectively rear children is reduced because societal intolerance often translates into public policies that create challenges with regard to child custody or visitation rights.

Finally, the hope for the future is that all gays/lesbians, but especially gays/lesbians as parents, will become better understood in the society. Future public policy will accurately reflect what is empirically known about homosexuals, homosexuality, and homosexual parenting families and, by so doing, help these families avert the needless pain so many of them had experienced in the past.

RECOMMENDATIONS FOR FURTHER STUDY

Although much has been written about gays/lesbians as individuals, as couples and as parents there is very little written about gays/lesbians and their children living as a unit in stepfamily relationships. In the last fifteen years there has appeared a virtual avalanche of interest and literature about stepfamily relationships. Unfortunately, however, gays/lesbians living as stepfamilies did not receive equal attention or literature. To better understand this unique subset of stepfamilies and better serve their equally unique needs, more research studies that focus on these families are needed.

The greatest need is for longitudinal investigations using multiple research methods and designs that will study these families over-time. Based upon the currently available literature, there are many questions about the functioning of these families that cry out for research. The following then are some brief suggestions for further research in this unresearched area. These suggestions are not intended to be exhaustive but are intended to stimulate discussion and thought and some future research about many of the unverified perceptions of these families.

1. While a few studies have examined the psychological development of children in lesbian stepfamilies, none to date have examined the adult adjustment of children who have been raised in homes parented by two gay/lesbian persons. Such studies are needed.

2. Since a majority of the available literature pertaining to homosexual parenting examines lesbian parenting, there is a critical need to study stepfamilies parented by gay males.

3. Many studies have examined the formation of heterosexual stepfamilies and have suggested ways to improve this process. Similar studies should be conducted for gay/lesbian stepfamilies.

NOTES

1. A national poll conducted in December 1985, revealed that although the nation's sympathy for homosexuals has increased (compared to 1973), most Americans continue to disapprove strongly of homosexuality. (*Sun News*, Las Cruces, NM, December 10, 1985, p. 6A).

2. During debate on an amendment forbidding placement of foster children in homes deemed to pose a psychological and social threat to them, Royal Switzer, a Massachusetts State Representative stated, "to knowingly place children with individuals who are known homosexuals is not in the best psychological interest of the children." (*Sun News*, Las Cruces, NM, May 24, 1986, p. 6A).

3. As evidence of this situation the AP Wire Service recently reported that the American Civil Liberties Union plans to actively seek elimination of legal barriers to gay/lesbian marriages. (*Sun News*, Las Cruces, NM, October 28, 1986, p. 5B).

REFERENCES

Ahrons, C. (1986, October 24). Divorce rancor often lingers, hurts children. *Sun News*, Las Cruces, New Mexico, p. 1A.

Baptiste, D. (1982). Issues and guidelines in the treatment of gay stepfamilies. In A. Gurman (Ed.), *Questions and answers in the practice of family therapy.* Vol. 2. New York: Brunner/Mazel, pp. 225–229.

____. (1984). Marital and family therapy with racially/culturally intermarried stepfamilies: Issues and guidelines. *Family Relations, 33* (3), 373–380.

____. (1987). Psychotherapy with gay/lesbian couples and their children in "stepfamilies": A challenge for marriage and family therapist. *Journal of Homosexuality, 14*, 217–232.

Bell, A., & Weinberg, M. (1978). *Homosexualities.* New York: Simon & Shuster.

Bernstein, B. (1977). Legal and social interface in counseling homosexual clients. *Social Casework, 58* (1), 36–40.

Bozett, F. (1981). Gay fathers: Identity conflict resolution through integrative sanctioning. *Alternative Lifestyles, 4* (1), 90–107.

____. (1985). Gay men as fathers. In S. Hanson & F. Bozett (Eds.), *Dimensions of fatherhood.* Beverly Hills, CA: Sage, pp. 327–352.

Burgess, E. (1973). The family as a unit of interacting personalities. In G. Erickson & T. Hogan (Eds.), *Family therapy: An introduction to theory and technique.* Monterey, CA: Brooks/Cole.

Cheers, M. (1983, March 28). Florida interracial couple loses custody battle. *Jet*, 36–38.

Einstein, E. (1982) *The stepfamily*. New York: MacMillian.

Glick, P. (1984). Marriage, divorce and living arrangements: Prospective changes. *Journal of Family Issues, 5* (1); 7–26.

Goffman, E. (1963). *Stigma*. Englewood Cliffs, NJ: Prentice Hall.

Goodman, B. (1980). Some mothers are lesbians. In E. Norman & A. Mancuso (Eds.), *Women's Issues and social work practice*. Itasca, IL, pp. 153–180.

Green, R. (1982). The best interests of the child with a lesbian mother. *Bulletin of the American Academy of Psychiatry and Law, 10* (1), 7–15.

Hall, M. (1978). Lesbian families: Cultural and clinical issues. *Social Work, 23* (5), 380–385.

Harry, J. (1983). Gay male and lesbian relationships. In E. Macklin & R. Rubin (Eds.), *Contemporary families and alternative lifestyles*. Beverly Hills, CA: Sage.

Hoeffer, B. (1978). Single mothers and their children: Challenging traditional concepts of the American family. In P. Brandt et al. (Eds.), *Current Practice in Pediatric Nursing*. St. Louis, MO, C. V. Mosby.

Hotvedt, M., & Mandel, J. (1982). Children of lesbian mothers. In W. Paul, J. Weinrich, J. Gonsiorek, & M. Hotvedt, (Eds.), *Homosexuality: Social, psychological and biological issues*. Beverly Hills, CA: Sage.

Jay, K. & Young, A. (1979). *The gay report*. New York: Summit Books.

Kirkpatrick, M., Smith, K., & Roy, D. (1981). Lesbian mothers and their children: A comparative survey. *The American Journal of Orthopsychiatry, 51*, 545–51.

Lewin, E. & Lyons, T. (1982). Everything in its place: The coexistence of lesbianism and motherhood. In W. Paul, J. Weinrich, J. Gonsiorek, & M. Hotvedt. *Homosexuality: Social psychological and biological issues*. Beverly Hills, CA: Sage.

Maddox, B. (1975). *The half parent*. New York: M. Evans.

_____. (1982, February). Homosexual parents. *Psychology Today, 12*, 62–69.

Martin, D. & Lyon, P. (1972). *Lesbian/Woman*. New York: Bantam Books.

Miller, B. (1978). Adult sexual resocialization. *Alternative Lifestyles, 1* (2), 207–238.

Nobel, J. (1981). *Where do I fit in?* New York: Holt, Rinehart and Winston.

Nobel, J., & Nobel, W. (1977). *How to live with other people's children* . New York: Hawthorne.

Palmore v. Sidoti, 426 So. 2nd 34 (Fla. App. 1982).

Richardson, D. (1981). Lesbian mothers. In J. Hart & D. Richardson (Eds.) *The theory and practice of homosexuality*. London: Routledge and Kegan Paul.

Riddle, D., & Arguelles, M. (1981). Children of gay parents: Homophobia's victims. In I. Stuart & L. Abt (Eds.) *Children of separation and divorce: Management and treatment*. New York: Van Nostrand Reinhold.

Robinson, D. & Barret, R. (1986). *The developing father*. New York: Guildford.

Ross, H. & Sawhill, I. (1975). *Time of transition*. Washington, D.C.: The Urban Institute.

Sager, C., Brown, H., Crohn, H., Engel, T., Rodstein, E., & Walker, L. (1983). *Treating the remarried family*. New York: Brunner/Mazel.

Schulenburg, Joy (1985). *Gay parenting*. New York: Doubleday.

Skeen, P. & Robinson, B. (1984). Family background of gay fathers. *Psychological Reports, 54*, 999–1005.

____. (1985). Gay fathers and nongay fathers. Relationships with their parents. *Journal of Sex Research, 21*, 86–91.

Visher, E., & Visher, J. (1979). *Stepfamilies*. New York: Brunner/Mazel.

Voellers, B., & Walters, J. (1978). Gay fathers. *The Family Coordinator, 27*, 149–157.

8

THE HETEROSEXUALLY MARRIED GAY AND LESBIAN PARENT

David R. Matteson

Households headed by a man and a woman are not "suspect" in the way that households with two adult women or two adult men living together would be. If the husband is gay, or the wife is lesbian, those not otherwise informed are likely to view the couple as an "ordinary" couple, making it easy for these parents to "pass" as nongay. In fact, in most cases, at the time of their marriage both spouses identified themselves as heterosexual. Even later, when they have come to terms with their homosexual inclinations, it is more descriptive to use the term "bisexual," at least in regard to their history, and in most cases their present behavior. The term "bisexual" will be used throughout this chapter, although it is recognized that married gays vary regarding whether they prefer the term "gay" or "bisexual" (Matteson, 1985), and give personal identity and political reasons for each choice.

Before discussing mixed-orientation couples and their children, the process of developing a bisexual identity will be clarified. This will be followed by a description of the phases undergone by couples in these marriages, based on research to date. Implications for the children in each of these phases are discussed, although these are somewhat speculative since few studies provide data regarding them (Miller, 1979a, 1979b; Matteson, 1985; Matteson, in process, a). The issue of disclosure of the bisexual lifestyle to children is also reviewed. Social changes that are presently affecting families of mixed-orientation couples are noted. Finally, the special needs of these families and their implications for professionals are listed, and priorities for future research are suggested.

BISEXUAL DEVELOPMENT

The development of a gay or lesbian identity has been discussed elsewhere (Cass, 1979; McDonald, 1982; Weinberg, 1978; see also Chapters 1 and 2). Bisexuals, like gays and lesbians, are generally reared in heterosexual homes by heterosexual parents and learn of their minority status only through their private fantasies or experiences. For the bisexual, these fantasies and experiences usually involve both sexes, making it even more difficult to unravel how one does and does not fit the heterosexual norm.

Because of this difficulty, as well as the lack of models for alternative lifestyles, it is likely that the majority of bisexuals drift into the "normal" heterosexual lifestyle before they fully identify themselves as bisexual. Joe, for example, was aware as an adolescent of some interest in men, but was comfortable dating women, fell in love with Nancy and married her with little thought about his "adolescent" experimentation with males. He felt good about his own childhood and knew he wanted to have a family. After marrying, fantasies and dreams about sex with men began to bother him. These "obsessions" finally led him to seek out gay bars and, eventually, to affirm the "gay side" of his sexual orientation.

Visual fantasies and dreams play an important role in discovering one's sexual orientation for a large portion of the bisexual married men studied (Matteson, 1985). Dan provides a prototype of this visual style:

> Dan was in his late twenties when I first interviewed him. He and his wife had good communication; both were sensitive persons, and well-educated. But Dan was worried that the majority of his sexual dreams and fantasies were of homosexual relationships. He joined a support-group for married bisexual men. Two years later I learned he had left his wife and was living in the gay community. Though most of his sexual activity was now with men, he reported that many of his fantasies and sexual dreams were now of women.

We can hypothesize that men whose arousal pattern is primarily visual, and whose sexual fantasies and dreams are exclusively of other men, have a clear inner response pattern that may aid them in moving to a gay identity. However, men who have a mixed pattern (either both visual and kinesthetic arousal, or arousal to both same-sexed and other-sexed visual stimuli) may not be able to clarify their sexual orientation until they have had considerable experience. A common pattern in my sample of thirty bisexual married men involved a kinesthetic "turn-on" to women, but a visual "turn-on" to men. Jim, one of the men in a support group for bisexual married men, stated, "I can be satiated with sex with my wife, but still be horny as hell for a man; it's like I have two different kinds of horny." These men frequently had thought of themselves as heterosexual because they were responsive sexually once they had an emotional relationship with a woman (kinesthetic). Only later, after their sexual inhibitions and homophobia decreased, did they recognize the fact that their visual interest was homosexual.

Most of the bisexual husbands in my study became aware of their homosexual interests through visual fantasies (Matteson, 1985). This contrasts sharply to the experience of most bisexual women in marriages, whose first awareness of lesbian desires emerged out of emotional attraction to a particular woman friend. This fits the sexual arousal pattern I call kinesthetic.[1] Shirley, the wife of a bisexual man in my study (Matteson, 1985), is a clear example of the kinesthetic pattern:

> Shirley is married to a bisexual man, but is herself completely heterosexual. . . . In her experience, sexual feelings emerge from a deep emotional relationship. She has no problem with others having gay or lesbian sex, though other women do not "turn her on." However, she finds it difficult to understand why someone would want to have sex with anyone except their primary partner, although she did, during her husband's bisexual coming out, explore extramarital sex.

For the person whose arousal is largely kinesthetic, emotional intimacy and physical touch with a close friend, or some other situation in which there is physical closeness (see Dixon, 1985), may lead to sexual experimentation and the discovery that same-sex arousal is part of one's repertoire. Lesbians are equally or more likely to have been previously married than their gay male counterparts (Bell & Weinberg, 1978; Masters & Johnson, 1979; Saghir & Robbins, 1973; reviewed in Wilson, 1986). This may be attributed to the fact that women generally marry earlier than men and have less opportunity to explore their sexual orientation than do men. Lesbians tend to have their first homosexual experiences at about age twenty, which is five years later than the average for gay males (Kooden et al., 1979). If the first lesbian experience was an outgrowth of a deep friendship, based on kinesthetic response, it would likely be perceived as a personal event; only after a number of such events is the woman likely to perceive the pattern and identify herself as bisexual or lesbian (Coleman, 1985b).

We can hypothesize that men tend to discover their sexual orientation first through visual experience, and women through kinesthetic experience. There is some evidence (though far from conclusive) that the privatized nature of masturbation in boys leads to the development of elaborate sexual fantasies that are far less common in adolescent girls, at least in our culture (Offer & Simon, 1975). Women in our culture often do not begin masturbation, or have explicit sexual fantasies, until they have had a fair amount of interpersonal sexual experience. They have a kinesthetic "awakening" and a kinesthetic "arousal pattern." The suggestion that the kinesthetic arousal pattern is more common for women and the visual for men is at best too simple, since many persons of each gender have a mixed pattern. The more important point is the distinction between the "kinesthetic" and "visual" components of sexual arousal.

Although Dan and Shirley are real persons (only the names have been changed), they are close to "ideal types." Dan has a visual arousal pattern; his fantasies and dreams led him to homosexual exploration and then back to bisexuality. For Shirley, however, the pathway to sexual arousal is emotional stimulation, physical touch, then arousal. (See Matteson, in process, b, for a more detailed discussion.)

The importance one places on each of these has implications for the person's experience of bisexuality. In our culture, men tend to value visual experience as the test of reality. (And most of the scientific experiments on sexual arousal, having been conducted by men, have used responses to visual stimuli as the criterion for sexual orientation). Some bisexual men question if they are really bisexual, because their visual responses are geared primarily to other men, even though they enjoy sex with the woman they love. They devalue the kinesthetic "turn-on." And some "pure visual" types, like Dan, do not experience their lives as complete unless they are having both male and female sexual partners concurrently. It is as if their visual expectations, which involve fantasies of both male and female partners, must be met.

On the other hand, some bisexuals are quite happy with monogamy. It makes very little difference if their lover is male or female. These persons are often sequentially bisexual, tending to alternate between male and female lovers. Such persons invariably emphasize a kinesthetic turn-on, and may experience bisexuality as a "choice": "I can live the heterosexual lifestyle, or I can live a lesbian lifestyle."

DEVELOPMENTAL PERIODS IN
MIXED-ORIENTATION MARRIAGES

A six-year longitudinal study of a nonclinical sample of forty-four spouses representing thirty mixed-orientation marriages provided the primary data on which this developmental schema was based (Matteson, 1985; Matteson, in process, a). Twenty-four of the couples had children. A comparison was made between couples in which the homosexual behavior of the husband was acknowledged and those in which it is secretive (in which only the husband was interviewed), based on data from detailed semi-structured interviews. Data from this study suggested personality and communication patterns that differentiated the couples who acknowledged the husbands' bisexuality from couples who maintained a "conspiracy of silence" (though not all couples fell neatly into these categories). Husbands in the acknowledged group were far more likely to develop positive gay or bisexual identities. Two years later, acknowledged couples and secretive couples were equally likely (66 percent) still to be married. When four more years had passed, none who were together at the two-year follow-up had separated. Some of the couples who had not acknowledged the bisexuality earlier had done so by the time of this six-year follow-up.

In what follows, information regarding the children is based on parents' reports; at present no data have been collected directly from the children of mixed-orientation marriages.

Phase 1: Entering the Marriage

Less than one-third of the bisexual husbands (Matteson, 1985) and less than one-third of the bisexual wives (Coleman, 1985b) in mixed-orientation marriages thought of themselves as gay/lesbian before marriage. A few of these spouses considered themselves bisexual but assumed that the homosexual desires would fade in the context of healthy marital sex. The majority presumed themselves heterosexual or believed their bisexuality would make monogamous marriage possible. The vast majority remained monogamous for a number of years after marrying. Thus, for most of the couples, the issue of homosexual behavior and the division into secretive or acknowledged marriages did not arise until some years into the marriage (see phase 3 below).

The reasons bisexual husbands gave for marrying are similar to those of most men who marry: they wanted a wife and family, and they loved a particular woman (interviews for Matteson, 1985; Ross, 1983). The bisexual wives also indicated love for their husbands and family pressures as the major reasons for marrying (Coleman, 1985b).

For a few, hoping to overcome their homosexuality through marriage, childbirth was an especially momentous occasion, one interpreted as confirmation of their heterosexuality.

> Going through natural childbirth with my wife, it seemed like I had crossed the bridge. I was very much in love with JoAnn, and . . . had confirmed that I was "normal" (Matteson, 1979).

The importance of having a family was especially clear for those men who were still in their marriages years later; they listed "children" as one of the best things about marriage, second only to "companionship" (Ross, 1983). That is not to say this opinion is unanimous. One father, highly invested in his profession, stated:

> I like (the children's) attention, but I frequently do not allow myself to enjoy it as I'm trying to do three things at the same time. And if I didn't see them for a week, it would be perfectly fine (Matteson, 1985).

Phase 2: Developing the Primacy of the Marriage

Data from the author's research suggests that, in those mixed-orientation marriages that became stable, the first five or more years of the marriage was a period of developing the primacy of the marital relationship (Matteson, 1985). It seems crucial that a high level of intimacy and trust be developed before extramarital relationships can be openly tolerated.

During this period of primacy, there is little reason to believe that the childrearing of these couples was any different than that of heterosexual couples. The bisexual spouses, for the most part, have accepted the heterosexual model of marriage and family.

Phase 3: Sexual Identity Crisis

However, some years into the marriage same-sex desires reemerged for almost all the husbands; these desires became compelling and were acted upon. The assumption that homosexual desires will decrease if the person marries and has regular heterosexual relationships is simply not supported by the research evidence (Bozett, 1982; Matteson, 1985; Miller, 1978; Ross, 1983). Studies of bisexual married men consistently have reported that most of the husbands experienced an increase in their homosexual inclinations during the course of the marriage. Usually a year or two of sporadic homosexual activity occurred before the husbands experienced a crisis regarding their sexual identity (Matteson, 1985). The limited data available suggests that this process is different for bisexual wives. Although most of the bisexual husbands had had some homosexual experience, at least in adolescence (Coleman, 1985a; Matteson, 1985), the majority of bisexual wives (60 percent) had their first lesbian experience after they were married (Coleman, 1985b).

Secretive couples.

Many spouses keep these desires and behaviors separate and secret from their heterosexual spouse and their children. Perhaps they drop hints and get feedback that their spouses are too dependent or too rigid to tolerate more complete disclosure. Often a conspiracy of silence begins, leading to a spiral of mistrust and distance, along with guilt, which often destroys the emotional reality of the marriage (Bozett, 1982). The outward appearance of a conventional marriage may be maintained. These chronically secretive relationships, common among bisexual husbands are not maintained very long by bisexual wives (Coleman, 1985b).

Closeted homosexual fathers.

In an early study of bisexual fathers, Miller (1978) found that those still living with their wives were in highly closeted lifestyles. Miller categorized these men as "trade husbands" (unwilling to acknowledge their homosexual orientation even to themselves) and "homosexual husbands" (acknowledging it to themselves, but not to others). The main reason these husbands gave for remaining with their wives was the children. They all considered the experience of fathering as central to their lives. One stated, "In this horrible marriage, [the children] are the consolation prize." Another said, "My children are the only humans I have ever loved. My parents, my brothers, my wife don't mean beans to me. I need my kids; they're what keep me going" (Miller, 1978, p. 216). Similarly, one of the husbands in the author's study, who had not disclosed his bisexuality to his wife, said nothing was good in his marriage, or in the sexual relationship between him and his wife. But when he talked about his daughter he became animated and cheerful (Matteson, 1985).

Even grown children were given as a reason for staying in the marriage: "Since the beginning, I've kept saying, 'next year I'm leaving as soon as the children are bigger.' Now that they are in college, I can't leave because they are my judges. They'd never forgive me for doing this all these years to their mother" (Miller, 1978, p. 217).

Two studies have shown an inverse correlation between the number of children a couple have, and how open the bisexual husband is about his homosexuality (Matteson, 1985; Ross, 1983). However, those couples with more children are older and married earlier, so it is likely that the inverse correlation has more to do with historical factors than with the children themselves.

Many of these men were married long before the beginnings of gay liberation and feel that "the male couple" lifestyle is not a real option. Brownfain (1985) interviewed sixty bisexual husbands regarding the "contradiction between their heterosexual public identity, which places them comfortably in the mainstream of society, and their stigmatized and forbidden homosexual desires and behavior" (p. 173). Most of these appear to have been secretive couples. These men tend to separate the psychosocial and affectional life (with their families) from their erotic and sexual life (with other men). Many "love their wives and children and would not choose to be other than married, yet (their) chief sexual pleasure is homosexual." One husband, age fifty-six, who had his first homosexual experience only two years ago, stated:

> It bowled me over. I've had a number of experiences since and they all bowl me over. But they don't take anything away from my marriage. I feel about homosexuality the same way I feel about New York City. I love to visit but I wouldn't want to live there (Brownfain, 1985, p. 185).

> Only rarely and inadvertently did the children (of these highly closeted bisexual fathers) learn about their fathers' bisexual inclinations, (though) when they did they appeared to assimilate this knowledge with equanimity (Brownfain, 1985, p. 186).

Internalizing homophobia and rejecting or denying a part of their own selves must have effects on the husbands' self-esteem. We can only speculate (lacking research data) that this would affect their parenting and their children. Similarly, the downward spiral of communication in many of these marriages must affect the couples' ability to coparent. We can only hope that the children derive some benefit from these fathers, many of whom describe themselves as "very devoted" to their children.

Closeted bisexual mothers.

As noted, there is only one study of bisexual wives in heterosexual marriages (Coleman, 1985a). These marriages do not appear to last. The mixed-orientation couples in which the wife is bisexual have fewer children (average of 1.2) than those mixed-orientation marriages in which the husband is bisexual (average of 2.0), probably due to the shorter length of the bisexual wives' marriages (Coleman, 1985a). Although it is rare for either bisexual men or women to have established a clear bisexual identity and to disclose it to their spouses prior to the marriage, this happens more frequently with bisexual men than with bisexual women (Coleman, 1985a). Bisexual husbands were also more likely to disclose to their wives their homosexual feelings during the course of the marriage. Very few marriages of bisexual women reach the point of acknowledgement and continue (Coleman, 1985a). Hence, it is unlikely that many of these women would have disclosed to their children their sexual orientation while still living with their husbands. Unfortunately, there is no direct research data on the subject of the children of bisexual women in heterosexual marriages.

Acknowledged couples.

Some spouses do share their personal struggle regarding sexual orientation with their husband or wife early in the process of exploring same-sex relationships. Husbands' decisions to disclose their gay feelings early seem to be related to generally more open communication in the marriage, a higher comfort level with their own homosexual feelings, and a perception that their wives are strong and independent enough to tolerate the disclosure (Matteson, 1985).

Whether homosexuality is hidden or disclosed, during this phase the bisexual spouse becomes absorbed in an identity process, which often takes precedence over spouse and family; psychological withdrawal from the spouse and family for a period is the norm. Depending on the age and the personalities of the children, and the role that parent has taken up to this point in childrearing, this withdrawal may be traumatic, experienced as abandonment, or it may hardly be noticed, since it appears no different than absence due to job pressures or other reasons.

Phase 4: Marital Crisis

The period immediately following the disclosure (or discovery) is usually tumultuous. At first, bisexual spouses are so involved in issues related to their own sexual identities that they may be insensitive, or at best only reactive, to their spouses' needs. In some cases the heterosexual spouse makes a decision to reject the "negative" characteristics they have now discovered in their mate and end the marriage.

It is infrequent that bisexual husbands move to end the marriages; they experience sexual needs their wives can't fulfill but continue to want the intimacy they have had with their wives and families and are afraid of losing close contact with the children should they seek separation (Matteson, in process, a). Usually both partners experience a period of ambivalence. The bisexual husbands hope things will work out, but are unwilling to surrender their newly affirmed gay life, and the wives are deeply hurt and long for support. There is a tendency, in this crisis, to blame the problems in the marriage on the gay issue. Marriage counseling (with therapists who are familiar with open marriages and who are not heterosexist), and peer support groups seem particularly useful at this phase.

The pattern appears to be rather different when the wife is the bisexual spouse. These marriages appear to be short-lived compared to similar studies of bisexual husbands (Coleman, 1985b). In Coleman's (1985b) sample of bisexual women who were or had been in heterosexual marriages, only four of the forty-five women were still in marriages. Schulenburg (1985) was able to locate twenty-eight gay or bisexual fathers still in marriages, but only one bisexual wife was married to a heterosexual man, and that woman was still very much in "the closet" (p. 59). The reasons for this are not clear. Coleman suggests that women's sex role socialization trains them to be less tolerant of secretive extra-marital sex or open marriage. Further, their nongay husbands may be less tolerant of bisexual lifestyles than are the wives of bisexual married men.

Another possible explanation focuses on the fact that women in our culture are better trained for intimacy than are men (Matteson, in press, b). Bisexual husbands depend on their wives and family for intimacy and are uncertain that they can develop as much personal intimacy with another man. Bisexual wives often find greater personal intimacy with another woman than with their husbands; thus many women, once a deep friendship with another woman has become sexualized, experience a combination of emotional and sexual intimacy that they've never experienced with a man. There is less reason to hang on to marriage.

During this crisis, we can assume that many children will sense uncertainty. Two mixed-orientation couples in therapy with me have reported a child asking direct questions about whether something was wrong. The parents reported that the children seemed reassured when told that the parents were struggling with a problem, but that it was not something the child was responsible for and that they would continue to be Mom and Dad for the child whatever happened.

Phase 5: Negotiation and Stabilization of an Open Relationship

After a year or so of marital crisis, if the wives are able to acknowledge and accept the husband's bisexuality, the mixed-orientation marriages with bisexual husbands typically move into a renegotiation stage (Latham & White, 1978), either toward defining the marriage as an acknowledged bisexual marriage (often with extramarital experimentation on the wives' side) or toward amicable divorce and friendship, with shared parenting.

Parents who separate.

Miller (1978) described those separated fathers who have told their wives but are closeted to the world at large:

> Few (of these fathers) live with their children; rather they have structured a regular visiting schedule with them. They do not have the financial resources either to persuade their wives to relinquish the children or to hire surrogate care for them while devoting needed time to rise in their careers. A minimum of openness about homosexuality exists with respect to their children. Typically, only older children are told, and it is not considered a topic of general discussion. There is some fear that, if it becomes widely known in the same community that he is gay, his ex-wife will become irked and deny him

visiting privileges or his employer will dismiss him (Miller, 1978, pp. 218–219).

However, husbands who have truly affirmed and are open about being bisexual or gay and whose separations are amicable (with the ex-wife also affirming his gayness), often move to joint custody, or with the husband maintaining primary custodial care.

> A number of (gay-affirming) husbands have full-time custody of their children and are living with a lover. In all cases, the children are aware of their fathers' sexuality. Problems with child-rearing are not foreign to (these) fathers; but they appear to be no more than those reported by single heterosexual fathers with custody . . .
> Those who live with their children and lover are more sedentary and more apt to have a close circle of gay friends, rather than being at the center of gay social institutions. Most of these (gay-affirming) husbands waged difficult battles to obtain custody of their children and express concomitantly high commitment to spending considerable time with them (Miller, 1978, 220–221).

Data on lesbian mothers who have previously been married, and have separated from their husbands and maintained custody of the children, has been represented in a previous chapter and won't be reviewed here.

Couples who stay together.

If the couple survives two years of this renegotiation phase and remains together, chances are they will stay together indefinitely (Matteson, in process, a).

It takes approximately four years from the time of disclosure for the couple to develop mutually acceptable guidelines, adhere to them, and redevelop a stable marriage with secure intimacy. My longitudinal study of married bisexual men showed that positive gay or bisexual identities and stable mixed-orientation marriages are possible when both spouses acknowledge the husband's bisexual orientation (Matteson, 1985).

In this process, the heterosexual spouse learns that one cannot control the other's activities, but that one can state one's own needs clearly and firmly, and set one's limits of tolerance, and find ways to care for and entertain oneself when the spouse is not available. The bisexual husbands whose marriages continued gradually moved through their identity issues and, as compared to bisexual husbands whose marriages split up, were significantly more likely to take the initiative to nurture their marriages, rather than relying on their wives to initiate interaction or to demand time (Matteson, 1985). These husbands were also significantly more empathic toward their wives and had an appreciation of the pain their wives had experienced during the tumultuous years (Matteson, 1985).

WHEN TO TELL THE CHILDREN

Once the relationship with the spouse or ex-spouse is on its way to restabilization, it is likely that the bisexual spouse can reinvest energy in the children. The issue of when and what to tell the children about one's bisexual identity may arise at this point. Several factors play a part in the decision. Probably the most important is the bisexual spouse's own level of acceptance of his/her gay sexuality. To what extent the bisexual spouse is comfortable compartmentalizing life, how private a person she/he is, the evaluation of risk to the family if the "secret" is out, and the wishes of the nongay spouse may all be factors in the decision.

Some of the fathers who are open to their wives still decide not to disclose their bisexuality to their children. One of the bisexual husbands I interviewed speaks of code words he and his wife use.

> When I tell my wife "I was at the Health Club," she knows I mean "Man's Country" (a gay bath), but I would never say that in front of the kids. They don't know anything about my gay life. Sometimes when I come home late they ask where I've been, but when I say "at the Health Club" they accept that. I expect they'll never know or guess. It has nothing to do with them . . . and nothing to do with the marriage. [Being with] another woman would violate monogamy, but my gay experience [does not] (Matteson, 1979).

Another respondent stated he wasn't sure he wanted his kids to know. When interviewed shortly after telling his wife, he stated, "At least I have no plans to tell them. It would be hard on them" (Matteson, 1979). When recontacted six years later, he still had no plans to tell the children, all of whom were adults except one who was a senior in high school (Matteson, in process, a). His wife considered the fact that they had shielded the children from this part of their struggle one of the really positive achievements of their rather negative marriage.

Some bisexual spouses feel it is up to the children to ask for information. "I didn't tell my wife until she asked directly. At present I haven't told my boys (age 8 and 4); I would tell them if they asked" (Matteson, 1979).

Often, however, these acknowledged gays want to be sure that their children do not enter life's commitments with the ignorance or prejudice that the fathers have had to fight in their own lives. In one of the most solid open marriages in my study the children began to ask questions about the husband's male friends when they were only five or six years old and were given honest answers, appropriate to their ability to understand (Matteson, 1979).

In one very open couple, the man's gay lover frequently stayed in the home, and the daughter was aware that sometimes they slept in the same bed. The seven-year-old daughter asked her father some questions about "Gene" (the lover), and the father answered them honestly, explaining that he loved Gene and he loved Mommy. The daughter did not seem concerned, but shortly afterward she asked her mother, "Do you still love Daddy?" Mother assured her that she did. "Do you love Gene?" the daughter asked. "He's my friend," her mother answered, "but I love your father." The daughter seemed to accept these answers happily. Mother commented to the interviewer, "So long as she sees the warmth and love between us, and between Gene and her dad, and so long as there's plenty of attention paid to her, I don't think there's anything lacking in her life." "She sometimes considers Gene a pain in the neck, and sometimes a nice person," mother continued. The daughter mentions Gene in conversations with friends, who have sometimes asked "Who's Gene?" She responds, "Well, sometimes he's like my brother, sometimes he's my friend, and sometimes he's just Gene" (Matteson, 1979).

Another bisexual father, who was separated from his wife, stated emphatically:

> My kids will be raised knowing about gays. I want to be an "uncle" to John's [his lover's] boy, and I want him to be an uncle to my kids. I sometimes wonder about what I will say when my kids ask me — but I think I'll just tell them. I want them to be able to understand both lives. And if my son asks, I want to be able to tell him the good and the bad (Matteson, 1979).[2]

Obviously, when the parents' separation has been bitter, the children may pick up the nongay parent's negative attitudes and use the issue of homosexuality to reject the bisexual parent. A nine-year-old son of one of the separated couples in my study (Matteson, in process, a) developed an interest in telling antigay jokes soon after the separation. Later, this behavior ceased completely.

It seems likely that the majority of separated couples tell the children about the bisexuality of the spouse, especially if the children are living with that spouse much of the time. Even then, in 20 percent of the cases the children had not been told, and many more of the parents admitted that they have only mentioned the matter; it had not been discussed in any depth (Schulenburg, 1985). Percentages in all of these studies must be considered questionable, since it is impossible to get representative samplings of these families.

A study of still-married bisexual husbands in counseling found that only one-third of the couples with children had discussed the husband's bisexuality with their children. The average age of the children when told was eighteen (Coleman, 1985a). However, in a study with a nonclinical sample, 50 percent of the acknowledged bisexual couples who had school-age children stated that the children were aware of their father's bisexuality (Wolf, 1985).

There is reason to believe that it is advantageous to disclose to the children before they enter their own sexual identity issues in adolescence (Epstein, 1979). The children's reactions to parents' disclosure have not been systematically studied. Schulenburg (1985) states that "daughters rarely expressed outright rejection of a bisexual parent, while sons tended toward initial rejection followed by later acceptance" (p. 44). This would fit the general cultural pattern of greater homophobia on the part of males; it would also fit the pattern that male youth are more likely than females to express negative or critical feelings toward parents (Matteson, 1975, Ch. 12). This should not be taken to imply that teenage daughters are typically comfortable with their fathers' bisexual lifestyles. One daughter in my study could comfortably discuss this issue with her father but firmly instructed him not to be seen with his lover in areas where her friends might observe them. My impression from both research and clinical interviews with bisexual fathers is that strong rejection is rare, even with sons. (See Chapters 3 and 4 on the children of gay fathers and lesbian mothers.) The age of disclosure probably makes a difference. Preadolescents may be comfortable with the issue generally but be very uncomfortable where it might threaten their peer relationships. And adolescents often prefer not to discuss issues of their parents' sexuality, even though they have appeared comfortable with such discussions earlier in their lives. The exception is the adolescent or youth who becomes involved in social causes, and may join the parent in gay pride parades, or may support gay issues in other ways.

It is important to remember that not all of the mixed-orientation couples that remain together have moved through open disclosure to a renegotiated relationship. A large portion seem to stabilize their marriages in an ongoing "mutual conspiracy of silence," with its concomitant emotional distancing. In a few of these marriages the bisexual spouse seems able to keep this part of his/her life compartmentalized and still continue a healthy marriage with open communication on other issues.

CHANGES EFFECTING
MIXED-ORIENTATION MARRIAGES

Gay-affirmative Attitudes

Maddox (1982) has suggested that the reasons homosexuals and bisexuals have married in the past may not be those of the present. At least two studies substantiate that the younger couples in samples of mixed-orientation marriages are much more positive in their reasons for marrying. These couples had faced more directly the importance of homosexuality in their lives and the impact this might have on the marriage (Matteson, 1985; Wolf, 1985). More open disclosure of bisexuality reflects recent more accepting social attitudes toward homosexuality; the bisexual partner is more willing to risk this disclosure, and the nongay partner more willing to accept the homosexual behavior (Wolf, 1985). The bisexual spouses in these younger couples typically have had considerably more gay experience, especially experience with self-affirming gays, than their older counterparts. This socializing with others who have affirmed their gayness has helped them to affirm their own gay desires and the gay aspect of their identity. These young bisexuals are much less homophobic than older married gays (Matteson, 1985; Wolf, 1985). Since these couples enter their marriages with their eyes open, they do not face the crisis of later discovery and disclosure. The particular difficulty for these couples is that they may not take time to develop the primacy of the marital relationship (Matteson, 1986). In some cases, a major reason for the marriage was the desire of the bisexual partner to have children. (See section above on "Developmental Periods" in these marriages for a discussion of the importance of developing primacy in the marriage as the foundation for a workable open marriage.)

The AIDS Epidemic

There is no doubt that the outbreak of AIDS (Acquired Immune Deficiency Syndrome) has had effects that have set back some of the social, as well as legal, gains of gay liberation. Probably many married men who have become aware of their homosexual desires have been pushed back into the closet because of the fear of contacting AIDS. Similarly, youth who might wish to explore their gay sexuality may avoid doing so due to AIDS. They may move into heterosexual marriages with the same lack of experience, and nourish the same naive assumptions that their feelings will go away, as did their predecessors in decades past. It is likely that the percentage of closeted bisexual marriages will increase whenever homophobia increases.

For already married bisexuals, AIDS presents a special dilemma. Monogamy as a method of reducing the risk of contacting AIDS is not a viable option for most married bisexuals. There is great risk of acquiring AIDS unless bisexuals are disciplined to have only "safe sex." The details of "safe sex" can be obtained by calling any gay hotline. For the bisexual who desires steady and intimate relationships, both with his spouse and with a gay lover, one of the most workable alternatives is to develop such a relationship with another married bisexual. Assuming that the nongay spouses are monogamous, that the bisexual spouses limit gay sex to each other, and that none of the four presently are infected, they form a "closed system"; logically there is no danger of infection. Feeling certain that the above assumptions are valid, particularly if one does not know the gay spouse's partner, is another matter. It is in the interest of one's own health, as well as one's spouse's, to limit gay sex to safe sex. The methods of transmission of the AIDS virus are now fairly clear, and it is important to be informed enough, and frank enough, to ask specific questions about a potential sexual partner's sexual history.

Social Confirmation for Bisexual Parents

Since parenting is invariably perceived as a link to the heterosexual community, all bisexual parents struggle with living between two worlds. For mixed-orientation married couples, the primary world of day-to-day living is usually the nongay world. As stated above, it is easy for a male-female couple to "pass" as nongay. But, like all "passing," this produces some inner incongruities — a sense of being phony or deceitful. The experience is somewhat different for the bisexual than for gays or lesbians. Gays or lesbians frequently experience the strain of "passing" on the job, but after work, when they go to a gay restaurant or bar, they experience a sense of relief at "belonging" and feeling congruent. The bisexual, however, while hiding one part of his identity when passing in the nongay world, also experiences a sense of incongruity in gay settings, for in that world the heterosexual component of one's identity is rarely affirmed. They have no community that is "their own." Even closest friends, unless they themselves are bisexual, often feel that the bisexual person would be more integrated if only they would "choose" one world and commit themselves to it. Indeed, some (kinesthetic) bisexuals can do so, at least for periods of their lives. But many cannot; they feel fulfilled only when they have sexual activity on "both sides."

Support groups for "gay and married men," which exist in most large cities in the United States, provide one of the few places where bisexual husbands feel accepted "on both sides." (It is unfortunate that such groups have not developed for bisexual married women. However, group experience may be more important for male self-acceptance regarding sexual orientation, since from early adolescence men treat sexuality as an important peer status issue, in a way that women do not.) My impression is that most of the men who become fully comfortable with their bisexual orientation have not only had support in the gay community but have also been open with their heterosexual friends, or with other married bisexuals. Having been open to both gays and nongays alike, they have ended the fear of phony acceptance, at least among those who matter most to them.

SPECIAL NEEDS OF THESE FAMILIES AND THEIR IMPLICATIONS FOR PROFESSIONALS

Although there is a broad range of lifestyles among couples in mixed-orientation marriages, they and their families have in common the following needs for respect in their interaction with professionals:

respect the uniqueness of each person's sexual orientation
respect each individual's attempt to meet his/her needs for intimacy and
    for sexual satisfaction in the way that is authentic for them

respect the boundaries and contracts the couple has worked out between
each other, and in relation to their families and their gay/lesbian
partners

respect the special need for privacy and confidentiality of all family
members in relation to the homophobic society in which we live

respect the client's choice of issues for which they are asking
professional help. Do not assume that the homosexuality, or a
marriage problem is the "real" issue. (For an expanded discussion of
each of these needs see Matteson, in press, c. For a discussion of the
special needs bisexuals have in counseling, see Coleman, 1985b, pp.
204–205; Gochros, 1985; and Matteson, in press, a.)

SUMMARY AND CONCLUSIONS REGARDING THE EFFECTS OF MIXED-ORIENTATION MARRIAGES ON THE CHILDREN

Given the lack of adequate research regarding children of mixed-
orientation couples, we are left with impressions from spontaneous
comments volunteered by parents in the course of interviews which did
not focus on the children. These indicate that no simple generalizations
are possible. It seems likely that the children are effected differently at
different ages, and at different phases of the marital relationship. The
quality of communication in the marriage, and the degree of distancing of
the gay spouse are expected to be important factors.

It is clear from the research on bisexual husbands that it is possible to
develop a positive bisexual identity and yet create a stable heterosexual
marriage when the bisexuality is openly acknowledged in the marriage;
these marriages are characterized by exceptionally good communication
and a deep acceptance of each other's differences, a lack of need to
control the partner, and an ability to set boundaries and care for oneself
(Matteson, 1985). Some of these families discuss the issue of bisexuality
openly, and the children are introduced to gay lovers. If the children are
aware that their parents have been able to communicate their needs and
negotiate differences, while dealing with this difficult problem, the
children have a healthy model to emulate. Further, the children's
recognition of the variety of lifestyles available may have positive effects
on their lives. Given the quality of these couples' communication, there is
reason to believe that they provide quality parenting for the children.

Other couples, who are open with each other about one spouse's bisexuality, deliberately protect the children from the issue, or give minimal information.

Some bisexual spouses handle their homosexual needs discreetly, without direct disclosure even to their wives; they maintain heterosexual marriages and a family life that appears "normal" to outsiders, and possibly to the children. Perhaps many mixed-orientation couples are able to raise their children without the uniqueness of their marital situation having any particular impact on the childrearing.

For bisexuals married before gay liberation, the process of affirming one's bisexual identity was rarely completed before the children were born. There is anecdotal evidence (from interviews, Matteson, 1979) to suggest that the bisexual spouse who, during the marriage, undergoes a crisis in sexual identity temporarily withdraws from spouse and children.

We can conjecture that if this withdrawal comes at a time in the children's lives when for other reasons they were particularly rejection sensitive, the effects on the parent-child relationship might be long term.

There is also tentative data suggesting that the age of children when the bisexuality of a parent is disclosed may be significant. If the disclosure of homosexuality comes at a time when the children are struggling with their own sexual identity, it may be especially difficult for them.

There is reason to believe that the spouses in secretive marriages are frequently involved in a downward spiral of rejection of self, and withdrawal from their spouses. Rejection of homosexuality by society in general may result in internalized homophobia which slows the process of forming a sexual identity. The data available on the children is too indirect; we can only speculate about how the disruption in the parents' communication and the negative self-image of the bisexual parent may effect the children. It is ironic that prejudice against gays, often justified in the name of "preserving the family," may end up hurting the children of these bisexuals whose self-acceptance is impaired or delayed.

The differences between the couples married before and after the advent of gay liberation (Matteson, 1985) suggest that as society becomes more accepting of homosexuality, youth are more likely to develop self-accepting sexual identities before entering marriages and having children. If they choose marriage knowingly, the children are less likely to experience the effects of a parent's rejection of self, and distancing from the family.

PRIORITIES FOR FUTURE RESEARCH

Bisexuality (male or female) has usually been researched using a subsample of "gays" in research designed to look at gay issues, rather than treating bisexuality as a legitimate research area in itself. It should be noted, by way of credit, that the *Journal of Homosexuality* has devoted three issues to research and theory about bisexuality (De Cecco, 1981; De Cecco & Shively, 1983; Klein & Wolf, 1985).

Specific aspects of bisexuality that need empirical research include two mentioned above. The first is in regard to differences between kinesthetic and visual arousal patterns and could best be pursued using physiological as well as psychological measurements (see Matteson, in process, b.) The second concerns the issue of the formation and self-acceptance of a bisexual identity. The hypothesis, discussed above, that self-acceptance is facilitated by disclosure to and acceptance from both gay and nongay friends deserves testing. Longitudinal research beginning in early adolescence regarding the formation of each of the sexual orientations/identities is also needed.

Most of the research regarding gay lifestyles focuses almost exclusively on men. Lesbians now and throughout history have been largely disregarded — a phenomenon of the patriarchal society that is, at best, a mixed blessing (Schulenburg, 1985, p. 8). Most obviously, more research is needed regarding lesbian and bisexual women in heterosexual marriages. It would be especially interesting to have data testing the hypothesis that bisexual wives are more likely than bisexual husbands to develop deep emotional intimacy with their lesbian lovers, pulling them away from the marriage. However, the difficulty of obtaining samples of bisexual women still in marriages has already been noted (Coleman, 1985a; Schulenburg, 1985).

Research directly observing the communication patterns of mixed-orientation couples and their families is also needed. This includes research concerning the processes that are used to handle relationships with multiple partners. Exploratory research was begun in this field in the 1970s with the popularization of the concept of "open marriage." The topic is still of importance to bisexuals. Research needs to go beyond the interview approach, extending to social psychology experiments simulating jealousy-evoking situations, in which the partner is "out with a lover," identifying processes of self-care and coping, reentry situations (returning to the primary partner after time out with gay friends), identifying mechanisms used to reconnect and to diminish jealousy; and other such critical incidents in the day-to-day management of these families.

All of the above suggestions focus on the parents in these families. Most striking is the lack of research that studies the effects of these issues on the children. The only social scientist who has reported a study that systematically interviewed bisexual married parents about their children is Miller (1979b), although Matteson's (1979) recorded interviews also included some material, and two journalistic works have included interviews with the children as well (Epstein, 1979; Schulenburg, 1985). Of particular interest would be interviews with children comparing the children's reactions to learning of a parent's bisexuality, taking into account the ages of the children, and the stages of the marriage. Longitudinal research that followed these children and observed changes in their feelings toward each parent over time would be ideal. Some objective indicators of stress (such as a drop in children's school grades) might be collected without directly involving the children, allowing comparisons among children from acknowledged mixed-orientation couples in which the children have been told, those in which the children have been "protected," and a control group such as children of families in which the husband has recently been promoted, made a career switch, or some similar identity change. Audiotaped or videotaped direct interaction studies using a problem-solving format (such as Matteson, 1974; Grotevant & Cooper, in press) can assess family interaction variables without overtly dealing with the marital and bisexual issues, again opening the possibility of comparing groups (including secretive couples) without breaching the confidence of the index subject, the bisexual.

NOTES

1. I am indebted to Bandler and Grinder (1979) for their work recognizing different "lead" and "representation" systems, which led to my recognition of the kinesthetic and visual patterns of sexual arousal.

2. Many gay-affirmative persons would argue that "uncle" is a euphemism that avoids acknowledging the true nature of the couple's relationship.

REFERENCES

Bandler, R., & Grinder, J. (1979). *Frogs into princess.* Moab, Utah: Real People Press.

Bell, A., & Weinberg, M. S. (1978). *Homosexualities: A study of sexual diversity among men and women.* New York: Simon and Schuster.

Bozett, F. (1982). Heterogeneous couples in heterosexual marriages: Gay men and straight women. *Journal of Marital & Family Therapy, 8,* 81–89.

Brownfain, J. J. (1982). A study of the married bisexual male: Paradox and resolution. *Journal of Homosexuality, 4,* 173–188.

Cass, V. C. (1979). Homosexual identity formation: A theoretical model. *Journal of Homosexuality, 4,* 219–236.

Coleman, E. (1985a). Bisexual women in marriages. *Journal of Homosexuality, 11,* 87–100.

_____. (1985b). Integration of male bisexuality and marriage. *Journal of Homosexuality, 11,* 189–208.

De Cecco, J. P., Ed. (1981). *Journal of Homosexuality, 6,* (3).

De Cecco, J. P. & Shively, M. G., Eds. (1983). Bisexual and homosexual identities: Critical theoretical issues. *Journal of Homosexuality, 9,* (2&3).

Dixon, J. K. (1985). Sexuality and relationship changes in married females following the commencement of bisexual activity. *Journal of Homosexuality, 11,* 115–133.

Epstein, R. (1979). Children of gays. *Christopher Street,* (June), 43–50.

Gochros, J. S. (1985). Wives' reactions to learning that their husbands are bisexual. *Journal of Homosexuality, 11,* 101–114.

Grotevant, H. D., & Cooper, C. R., (in press). Individuation in family relationships: A perspective on individual differences in the development of identity and role taking skill in adolescence. *Human Development.*

Klein, F., & Wolf, T. J., Ed. (1985). Bisexualities: Theory and research. *Journal of Homosexuality, 11,* (1&2), New York: Haworth Press.

Kooden, H. D., Morin, S. F., Riddle, E. I., Rogers, M., Sang, B. E., & Strassburger, F. (1979). *Removing the stigma: Final report, task force on the status of lesbian and gay male psychologists.* Washington, D.C.: American Psychological Association.

Latham, J. D., & White, G. D. (1978). Coping with homosexual expression within heterosexual marriages: Five case studies. *Journal of Sex and Marital Therapy, 3,* 198–212.

Maddox, B. (1982). *Married and gay.* New York: Harcourt Brace Jovanovich.

Masters, W., & Johnson, V. (1979). *Homosexuality in perspective.* Boston: Little, Brown.

Matteson, D. R. (1974). Alienation vs. exploration and commitment: Personality and family correlates of adolescent identity statuses. *Report from the Project for Youth Research.* Copenhagen: Royal Danish School of Educational Studies.

_____. (1975). *Adolescence today: Sex roles and the search for identity.* Homewood, Ill.: Dorsey Press.

_____. (1979). Audio-recordings of interviews (unpublished) for the first data wave of the longitudinal study published as Matteson (1985).

_____. (1985). Bisexual men in marriages: Is a positive homosexual identity and stable marriage possible? *Journal of Homosexuality, 11,* 149–173.

_____. (in press, a). Counseling bisexual men. In M. Scher, *The handbook of counseling and psychotherapy with men.* Beverly Hills, Ca.: Sage.

_____. (in press, b). Identity: The alienated self, the merged self, and the intimate self. In *Psicológica de Professores*. Braga, Portugal: University of Braga.

_____. (in press, c). Spouses in mixed-orientation marriages. In B. Kus (Ed.), *Helping your gay or lesbian client*. Boston: Alyson.

_____. (in process, a). Bisexual men in marriages: A Six year followup.

_____. (in process, b). When is bisexuality a choice? Exploratory research on two types of arousal patterns.

McDonald, G. J. (1982). Individual differences in the coming-out process for gay men: Implications for theoretical models. *Journal of Homosexuality, 8*, 47–60.

Miller, B. (1978). Adult sexual resocialization: Adjustments toward a stigmatized identity. *Alternative Lifestyles, 1*, 207–234.

_____. (1979a). Unpromised paternity: The lifestyles of gay fathers. In M. P. Levin (Ed.), *Gay men: The sociology of male homosexuality* (pp. 239–252). New York: Harper & Row.

_____. (1979b). Gay fathers and their children. *Family Coordinator, 28*, 544–552.

Offer, D., & Simon, W. (1975). Stages of sexual development. In A. M. Freedman, H. I. Kaplan, & B. J. Sadock, *Comprehensive textbook of psychiatry -II*; vol. 2, 2nd edition. Baltimore: Williams & Wilkins.

Ross, M. W. (1983). *The married homosexual man: A psychological study*. Boston: Routledge & Kegan Paul.

Saghir, M. T., & Robins, E. (1973). *Male and female homosexuality: A comprehensive investigation*. Baltimore: Williams & Wilkins.

Schulenburg, J. (1985). *Gay parenting*. Garden City, N.Y.: Anchor Books.

Weinberg, T. S. (1978). On "doing" and "being" gay: Sexual behavior and homosexual male self-identity, *Journal of Homosexuality, 4*, 143–156.

Wilson, M. (1986). Gay and married. *Windy City News, 1*, (36–38) June 5, 12, 19, pp. 2 ff. Chicago, Ill.

Wolf, T. J. (1985). Marriages of bisexual men. *Journal of Homosexuality, 4*, 135–148.

IV

PSYCHOSOCIAL IMPLICATIONS AND LEGAL ISSUES

9

CONSIDERING PARENT-HOOD: PSYCHOSOCIAL ISSUES FOR GAY MEN AND LESBIANS CHOOSING ALTERNATIVE FERTILIZATION

Cheri Pies

Within the last fifteen years, there has been an increasing awareness in the lesbian and gay communities that being gay does not rule out the possibility of being a parent. Consequently, may lesbians and gay men are considering parenthood after coming out (Pies, 1985). Many think about adopting a child, others consider becoming the nonbiological parent to children conceived by a partner. More recently, however, increasing numbers of lesbians and gay men are considering the possibility of conceiving a child through the use of artificial insemination (also known as alternative fertilization and woman-controlled conception). Whatever the plan, for most, this is not an easy decision; it is a deliberate and intentional decision demanding intricate and advanced planning.

Each parenting option raises significant psychosocial concerns, all of which need exploration and clarification. The purpose of this chapter is to identity and describe the range of psychosocial issues that arises for lesbians and gay men considering parenthood through the use of artificial insemination. The effect of society's perception of lesbians and gay men as potential parents will be discussed initially, followed by an exploration of specific social, psychological, and ethical issues unique to lesbians and gay men considering parenthood through artificial insemination. The issue of AIDS in relation to the use of artificial insemination will also be addressed. Finally, the chapter will conclude with a discussion of the implications for professional practitioners and will highlight areas for further research.

THE SOCIAL CONTEXT

Contemporary society continues to perceive the two-parent heterosexual family as the norm. Lesbians and gay men are creating family configurations that challenge that norm. The possibilities for these family forms are numerous. In fact, there is no typical lesbian/gay family, and there is probably no easy way to describe the various relationship arrangements that lesbians and gay men have developed over the years (Schulenberg, 1985). Many lesbians choose to parent without the involvement of a man. In other instances a family will consist of one lesbian and one gay man, both of whom are biological parents to the child. In still others, a lesbian and her partner will contract with a gay man to parent together, but that gay man may not be the donor or biological father to the child. One person from a lesbian couple and one from a gay male couple may conceive a child and yet both partners in both couples have an equal role and responsibility in parenting the child. The combinations are varied and creative.

Because they are creating new family forms, lesbians and gay men are sometimes seen as contributing to the erosion of the traditional family. Their parenthood calls into question the institution of marriage, the necessity of male-female sexual relations to bring children into the world, and the traditional model of the heterosexual couple as ideal parents. Since this questioning has the potential to redefine the notion of family, lesbians and gay men face disapproval by those who do not welcome alternative, nontraditional family choices.

Western society has traditionally viewed lesbians and gay men in terms of their sexuality, rather than in terms of their skills, capabilities, and personal qualities. Negative attitudes about homosexuals in general, and often incorrect assumptions about their attitudes toward children, frequently lead others to assume lesbians and gay men will not be good parents. As a result, there is a prevailing societal attitude that lesbians and gay men should not be parents.

Many lesbians and gay men have taken on the fear, dislike, and negative judgments of homosexuals that are identified as homophobia. It is difficult to avoid internalized homophobia in a culture that perpetuates myths about lesbians and gay men. Having been raised with these societal attitudes, many lesbians and gay men question their own ability to be "good" parents, have negative assumptions about themselves as potential parents, and feel they must become more than simply "ordinary" parents.

Any lesbian or gay man considering parenthood must be prepared for numerous personal and sometimes startling questions. These questions range in intensity from the seemingly harmless "How will you do it?" or "Why do you want to be a parent?" to the more threatening "What right do gay people have to be parents?" or "How can you bring a child into *that* kind of family?" Lesbians and gay men are expected to have coherent answers to these questions and are expected to be able to explain why homosexuals want children in their lives.

FAMILIES OF ORIGIN

Parents and family members are usually among the first to ask some of the more difficult questions. For most lesbians and gay men, just the anticipation of talking with their families about plans for parenthood creates tremendous anxiety. If the individual has not "come out" to the family, the issue of homosexuality may surface simultaneously with that of parenthood, thereby generating greater tension.

For some lesbians and gay men, talking with family members is emotionally charged and painful. Families can be hurtful. Parents and other family members may not be as supportive of the idea of parenting as one wants them to be. However, in other situations, families do embrace the idea of a lesbian daughter or gay son parenting a child. Regardless of the possible reaction, careful attention is often paid to how, when, and where to tell parents and family members about plans for parenting. It is not a casual conversation.

Not surprisingly, parents and other family members often worry about how they will explain the arrival of a grandchild or niece/nephew to their friends and other relatives. They may be confused about how to explain their adult child's life choices. They may be thinking "How will I explain this child to my friends?" "What will I tell them?" "To whom do I say this child belongs?" "Who do I say is the father?" A family member may also fear "coming out" as the relative of a lesbian or gay person. And, if the son or daughter is the nonbiological parent, questions will undoubtedly arise about how the family is to relate to this child. Who is this child to them? Are they expected to recognize the child as a family member, and their lesbian or gay son as the parent?

FAMILY PLANNING WITH A DIFFERENCE

For lesbians and gay men, the act of planning a family is not the preassumed endeavor that it is for some heterosexual couples. Many practical questions need to be answered: Who will be the biological parents? Will there be a known or unknown donor? Will there be a surrogate mother? Will the child be able to know both biological parents? Is the donor or surrogate mother also a person who will parent the child? How many parents will this child have? Will the donor's partner have a relationship to the child? What kind of relationship will the biological mother's partner have to the child? Will there be a legal contract between parenting parties? The list of questions often seems staggering. There are often no right or wrong answers, and usually few role models. Lesbians and gay men who are thinking about becoming parents must take time to explore these complex questions with one another, carefully identifying the inherent problems and pitfalls, some predictable, others quite unpredictable.

ARTIFICIAL INSEMINATION: ISSUES OF SPECIAL INTEREST

For most lesbians planning to use artificial insemination, deciding whether to use a known or unknown donor and then finding a donor are the most difficult tasks (Hornstein, 1984). Within the past few years, commercial sperm banks have become more willing to inseminate single women and/or lesbians, thus increasing access to semen. Many lesbians however, have located donors through friends or acquaintances (Pies, 1985).

For gay men wanting to become fathers through artificial insemination, finding a woman with whom to parent may be difficult. Perhaps they have already discussed the topic with a woman friend and both parties are willing to pursue the possibilities. Or, they may have made a concerted effort to meet lesbians who are interested in building a family with a gay man, spent time exploring the possibilities, and taken concrete steps to create a family.

Using donor semen for artificial insemination, however, is more complex than it once was. Today, there is growing concern about the transmission of the AIDS virus through artificial insemination. The incidence of AIDS in the gay community has had a tremendous impact on the use of gay men as donors and on the options for lesbians and gay men wanting to be parents. AIDS is known to be transmitted through body fluids, mainly blood and semen. As of December 1986, there have been no reported cases of AIDS in women who have been inseminated, and none in their babies. However, in July 1985, a report from Australia indicated that four women, inseminated by an asymptomatic virus carrier, were found to be infected with the AIDS virus (Stewart, 1985). This report suggests that transmission of the AIDS virus can occur through insemination. Further research is currently being done in California to determine whether lesbians who have been inseminated with semen from gay and nongay men have been exposed to the AIDS virus.[1]

Since the AIDS virus can be transmitted through semen, and since it is not yet known how frequently transmission occurs through artificial insemination, it is strongly recommended that anyone who has engaged in behaviors that would put them at risk of exposure be screened for antibodies to the AIDS virus. Suggested screening techniques also include both a careful risk assessment of the potential parent(s) and a thorough medical/sexual history.[2] All sperm banks and private physicians have been advised by the Centers for Disease Control (1985) to test all semen donors for antibodies to the AIDS virus.

Who is the "Real" Parent?

Once it has been decided how a child will be conceived in a given situation, questions arise about who the "real" parent(s) are. Society gives little credibility to the parent who cannot demonstrate a biological or legal connection to a child. Lesbians parenting children together, or a combination of lesbians and gay men parenting together, have biologically asymmetrical relationships to their child; this can create enormous strain on any family or coparenting relationship. If people who are not biologically related to a child are equally responsible for the care of that child, are they equal parents with the biological parent(s)? The nonbiological parent(s) may be repeatedly confronted by the painful reality of being unacknowledged as a "real" parent by family, friends, community, and society at large. Even the child may question whether the nonbiological parent is a "real" parent because of the pressure for children to have one identifiable mom and one identifiable dad.

Legal Issues

Regardless of who is the biological parent, lesbians and gay men need to understand the relevant laws in their state in order to protect their rights as parents, the rights of their children, and their parenting relationships. Attorneys have developed some guidelines for protecting lesbian and gay parents; however, the laws vary from state to state concerning artificial insemination by donor. As Hitchens (1984) comments, "Many states do not have any statutes covering artificial insemination by donor, nor do they have any court opinions that define the rights of the mother, donor, or the child conceived through artificial insemination by donor." Some states do have laws, adapted from the Uniform Parentage Act, that address these concerns. These laws are often limited to covering a marital situation or a situation in which a licensed physician performs the insemination procedure. For lesbians seeking to conceive and then parent without the involvement of the donor, these laws are of utmost importance. The statutes clarify that when a physician performs the insemination, the man who donates the semen has no legal rights to the child, unless he is the recipient's husband.

Hitchens (1984) advises that lesbians and gay men planning parenthood through artificial insemination enter into agreements to "clarify the intent of the donor and recipient, and to clarify their relationship." She goes on to explain that "the most important reason for writing an agreement is so that both the known donor and the woman will be clear with each other as to their expectations." When the donor and recipient are known to one another and their intention is to parent together, the agreement should state this. In the event of the biological parent's death, such agreements also help to clarify the relationship of the nonbiological parent to the child.

Attending to the various legal questions requires perseverance and regard for detail. Because of the ever present threat to lesbians and gay men of the possibility of losing rights to their children, a thorough analysis of the laws in one's state and consultation with a lawyer are recommended and encouraged.[3] The decision to become a parent through artificial insemination must be undertaken with foresight and understanding of all the implications of this decision.

Some Ethical Concerns

The concerns of society regarding homosexual parenting — in both the literature and public debate — are couched in the framework of an ethical consideration for the well-being of the child. There are four commonly asked questions that reflect the depth and breadth of these ethical and social concerns:

Would the absence of a male or female role model adversely affect a child's acquisition of appropriate sex role behavior and traits?

If a child is raised by homosexual parents, will that child become homosexual?

Will a child be harmed or stigmatized by having homosexual parents?

What right do children have to know their biological parent(s)?

The first three questions have been discussed in the psychological literature on lesbian and gay parenting (Green, 1978; Herzog, 1968; Kirkpatrick, 1981; Lewis, 1980) and are addressed further in this volume. The last question is most often associated with the use of artificial insemination to conceive.

The issue is whether it is acceptable to bring children into the world when they may not be able to know their biological parents. Is there a moral imperative to provide a child with information about the biological parent? Is the desire to know one's biological parents the result of culturally bound social pressures, or is it a true biological desire of the individual to know their origins?

These questions are frequently difficult to answer in the abstract. Some lesbians and gay men want their children to be able to know both biological parents, while others are fearful of the possible custody battles that could ensue between two people who had no intention of parenting together. Still others feel that children who do not have access to both biological parents will adjust to that situation without undue stress and difficulty. It may be a number of years before researchers are able to determine the impact of these choices on children's lives.

IMPLICATIONS FOR PROFESSIONAL PRACTITIONERS

Lesbians and gay men considering parenthood through artificial insemination will undoubtedly come in contact with a variety of professional practitioners, including attorneys, clergy, educators, midwives, nurses, physicians, therapists, and others. It is imperative that these practitioners possess a thorough and succinct understanding of the many practical, psychosocial, and ethical issues involved in this parenting option. A careful reading of the available professional literature, as well as lay literature (gay/lesbian press, gay/lesbian newspapers, women's publications, and others), will serve to increase one's familiarity with the subject and clarify various points of view.

When working with this population, professional practitioners need to be attentive to their own questions and attitudes about the phenomenon of lesbianS and gay men as parents. They must be encouraged to pay attention to their reactions to clients considering parenthood, being conscious of their personal decisions about parenting, and being aware of the issues this decision raises for their own lives.

Because of the nontraditional and complex nature of lesbian and gay parenting, there is a need for a range of support services addressing this issue. Educational and support groups have been helpful in encouraging lesbians and gay men to identify and explore the various issues associated with the decision to parent.

Enabling clients to explore their questions about parenting in a nonjudgmental, nonthreatening environment is a challenging and exciting task. Professional practitioners are frequently given the opportunity to undertake this task and are encouraged to see themselves as a valuable and essential resource in the decision-making process around parenting.

CONCLUSIONS

Parenting is a human right — a reproductive right of all women and men, regardless of their sexual orientation. Deciding to parent is a complex decision for most people, and that complexity is often compounded for the lesbian or gay man considering parenthood. Lesbians and gay men, as well as the professional practitioners to whom they may turn for assistance, should understand the decision-making process and the psychosocial issues involved in that process.

SUGGESTIONS FOR RESEARCH

There is still a great deal of research needed in order to learn more about the phenomenon of lesbian and gay parenting. However, any research that is undertaken must be designed to protect the integrity of all participants and must serve to clarify the issues around lesbian and gay parenting, not exploit those who have chosen this family form. There is often some reluctance among lesbian and gay parents to participate in research. Questions concerning who is doing the research, how the data will be analyzed, and why this research is being done at this time are of particular concern. Any social science research conducted within the lesbian and gay communities must responsibly address these questions.

It would be of interest to have an actual estimate of the number of lesbians and gay men who become parents after coming out. In addition, there is a great deal to be learned about the experiences of children born through artificial insemination to lesbian and gay parents. Certainly a wealth of questions abounds concerning the effect of knowing or not knowing the donor, both as a phenomenon in itself, and in comparison to children who have been adopted and do not know their biological parents. Longitudinal studies comparing the relative mental, emotional, and sexual health of children of lesbians and gay men with that of children of nongay families would be of value as well. Finally, in an effort to clarify that sexuality is not an appropriate yardstick by which to measure one's skill as a parent, research, comparing parenting styles of lesbians, gay men, and nongay parents would be timely.

NOTES

1.   The Lesbian Insemination Project is a research study funded by the University of California, University-wide Task Force on AIDS. It is a statewide study designed to determine whether lesbians who use artificial insemination with semen from gay, bisexual, or heterosexual donors are at risk of exposure to the AIDS virus. For further information, contact Lesbian Insemination Project, 520 Castro, San Francisco, California 94114.

2.   For further information about AIDS and/or the AIDS antibody test, contact the National Gay Task Force Crisis Line for the AIDS organization in each state. In New York, Alaska, and Hawaii: (212) 807-6016. All other states: (800) 221-7044.

3.   For further information concerning the various complex legal implications of the decision to become a parent through artificial insemination, consult *Legal issues in donor insemination* (1984), a publication of the Lesbian Rights Project, 1370 Mission Street, San Francisco, California, 94103.

The author would like to thank Nancy Adess, Mary O'Donnell, and Nancy Shaw for editorial assistance with this chapter.

REFERENCES

Centers for Disease Control. (1985). Testing donors of organs, tissues, and semen for antibody to human T-lymphotropic virus type III/lympadenopathy-associated virus. *Morbidity and Mortality Weekly*, May 24, 1985, 294.

Green, R. (1978). Sexual identity of 37 children raised by homosexual and transsexual parents. *American Journal of Orthopsychiatry* (135), 692–697.

Herzog, E., & Sudia, C. E. (1968). Fatherless homes: A review of research. *Children* (15), 177–182.

Hitchens, D. J. (1984). *Legal issues in donor insemination*. San Francisco: Lesbian Rights Project.

Hornstein, F. (1984). Children by donor insemination: A new choice for lesbians. R. Arditti, R. D. Klein, & S. Minden (Eds.), *Test-tube women: What future for motherhood?* London: Pandora Press.

Kirkpatrick, M., Smith, C. & Roy, R. (1981). Lesbian mothers and their children: A comparative survey. *American Journal of Orthopsychiatry* (51), 545–551.

Lewis, K. G. (1980). Children of lesbians: Their point of view. *Social Work* (25), 198–203.

Pies, C. (1985). *Considering Parenthood: A workbook for lesbians*. San Francisco: Spinsters Ink.

Schulenberg, J. (1985). *Gay parenting: A complete guide for gay men and lesbians with children*. New York: Anchor Press.

Steward, G. T., Tyler, J. P. P., Cunningham, A. L., Barr, J. A., Driscoll, G. L., Gold, J., Lamont, B. J. (1985). Transmission of human T cells lymphotrophic virus type III by artificial insemination by donor. *Lancet* (2), 581–585.

10

COUNSELING GAY HUSBANDS AND FATHERS

Brian Miller

Gay husbands and fathers experience the same kinds of psychological difficulties that other people do (phobias, loneliness, substance abuse, and so on), and there is no evidence that there is a disproportionate amount of psychopathology among this group. The fraction of gay husbands and fathers who do enter therapy, however, exhibit a rather unique constellation of behavior patterns. Understanding these patterns and effective interventions will help the experienced clinician better serve this special client population.

When these men enter therapy their presenting problems center on five areas: (1) Relationship to Self, (2) Relationship to Wife, (3) Relationship to Children, (4) Relationship to the Heterosexual World, and (5) Relationship to the Gay World. This chapter outlines the concerns experienced in these areas and discusses therapeutic techniques toward resolution. Although gay husbands and fathers in therapy display a variety of feelings, central trends emerge and it is the *modal* experiences that are described (Miller, 1979, 1983, 1986).

RELATIONSHIP TO SELF

When gay husbands and fathers first enter therapy, they often evidence the distress syndrome (depression, anxiety, guilt, nervousness) and concomitant physical problems (gastrointestinal irregularities, eating and sleeping disorders, fatigue). Typically, these symptoms are their bodies' responses to years of neglecting psychosexual issues. This becomes clear when the men are asked about their sexual identity and they have difficulty answering. For years, they have avoided confronting the question, "Who am I?" They report Jeckyl and Hyde feelings and extreme ambivalence about homosexuality. Many view their gay feelings not as a sexual orientation, but rather as a compulsion: "I don't want to do gay things, but I'm driven to do them." Gay family men have unstable self concepts. They try to view their homosexual behavior as nothing more than a genital urge and are reluctant to label themselves homosexual. They have difficulty in seeing themselves simultaneously as good, worthwhile people *and* as gay. Their social isolation from others who share their lifestyle burdens them with "I'm-the-only-one-in-the-world" feelings. Realizing that their behavior is inconsistent with their publicly presented heterosexual identity, these men try to reduce cognitive dissonance by compartmentalizing gay and nongay worlds with elaborate rendezvous strategies and facades. Stripping away the denial and having the men discuss their genuine feelings is an important clinical task.

In initial sessions, gay husbands and fathers typically talk negatively about homosexuality. They are filled with self-loathing and despair; they are also scared and confused. Although suspecting they are homosexual, they hope not. The men's anxiety is not over their homosexual behavior per se (some have done little more than think about homosexual acts), but rather their inability to either embrace it or reject it. Since homosexuality figures so highly in their consciousness ("ruminative obsessions"), they are sometimes described as having "homosexual panic."

Because the men have considerable financial, domestic, career, ego, and social investment in being perceived as heterosexual, they see homosexuality as something that could ruin their lives. Consequently, the men often try on several possible interpretations to neutralize and explain away their desires. "I'm just oversexed"; "It's simply a passing phase"; "I go out for it only when I'm depressed and too drunk to know better"; "So I get my rocks off with another guy, that's not gay, that's just relieving myself"; "I'd be okay if my wife learned to give good blowjobs."

An especially common account is the "Eichmann dodge." Men may claim, like Eichmann, that they are the victims of other men's desire, inadvertently caught up and swept along by the events thereby absolving themselves of responsibility. Men stating this rationalization, however, are often skilled at seducing others into making the first move. Some gay husbands and fathers claim that they limit themselves to one special "friendship" and that no one else of their sex could excite them. If they think of homosexuality at all, they conceive it as promiscuous behavior done by degenerates, not by people like themselves who are loyal and who look conventional. Dismantling these myths is a prerequisite in order for the men to examine honestly their sexuality.

Frequently gay husbands and fathers justify their continued closetedness by citing evidence that the world at large is virulently antigay. This is usually a projection of their own self-hatred about homosexuality onto others. Certainly there is homophobia in our society, but there are also many people (both gay and nongay) who are quite accepting. An important clinical task, therefore, is to desensitize the men's fear of negative societal consequences before they can live openly with their sexual orientation. Bibliotherapy using Brown's *Familiar Faces, Hidden Lives* (1976), Clark's *Loving Someone Gay* (1977), and the Gay Fathers of Toronto book, *Gay Fathers* (1981) is a useful starting point.

Self-acceptance is helped if these men can politicize their status, if they can see their difficulties stemming from social injustice and society's homophobic conditioning rather than personal inadequacy and if they can redefine themselves, not as deviants, but as an oppressed minority. This helps externalize their anger (anger about prejudice and about wasting their precious early years in the closet), lift depression, and ease acceptance of their homosexuality.

RELATIONSHIP TO WIFE

For those gay husbands and fathers who are not disclosed to their wives, keeping homosexuality secret is a major psychological strain. Although some men learn to routinize passing strategies, even the most skilled passer becomes complacent at risk. Passing is facilitated for some men by presenting themselves to their wives (and others) as heterosexual to a fault. Humphreys (1975) comments on this phenomenon:

In donning the breastplate of righteousness the covert deviant assumes a protective shield of superpropriety. His armor has a particularly shiny quality, a refulgence, which tends to blind the audience to certain of his practices. To others in his everyday world, he is not only normal but righteous — an exemplar of good behavior and right thinking. His whole life style becomes an incarnation of what is proper and orthodox. In manners and taste, religion and art, he strives to compensate for an otherwise low resistance to the shock of exposure (p. 135).

This brittle posture smokescreens the men's homosexuality through a combination of over control and distractability gestures.

Other gay husbands and fathers announce a heterosexual identity in such an eccentric, "devil-may-care" style that they disarm wives' suspicions equally well. They may present themselves as quirky creative types, as academicians consumed by esoteric interests, or as bohemian free-thinkers of a sort. This pose is typically one of mixed messages so the husbands and fathers resemble, as one man states, "a crazy-quilt of contradictions." Their eccentric role trivializes their homosexuality if not smokescreens it entirely, and it becomes the least of their peculiarities.

The two poses of righteousness and eccentricity are often resistant to change even in therapy. Continued posing, however, keeps the men alienated from their feelings, from others, prevents the development of intimacy, and creates tremendous loneliness.

There are other less complex ways that the men keep homosexuality secret from wives. For example, many men keep a stash of hidden gay magazines. They "beef up" their fantasies so they are less likely to experience sexual dysfunction during coitus, a common marital problem. Others have address book codes so gay activities can be secretly recorded and have separate apartments reserved for gay use.

A common defense strategy is the workaholic role. It allows the men to avoid time with the spouse, to have alibis for secret cruising forays, to gain family sympathy for apparent sacrifice to overwork, and to emphasize occupational identity so that it smokescreens awareness of sexual orientational identity. Moreover, the workaholic role, unlike the homosexual role, is accorded a degree of social respectability.

When homosexual activity and work crowd out husband and father duties, these men often compensate by buying their wives and children "penance gifts," in what may be called a guilt expiation ritual. Using credit cards to manage guilt has many of these men in serious debt. Guilt is also responsible for many gay fathers giving ex-wives excessive alimony settlements and child support payments. Encouraging the client to stop the deceit that feeds his guilt short-circuits the guilt-punishment cycle and is a major step in moving the client toward a happier adjustment.

Complicated family dynamics, however, play a central role in whether homosexuality is confronted (Ross 1983, p. 36). For example, Neill, Marshall and Yale (1978) investigated twelve husbands of obese women who had intestinal bypass surgery. Twenty-five percent became openly homosexual after their wives' weight loss. The possible explanation may be that a closeted homosexual (unconsciously) chooses a wife who is obese because she is less likely to question infrequent sex. After weight loss, her esteem improves, she becomes more sexually assertive, and the man is forced to confront his disinterest in coitus and his gayness. Besides weight loss, three additional factors that create a disequilibrium in the marital dynamics and often unmask the homosexuality are residential relocation, involvement in swinging, and the wife securing independent employment and income.

There are also *direct* ways that the homosexuality is uncovered. Men may be arrested by vice officers, be blackmailed, or give the wife a venereal disease — an especially dangerous occurrence in this age of AIDS. Such exposure is frequently devastating. Most often the precipitating incident for the family's discovery, however, is the husband's establishment of a love relationship with another man.

Regardless of these occurrences, many men continue to deny wives' knowledge about their homosexuality: "I don't think my wife knows. She's only mentioned it a couple of times, and only when she was too drunk to know what she was saying." This is an example of self-protective denial. If these men faced the fact that their wives are truly suffering, they would be overwhelmed by even more guilt and remorse. Sometimes wives also engage in denial in a mutual conspiracy of silence: "We both know, but let's pretend we don't." In the short run, anger and depression are oscillating responses to the collapse of the denial facade and a supportive therapist can do much to minimize the pain of this period.

The initial shock of exposure may give way to a feeling of couple solidarity, that "we can conquer the problem together." When this is the adaptation, the men do not come out of the closet so much as take their wives into the closet with them. Wives who had previously blamed themselves for lackluster marriages, for their husband's irritability, for his late nights, for his workaholic conduct, and for his hyperactive busyness now have an explanation of heretofore incomprehensible behavior. Homosexuality can be used as a scapegoat to explain away numerous, unrelated marital problems. Feeling "betrayed," wives often exhibit a variety of physical, as well as emotional, reactions — hearing loss, bleeding ulcers, suicide attempts. If therapy with the husband is to be effective, it is often essential that the wife also be in therapy — either individual or conjoint family therapy.

Couples try a variety of strategies to shore up the marriage. Gay celibacy via religious conversion, via family surveillance, and via therapy is one of the most common. Some men generously offer wives the freedom to experience extramarital affairs too, although it appears this is done mostly to relieve client's guilt since they know that wives are unlikely to take them up on the offer. When wives do not put the offer to the test, clients console their guilt by interpreting this as evidence that the wives are "frigid," but data from the wives dispute this characterization.

Some couples try instituting new sexual arrangements: menage a trois, or the husband is allowed out one night a week with gay friends. In the former interaction, wives tend to report feeling "used" and in the latter, men tend to report feeling they are on a "long leash." Sexual conflicts spill into other domestic areas. One man calls this compromise period "white-knuckle heterosexuality."

By negotiating ground rules that reinstate partial denial and by intellectualizing the situation, some couples maintain the compromise period for years. For example, the most frequent of these techniques is a bisexual announcement. Among upper-middle class clients, some come to regard themselves as part of a latter-day classical Greek revival or believe they are among the avant garde/cognoscenti.

This account is strengthened by the couple aligning themselves with tolerant liberals who view bisexuality, not as a stigma, but as a quaint eccentricity. The worlds of the visual and performing arts, especially music, dance, and theatre, offer supportive contexts. Some men bring their boyfriends into the marital household. The irony here is that men say they are bisexual and can love both men and women, when the facts suggest their spread-too-thin lifestyle allows them to deeply love neither and may be even a flight from intimacy. Indeed, their relationships fail to meet two requirements of intimacy — intensity and continuity. Because they are often simultaneously involved with several people, the intensity of their relationships is necessarily limited. Also, because they move back and forth between the sexes, the continuity of their relationships is impaired.

The uneasy truce of bisexuality ends if ground rules are repeatedly violated and when the wife realizes that her husband finds men sexier than herself, that he is unalterably gay, and that her primary place as object of permanent affection is challenged.

During marriage, many men attempt trial separations to test their sexual orientation. These experiments are almost certain to fail in that they are unintentionally fixed to guarantee a negative gay experience. For example, the men often move into cheap, ill-equipped flats and try to achieve in a few months the kind of gay acculturation and adjustment that single gays take years to achieve. Such trial separations may be repeated every few years as doubts arise usually with consistent results. It is often helpful to clients to point out to them this pattern of structured failure.

The marriages are further stabilized by the men's inability to answer two questions: "Am I certain that a gay lifestyle is what I want?" and "Is it what I will always want?" Answering such questions with the limited gay knowledge available to largely covert men is especially problematic.

Other conditions that keep the men married are family pressure, poor health, wives' dependence, homophobia in clients or community, perceived lack of support from other gays, economic difficulty, and religious scruples. These men tend not to have rejected divorce but rather have an indefinite postponement of it. They continue not disturbing the status quo now but holding to the dream that some day, if they meet Mr. Right, they may live openly gay.

For the man who divorces, the quality of the separated relationship with his wife depends on the anger of the split, the ages of the children, how well the wife adjusts away from her husband, and how well he adjusts to the gay world. Even in the most amicable divorces, however, a distancing and cooling off period is usually necessary before the couple can comfortably renew interaction. In spite of the relief of having the divorce finalized, both parties often experience the usual stages of mourning and grief for the dead marriage. Sometimes loneliness, depression, and self-recrimination set in, and the therapist may be called upon to provide active support after separation from the wife. Coming out groups may also be helpful at this time.

RELATIONSHIP TO CHILDREN

If gay fathers are to have a warm, intimate relationship with their children, disclosure of homosexuality is essential. Children are never too young for this information and should be told whenever the father feels comfortable with his sexuality. Children will absorb only as much as their development allows them to understand. As they become older, further details may be added so they gradually become educated about the varieties of gay experience.

I am a strong advocate for *planned* disclosure. All too often gay fathers come out to their children by default. There is a sudden, unexpected confrontation by the children; or a friend is careless in the children's presence and everyone is thrown into a flap. Planned disclosure can make the difference between a growth experience and a calamity.

When telling children, choose a quiet place where you will not be interrupted. Keep your tone upbeat and sincere, not heavy and maudlin. Make sure there is plenty of time for explanations and expressions of their feelings. Let your children know that this disclosure does not change your relationship with them except to make it more honest. The following are some questions children ask and some suggested answers:

Why are you telling me? My emotional life is important and, by example, I can teach you to value yours too. If I'm secretive about sex, you might get the idea that sex is frightening and something to be hidden. Homosexuality is not contagious. Fear and shame are.

What does being gay mean? Being gay means being attracted to another man. It means being attracted so much that you might fall in love with him and express the love sexually.

What makes a person gay? There are lots of theories, but no one knows exactly what makes some people attracted to men and some attracted to women. (Caution: The child might be really asking, "Will I be gay?" or "How will I know if I'm gay?")

Will I be gay? You will not be gay just because I am. You are a separate person. You will be whatever you are going to be because of your own makeup and life experiences. I hope you will find loving relationships and that you will be open to whatever your life has to offer.

Do you hate women? This question might mean, "Do you hate Mom?" Coming from daughters, this question usually means, "Do you hate me?"

Did your lover make you gay? My gayness is a fuction of my own sexual orientation, not something that was forced on me by anyone else. My lover, however, has helped me to express my warm and tender gay feelings.

What should I tell others about this? If you have friends that you want to tell, try it out. If you have a bad experience, let us talk about it. We can learn together the best ways of sharing this.

The younger that children are told, the more accepting they tend to be. Also, children who feel secure about their own sexuality react better. Family counseling with an informed therapist can be an important support should the need arise. Keep communication lines open and talk about your gay identity as often as it seems appropriate. If there are support groups available for gay fathers and their children, investigate them. But most important, trust yourself. You are the world expert on your father-child relationship. Use that knowledge to strengthen the love and honesty between you.

RELATIONSHIP TO THE HETEROSEXUAL WORLD

While in the closet, gay husbands and fathers often fall in love with heterosexual men. (This is understandable given the isolation of gay fathers from openly gay men.) The love, being unrequited, however, causes pain and bitterness in both parties. Continued attraction to heterosexual men sometimes is construed as evidence that the gay husband and father is not really gay: "Gays weren't good enough for me." "How could I be gay if just straight guys turned me on?" Adherence to this denial ensures the gay father an unsatisfying love life. Attraction to men who are sexually and emotionally unavailable is also a way for the gay husband and father to punish himself for his guilt about being gay.

This guilt often persists even after the men come out, especially if there has been a community scandal, an arrest, or if the wife has spoken negatively to friends. Sometimes the prospect of coming out to heterosexuals, people who have been lied to for years, is so intimidating that the gay father just bolts. He may quit his job and move to another city, try to bury his past and start fresh in a new place. This is a common pattern, but it is self-destructive, and such a sudden break often precipitates an emotional breakdown.

Another common but self-destructive pattern is the gay husband and father who comes out in a flurry, indiscriminately telling everyone. When significant others do not share the gay father's enthusiasm and react negatively, the man often becomes depressed or angry and rejects heterosexuals, fleeing and burning his bridges. It is important to point out to the client that, just as it took him time to come to terms with his homosexuality, it also takes significant others time to adjust, and demanding their instant acceptance is an exhorbitant expectation.

The bitter struggle to come out sometimes results in a separatist ideology with the men adopting extreme postures to both gays ("We are superior") and to nongays ("Straights can go fuck themselves"). This stance buttresses in the gay father's mind the correctness of his sexual identity and discounts any misgivings he may have about relinquishing heterosexual status and prestige. (Extreme postures are also adopted by teenagers as they develop identities. The process of gaining a new identity seems to necessitate "going overboard.") As therapy progresses and the man develops a support network and becomes more comfortable with his gay lifestyle, this posture mellows and he is able to integrate both gay and nongay worlds without feeling a threat to his homosexual identity (McWhirter and Mattison, 1984).

RELATIONSHIP TO THE GAY WORLD

While married, gay husbands and fathers tend to have an approach-avoidance conflict with the gay world. They eroticize it and exoticize it, but they are angry at the unacceptable feelings it arouses in them. They are drawn to what they perceive as a mysterious community ungoverned by the rules of everyday life. The men are both attracted and repelled by what they view as a world of perpetual, easy sex with no responsibility. They tend to see themselves as more "responsible," more "sensible," more "practical" than openly gay people. These perceptions psychologically distance the men from the gay world and from other homosexuals and insulate them from full gay identity.

While married, many gay husbands and fathers structure their lives so that they selectively perceive only the negative aspects of gay life. Furtive forays into the gay world for quick, genitally-focused sex and then back to their heterosexual friends does not allow the men to make gay friends or to view the gay world as a warm hospitable place.

Operating on the margins of the community also leads to many painful experiences: One client was hospitalized when attacked by gay bashers while cruising a city park. Another was caught by police flagrante delicto in a public washroom and convicted after an expensive and humiliating trial. And another was stabbed by a hitchhiker he solicited for sex. Even those men who glimpse positive aspects of the gay world often do not question their generally negative perceptions but merely regard these aspects as "exceptions" and continue to subscribe to generally negative assessments.

After divorce, acculturation into the gay world is problematic for gay husbands and fathers. The difficulties cluster around four areas: (1) disadvantage of late arrival on the scene; (2) the necessity of learning new social definitions and skills; (3) the need to reconcile prior fantasies to the realities of the gay world; and (4) integrating gay and father roles.

First, many gay husbands and fathers fear their age or appearance might disqualify them from gay life and that this would make them double failures: not being able to succeed in either the gay or nongay world. Many cope with their apprehensions by becoming physically fit and adopting more flattering clothing and hairstyles, thereby boosting their confidence.

Second, gay husbands and fathers often report awkwardness in approaching and conversing with other gays because they feel deficient in gay social skills. Their homophobia may cause them to perceive other gays as merely sex objects and they may not be able to relate to gays socially and intellectually. Finding new friends in the gay world, therefore, may require new social approaches and techniques. Some gay skills may be acquired through books, through support groups, and through trial-and-error. Assertiveness training can also be helpful for newly-emerging gays. Because of their hit-and-run sex during marriage, many men eroticize furtiveness so that they experience sexual dysfunction with gays when in a calm context. Learning to eroticize gay coupledom and achieve intimacy are other skills that these men may need to learn before feeling at home in the gay world.

Third, a high proportion of men report a dissonance between the newly encountered realities of the gay world and the fantasies that enticed and sustained them during the marital conflict and divorce. Gay institutions, which they saw only on rare and furtive pilgrimages, were viewed as temples of sexual and social celebration. In short, they romanticized the gay world. When the idealized fantasy collapses (after rejection by a lover, for example), many men consider retreating back to the more familiar and socially approved heterosexual life. The astute therapist can help the client reconcile the disparity between his gay fantasies and his gay reality.

Fourth, clients may fear their father and ex-husband status could distance them from single gays. Consequently, they tend to disclose only to those they feel will react favorably. Often they think gays regard them with curiosity, pity or confusion, and even as the gay movement's "Uncle Bruces." For those gay fathers who live with their children after divorce, acquiring a lover may seem like an impossible dream. There may be few single gays who want to accept them as a "package deal" and the gay father may feel that he has not enough time and energy to attend to both children and a lover. Therapy can help gay fathers sort out the difficulties in restructuring their new life in the gay world.

SUMMARY

Counseling gay husbands and fathers centers on five areas: (1) Relationship to Self, (2) Relationship to Wife, (3) Relationship to Children, (4) Relationship to Heterosexual World, and (5) Relationship to the Gay World. While this counseling can be as individual as the people involved, a general outline has been presented to give examples of common patterns. There are points of adjustment along a continuum ranging from remaining married in a monogamous relationship to separation to living in a monogamous gay relationship with or without children. Since it usually takes years to come to terms with homosexuality, the levels of adjustment shift over time until a mutually acceptable accommodation is reached with the man and his various significant others.

Paralleling this development are three shifting goals in therapy. Initially, gay fathers often want therapy to rid themselves of gay feelings, to become totally nongay and have a conventional marriage. When they try and fail at this, the men shift to wanting to integrate their homosexuality into their existing marriage. They want their wives to accept a mixed-orientation marriage. This is particularly difficult for middle class wives to accept, although working class and upper class wives tend to better tolerate this accommodation. A third shift often takes place in therapy. The gay fathers seek therapy to help them end their marriages with a minimum of pain and to live openly gay. This is more often the case for men who have established a reciprocal gay love relationship.

Usually the initial stages of therapy involve education about homosexuality and support during the later stages. Specifically, debunking antigay stereotypes via bibliotherapy, giving permission to be less inhibited in expressing feelings, desensitizing expected negative social reactions, resolving denial and guilt, and encouraging the men to meet conventional gays in the community are important psychological steps in the men coming to terms with their gay-father status. Teaching intimacy skills, assertiveness training, communication techniques, and effective group interaction move the men into more comfortable adjustments.

REFERENCES

Brown, H. (1976). *Familiar faces, hidden lives*. New York: Harcourt Brace Jovanovich.

Clark, D. (1977). *Loving someone gay*. Millbrae, CA: Celestial Arts.

Gay Fathers (1981). *Some of their stories, experience, and advice*. Toronto: Gay Fathers of Toronto.

Humphreys, L. (1975). *Tearoom trade: Impersonal sex in public places (Expanded ed.)* . Chicago, Aldine.

McWhirter, D., & Mattison, A. (1984). *The male couple: How relationships develop* . Englewood Cliffs, NJ: Prentice-Hall.

Miller, B. (1979). Gay fathers and their children. *Family Coordinator, 28,* 544–552.

_____. (1983). *Identity conflict and resolution: A social psychological model of gay familymen's adaptations*. Unpublished doctoral dissertation, University of Alberta, Edmonton.

_____. (1986). Identity resocialization in moral careers of gay husbands and fathers. In A. Davis (Ed.), *Papers in honor of Gordon Hirabayashi*, Edmonton, Canada: University of Alberta Press.

Neil, J. R., Marshall, J. R., & Yale, C. E. (1978). Marital changes after intestinal bypass surgery. *Journal of the American Medical Association, 240,* 447–450.

Ross, M. (1983). *The married homosexual man*. London: Routledge and Kegan Paul.

11

LESBIAN MOTHERS: MENTAL HEALTH CONSIDERATIONS
G. Dorsey Green

Lesbian mothers have the same mental health needs as all mothers. They also have additional needs generated by living in a predominantly homophobic society. Our culture especially does not like to see mother and lesbian in the same sentence. The author's goal is two-fold. First, it is her hope to educate the reader about the mental health needs of lesbian mothers. The second is to provide normative information about lesbian mothers in light of these needs.

COMING OUT

Before coming out can be appreciated fully, it is important to understand what a person comes out to. Homophobia is what it sounds like: homo, prefix meaning homosexual and phobia, meaning "an exaggerated, usually inexplicable and illogical fear of a particular object or class of objects" (Webster's Seventh New Collegiate Dictionary, 1983). Thus, homophobia is the illogical fear of homosexuality in oneself as well as in others. This phobia has become entrenched in society to such an extent that lesbians and gay men are systematically discriminated against emotionally, economically, spiritually, and socially. Most people are homophobic, including lesbians and gay men. Their homophobia is called internalized homophobia.

Heterosexism is another reality of our culture. It refers to our collective assumption that all people are heterosexual, unless blatantly not so. It also pertains to our bias that people *should* be heterosexual.

Anyone who comes out in the United States faces homophobia and heterosexism in themselves and others. Add to this stress the issues of motherhood and the reader may get a sense of the needs of these women.

MOTHERS WHO HAD THEIR CHILDREN AS HETEROSEXUALS

When a woman decides she is a lesbian she comes out in two ways, to herself, and to other people. Coming out to oneself usually involves a sense of disorientation as the woman readjusts her sense of identity to fit the new data about herself (Moses & Hawkins, 1982; Woodman & Lenna, 1980). Many women try to discount their attraction to other women, and they often work very hard to live a heterosexual life. If the feelings and awareness persist, the woman may decide she is a lesbian and then move on to deciding what this means to her lifestyle.

Many lesbians stop the coming out process because of their fear of reprisal from the nongay world. They worry realistically about losing family, friends, jobs, and money so they stay closeted. Other women first become aware of their lesbianism in the context of a sexual relationship with another woman. Usually this sexual involvement evolves from a close friendship that the woman labelled as special — not lesbian. Sometimes a woman ends this involvement without calling herself bisexual or lesbian; sometimes she decides that she is a lesbian (or bisexual). She may also decide to continue her coming out process to the rest of the world. When lesbians do choose to come out to other people they often then do lose jobs, family, and friends as the trade-off to living a lifestyle more congruent with their lesbian identity. When the woman coming out is a mother, her pain and fears are multiplied because of her concern for her children and the threat of reprisal against her and the children.

No matter which route a lesbian chooses, she is under considerable stress. This often translates into depression, mood swings, sleep and eating disturbances, bursts of anger, and somatic difficulties. There are also two compounding problems. One is that most newly defined lesbians feel isolated and cannot talk about their fears, joys, or changes. The other problem is that most newly defined lesbians have doubts about their lesbianism: this is their internalized homophobia. This phenomenon makes it impossible for them to evaluate clearly their coming out, getting divorced, or having a lover. They have to contend with an inner voice telling them that they are wrong or sick. This magnifies the other symptoms.

DIVORCE

A woman often decides to separate from her male partner or husband after she has begun to identify as bisexual or lesbian. In either event she faces the same issues of separation and/or divorce that all women do. It is likely that her economic status will drop substantially, although she may have had to return to work outside the home. She usually needs to find housing of a standard lower than that she has been used to. She must cope with raising children as a single parent much of the time. She also must say goodbye to someone she shared a family with and may still love. New lesbians who separate from their husbands may do so out of relief, or they may do so reluctantly if they still care for them. They may separate out of honesty rather than out of dislike.

These women also have to decide whether to come out to their husbands. The amount of stress this decision engenders is immense. If they do not come out the husbands often cannot understand why their wives *have* to leave. If they do come out there is a strong possibility of a custody battle. When men contest child custody they win 70 percent of the time (Chesler, 1986). When the mother is a lesbian this figure rises dramatically (Lesbian Mothers National Defense Fund, personal communication, September 30, 1986). Not coming out to the children's father may also mean not coming out to the children; they might tell their father on their own if they know. Not being out to the children may mean not being out at home. Imagine for a moment what it would be like to have to hide your feelings for a lover in your own home. Couples break up over this; mothers can get very anxious, depressed, or at the least, jumpy. The children, of course, do not know what is wrong and will frequently ascribe the problem to themselves. They may withdraw, act out their confusion, or use some other way of communicating their pain. Coming out is usually a better choice for the mental health of the mother and the family in the long run if the parents can work out custody issues in a mediative style rather than an adversarial one. But of course there are no guarantees and many women stay closeted out of fear.

Since her children are probably heterosexist and homophobic, a newly defined lesbian mother will probably have to reeducate them. They may already be angry at her because of the divorce and may want to hurt her in retaliation. They may want to stay away from her and from her lover (if she has one) or demand that she hide her sexual orientation. Lesbian mothers' own homophobia makes them vulnerable to their children's attacks and attempts to make them feel guilty.

Some mothers have women lovers as they come out of their heterosexual relationships. Thus, they have another set of decisions to contend with. Do they live together? Does the lover take a parenting role? How does she explain the lover to the children? Lovers who have never had children often do not understand how important the mother's children are to her.

Even a lesbian mother who is out may have trouble finding friends who can comprehend her situation. A complicating problem is that many health care providers will caution the lesbian mother to stay closeted to protect the children. Their opinions are usually based on their own homophobia and not on factual knowledge. Thus, mothers have few places to turn for supportive help in coping with the many stresses of being a lesbian parent.

Many lesbians do stay married after discovering they are lesbian. Some choose not to act on their attraction to women, some choose to have discreet affairs, and a small minority tell their husbands and reach an agreement with them to stay married and for both to seek outside sexual partners. It is most likely that of these options only the mutual choice between wife and husband will give them support within the relationship. The other two choices are more stressful from the standpoint that the wife/mother must forego open expression of intimacy, both sexually and emotionally, in order to stay married.

The author's bias is that the more open and honest choices are the least stressful. A number of authors (Berzon, 1978; Clunis & Green, in press; Moses & Hawkins, 1982; Schulenburg, 1985) suggest that coming out is much healthier for children because it clears up doubts and opens channels for honest communication. A lesbian mother who does come out will still have concerns as she continues her coming out to new people, especially the people important in her children's worlds, such as teachers and friends' parents. Children's discomfort with their own sexuality makes acceptance of a sexual issue even more difficult. Clearly all of these stresses create extreme problems for the married lesbian mother, most of them associated with the coming-out process, and this stems from society's refusal to acknowledge the legitimacy of a lesbian lifestyle.

MOTHERS WHO HAD THEIR CHILDREN AS LESBIANS

Lesbian mothers who have children after they come out as lesbians have some different mental health needs than their counterparts who have children as married heterosexuals. Usually these women have a developed social support network who know about their lesbianism. They have also had time to work out at least some of their internalized homophobia before they have to face the stresses of parenting.

Lesbians who choose to become pregnant can do so in one of two ways; they can have intercourse or use artificial insemination (AI). Increasingly lesbians are choosing AI for two reasons: The lesbian mother will be protected from paternity and custody battles, and most lesbians prefer not to have heterosexual intercourse. Whether a woman chooses intercourse or AI selecting a biological father is complicated. There are legal, hereditary, and emotional issues. Women who choose AI must be concerned about the health of the donor. If the donor is anonymous — through a sperm bank, physician or other intermediary — this concern has to be answered by a third party. If the donor is known, the mother and he must decide on whether he is to be involved in parenting. There are so few reports of these arrangements that most lesbian mothers are on their own in making these decisions. Although Pies' book *Considering Parenthood* (1985) and Schulenburg's *Gay Parenting* (1985) are excellent resources, at this stage these women also need the advice of health care providers who can help them through these decisions in a supportive, nonjudgmental way. But once a lesbian is pregnant she has immediate health care needs for herself and the developing baby. She is vulnerable emotionally. She needs prenatal care that is supportive and respectful of her lifestyle. Any other kind of care is destructive to her. The same is true of her birth and postnatal care.

When the baby has arrived there are new needs for the lesbian mother. If she is closeted she has to cope with people's assumptions that she is heterosexual and became pregnant by accident or that she voluntarily chose single motherhood. If she is out she very likely will have to educate and reeducate people about lesbians who parent. She must in general rely on the health care provider's good will.

Another related issue is what happens within the lesbian mother's family when she is confronted with the decisions of how to interface with her children's worlds. As the children get older they interact with more and more of mainstream society. This opens up whole new worlds of primarily heterosexist and homophobic institutions for the lesbian mother to deal with. She either stays closeted or has to come out over and over again. Over time it does get easier but coming out is extremely stressful when any stranger's prejudices can hurt her children. Ideally, lesbian mothers should be able to expect the same kind of support from mainstream society as nongay mothers, but this is not the case.

If a lesbian remains closeted she has to hide parts of herself even within her own home. This kind of strain hurts a family and can lead to a buildup of resentments. If the biological mother has a partner who also parents the children, being closeted negates the family itself. Closeted lesbian mothers often break up over the strain of trying to pass as nongay so that their children can survive the system. If the couple *is* out to the rest of the world, they are constantly faced with educating people and with the inevitable discrediting of the nonbiological mother's role ("She's not *really* your mom"). Luckily, there are a few pioneers who have survived the systems that are supposed to serve them, and who have begun the process of education. It is also important to acknowledge the many professionals who have responded supportively and have become allies in helping these mothers cope.

Because of the strain of being semi-invisible, lesbian mothers have a great need of support groups. They need to know they are healthy and not alone. They need to share coping mechanisms and resources that are useful to them as women and mothers. Mental health providers can facilitate these groups only when they have worked through their own homophobia and heterosexism. Once they do, however, they can be a tremendous resource for lesbian mothers.

Since lesbian couples cannot legally marry they always appear to be single women on "official" forms. As a result, all lesbian mothers are officially listed as single parents and this is a disservice to all single parents. Single parents have a difficult job to begin with because parenting is a full-time job and most of these people work outside the home as well. Lesbian mothers face these pressures in addition to the pressures of being lesbian. When lesbian mothers are supported in all their roles (wage earner, mother, lesbian, woman, lover, friend), they are happier, function more productively, and contribute much more toward raising healthy children. Anything less than this invites trouble. If she is out she may have a community supportive of both her parenting and lesbian roles.

Lesbian couples who share parenting at least have each other for support whether or not they are out. They also usually have more income, childcare capability, and extra hands to relieve each other when one needs a break. What these women face is the constant attack on the nonbiological mother as not being a "real parent." It is almost impossible for a person to absorb this negation without some reaction. It is not uncommon for these women to become angry, depressed, hostile, or withdrawn. They certainly often need help understanding what is happening to them.

LEGAL VULNERABILITY

A brief word needs to be added here about the legal vulnerability a *nonbiological* lesbian mother faces. If the biological mother dies, there is no guarantee that the nonbiological mother will retain custody, regardless of the length and quality of the parenting relationship. One judge in Colorado in 1986 gave custody to a child's grandparents in spite of the surviving mother's history as an excellent parent and the grandparents' history of only slight involvement with the child. The more closeted a couple is the more likely the survivor will be overlooked as a real mother but the more likely she may obtain custody as a nongay parent. This can be a no-win situation for the children and mothers. All lesbian mothers need legal advice and support.

Although Chapter 6 in this book deals with gay and lesbian parents and adoption, it is important to acknowledge here that there are two specific mental health issues for lesbians who adopt children. The adoption can be difficult because of two unknowns: the waiting period, and the money it costs. However, lesbians who adopt a child also must confront yet another homophobic institution — the adoption agency. Most agencies will not consider lesbians if they know the applicant is lesbian, so the woman must decide whether she is willing to take the risk of being rejected because of that bias. If she decides to remain closeted, she must negate herself for the screening, waiting, and probationary periods. This can take its toll.

If it is a lesbian couple who wants to adopt, it is highly unlikely that they both can become legal parents. They must decide who will be the *legal* parent as well as whether they will tell the agency about the true nature of their relationship. This can sorely test a relationship. They may both parent for years, break up, and the nonlegal parent could find she has lost all contact with the child, depending on the goodwill of her partner and the modernity of the courts.

ROLE OF PARTNER

Before a couple ventures into mainstream society as two lesbian mothers, they should work through with each other and the children just what everybody's role is. Will both women parent equally or will one be primary and the other secondary? Heterosexual parents usually assume that the mother will do most of the day-to-day work but both assume they are equally responsible. Most lesbians who have children together also assume equal status, but they need to be able to articulate that to the outside world. The couple has to figure out who will deal with teachers, physicians, Boy Scouts, and so forth. Often couples will need help in making some of these decisions since most of society has never had to tell outsiders who does what inside the family structure. The helper at this point should assist the couple to make their own decision, giving input on what the obstacles and supports are realistically.

FAMILIES OF ORIGIN

One of the lesbian mother's greatest strains is in her relationship with her family of origin. If she comes out after marriage her family is almost always hostile, terrified, and angry. This is another area where health care professionals can indirectly aid the lesbian mother. When her family asks questions, and they frequently do, health care providers can refer them to Friends and Families of Lesbians and Gays, give them book lists, and/or generally be supportive of their pain while challenging the homophobia. When this is done, everyone's mental health is improved.

Most of the mental health considerations of lesbian mothers stem from a homophobic and heterosexist society. As individuals lesbian mothers are subject to the same problems all women and mothers have. Even knowing this, however, a surprising number of lesbian mothers fall prey to the same doubts the nongay society has. People always ask about the children's psychosexual development; they assume that a mother's lesbianism somehow influences her child's developing sexuality. Green (1978); Golumbok, Spencer, and Rutter (1983); Kirkpatrick, Smith, and Roy (1981) and others have found that children of lesbians show normal development when compared to children of nongay mothers (see Chapter 5).

Another worry of lesbian mothers is how their children will fare in school. Hanscombe and Forster (1982) and the movie *In the Best*

Interests of the Children interview children of lesbians. It seems that these children have the same kinds of problems as their peers. Sometimes the youngsters report being more cautious about choosing their friends, but they also think they have better friends as a result. It would be unreasonable to tell a parent that her children will have no trouble in school because of her lesbianism, but it is also irresponsible to suggest that the children will be irrevocably hurt by it. Most clinical data seems to indicate that the more honest the lesbian mother is with her children the better adjusted they are and the better they are able to cope with school pressures of all kinds.

Another area of concern is whether a lesbian mother should show affection toward her partner in front of her children. Since women have differing value systems about public affection, they need to trust their own values. There is, however, no data to suggest that affection in front of children such as kissing, hugging, or holding hands is detrimental. On the contrary, if a lesbian mother is out to her children, she is going to feel better and be a better parent if she can be herself with her family.

One other general concern that lesbian mothers have is other lesbian mothers. Who are they? Where are they? How many are there? How can I meet some others? Isolation is perhaps the most pervasive concern for all of these women. Lesbian mothers often know no one like themselves, and their children have no peers like them. There is not much literature for these women and what there is is often professional (Goodman, 1980; Hall, 1978; Hotvedt & Mandel, 1982; Kirkpatrick, Smith, & Roy, 1981; Lewin & Lyons, 1982; Lewis, 1980; Pagelow, 1980; Richardson, 1981). Hanscombe and Forster (1982), Schulenberg (1985), and Pies (1985) do a good job of discussing the lesbian mother without using professional jargon. However, unless a lesbian has access to bookstores that carry such progressive works she may never find normative data about herself. As a result, these women will turn to health care providers to make sense of a problem that they think may be due to their lesbianism. Usually parenting problems of lesbians are just that — parenting problems. It is important for care-givers to learn when homophobia is the real problem so that they do not unwittingly compound the issues.

As one reads about and works with lesbian mothers it is crucial to evaluate what are the woman's individual issues, what is a parenting problem, what is a family issue, and what is homophobia. A mother may be depressed because that is how she copes with anger, because her son is failing in school, because the children are fighting too much, or because the girl's soccer coach will not let her help out because she is a lesbian. Homophobia can make all other symptoms worse without anyone realizing that it is an issue.

CONCLUSIONS

Most of the mental health issues that lesbian mothers face stem not from intrapsychic problems but from the interface of the mothers with society. If society and its primary institutions were less heterosexist and homophobic, these mothers would be able to spend more attention on productive issues rather than trying to cope with these pressures from society.

REFERENCES

Berzon, B. (1978). Sharing your lesbian identity with your children. In G. Vida (Ed.), *Our right to love: A lesbian resource book.* Englewood Cliffs, NJ: Prentice-Hall.

Clunis, D. M., & Green, G. D. (book in preparation). *Lesbians in couples.*

Chesler, P. (1986). *Mothers on trial: The battle for children and custody* . New York: McGraw-Hill.

Golumbok, S., Spencer, A., & Rutter, M. (1983). Children in lesbian and single-parent households: Psychosexual and psychiatric appraisal. *Journal of Child Psychology and Psychiatry, 24*, 551.

Goodman, B. (1980). Some mothers are lesbian. In E. Norman & A. Mancuso, (Eds.), *Women's issues and social work.* Itasca, IL: Peacock.

Green, R. (1978). Sexual identity of 37 children raised by homosexual or transsexual parents. *American Journal of Psychiatry, 135*, 692–697.

Hall, M. (1978). Lesbian families: Cultural and clinical issues. *Social Work, 23*, 380–395.

Hanscombe, G. E., & Forster, J. (1982). *Rocking the cradle.* Boston: Alyson.

Hotvedt, M., & Mandel, L. G. (1982). Children of lesbian mothers. In W. Paul, J. Weinrich, J. Gonsiorek, & M. Hotvedt (Eds.), *Homosexuality: Social, psychological and biological issues.* Beverly Hills: Sage.

Kirkpatrick, M., Smith, C., & Roy, R. (1981). Lesbian mothers and their children. *American Journal of Orthopsychiatry, 51*, 545–551.

Lewin, E., & Lyons, T. (1982). Everything in its place: The coexistence of lesbianism and motherhood. In W. Paul, J. Weinrich, J. Gonsiorek, & M. Hotvedt (Eds.), *Homosexuality: Social, psychological and biological issues.* Beverly Hills: Sage.

Lewis, K. G. (1980). Children of lesbians: Their points of view. *Social Work, 25*, 198–203.

Moses, A. E., & Hawkins, R. O. (1982). *Counseling lesbian women and gay men*. St. Louis: C. V. Mosby.

Pagelow, M. (1980). Heterosexual and lesbian single mothers: A comparison of problems, coping, and solutions. *Journal of Homosexuality, 5*, 189–204.

Pies, C. (1985). *Considering parenthood: A workbook for lesbians*. San Francisco: Spinsters Ink.

Richardson, D. (1981). Lesbian mothers. In J. Hart & D. Richardson (Eds.), *The theory and practice of homosexuality*. London: Routledge and Kegan Paul.

Schulenburg, J. (1985). *Gay parenting*. Garden City, NY: Doubleday.

Webster's Ninth New Collegiate Dictionary (1983). Springfield, MA: Merriam-Webster.

Wood, N. J., & Lenna, H. R. (1980). *Counseling with gay men and women*. San Francisco: Jossey-Bass.

12

LEGAL ISSUES IN GAY AND LESBIAN PARENTING

Rhonda R. Rivera

THE GENERAL PROBLEM OF DISCRIMINATION IN CHILD CUSTODY LAW

Parents who are gay exist in the shadow of a legal guillotine that lingers until the eighteenth birthday of their children. At any time during this period, the blade may fall and sever the parent-child relationship. This situation results from a combination of the legal system's homophobia and the peculiar nature of American domestic relations courts.

Systematic and widespread disapprobation of homosexuality is reflected in numerous court decisions and in many statutes. Criminalization of sexual activity between persons of the same sex has existed in various forms from the inception of the nation.[1] However, since 1961 a continuous trend has emerged in the United States to decriminalize adult, consensual, private sexual behavior. Stimulated by the publication and adoption of the Wolfenden Report in England,[2] Illinois adopted the Model Penal Code in 1961[3] and signaled a new perspective in public attitudes toward "victimless crimes." The Model Penal Code of the American Law Institute eliminated criminal penalties for all sexual behaviors except those involving minors, coercion or force, and public indecency. The Wolfenden Report in Great Britain urged the decriminalization of male homosexual behavior, a conclusion accepted by the British parliament. Not only have a large number of state legislatures decriminalized adult, consensual, private sexual conduct,[4] but a significant number of state supreme courts have declared statutes that criminalized such behavior contrary to state constitutions.[5] Reasons for the constitutional invalidity of the statutes have varied from violations of the right to privacy to denial of equal protection.[6] To date twenty-six states have decriminalized private, consensual, adult sexual relations while twenty-four states and the District of Columbia still retain such laws.[7] Most of the latter criminalize both heterosexual and homosexual acts; however, five states have statutes that criminalize only same-sex behavior.[8]

Until 1986, the question of whether these statutes were valid under the U.S. Constitution was open. The trend in the development of the constitutional right of privacy led most legal experts to believe that the right of privacy protected all intimate sexual acts of adults in private. However, in the case of *Bowers v. Hardwick*,[9] the U.S. Supreme Court, in a 5–4 decision, disabused legal experts of their opinions and to some extent shocked the public. In a case involving the arrest of a gay man in his own bedroom, the Court found permissible the criminalization of a broad range of sexual behaviors. While the majority opinion focused on homosexuality, the opinion did not forbid the criminalization of nonmarital heterosexual behavior. The *Hardwick* decision does not technically affect the status of homosexual persons in those states that have decriminalized sodomy. Those states are not required to recriminalize such behavior, and most experts believe they will not.

Nor does the decision affect in a technical sense those states that have such laws. The *Hardwick* decision simply allows states to retain sodomy laws free from a constitutional challenge based on federal constitutional privacy doctrines. Those states could decriminalize through either legislative action or through court action based on state constitutional grounds or nonprivacy federal constitutional grounds.[10] Indeed, the U.S. Supreme Court itself has yet to address the constitutional issues of equal protection and due process in this context.

The U.S. Supreme Court decision in *Hardwick* does, however, have a significant effect beyond its mere technical limitations. The language of the opinion made it clear that five Justices of the highest court in the land have a significant distaste for homosexuality and sexual practices that they dislike shall not during their tenure secure the protection of the right of privacy. This benediction of homophobia will reinforce the prejudices of lower court judges and encourage lay persons to use homosexuality as a legitimate tool in litigation with gay persons. In custody litigation, which we will discuss infra, the potential criminality of the gay parent in those states having sodomy laws has been used successfully to influence judicial decisions.[11] In the past, lawyers representing the gay parent could cast significant doubt on the validity of such laws. Given the decision in *Hardwick*, the Supreme Court has placed its imprimatur on discrimination against gay persons, including gay parents.

In the civil area, discrimination against gay persons has been pervasive. In particular, employment discrimination has been rampant.[12] At common law, a private employer is free to hire and fire at will. The only limitations on this right are created by statute. For example, Title VII of the Civil Rights Act of 1964 prohibits discrimination on the basis of sex, race, ethnicity or nationality. Other federal laws protect the handicapped and persons over forty. No federal law forbids employment discrimination on the basis of sexual orientation. One state and a number of cities, counties, and towns do forbid employment discrimination on the basis of sexual orientation,[13] but in general, most gay employees of private employers are not protected. This lack of protection becomes relevant in custody cases in two ways. First, an implied sanction of discrimination occurs. Secondly, the gay parent's ability to fight openly is limited if he or she fears correctly the loss of employment as a consequence of a custody suit fought on the issue of homosexuality.

Gay persons employed by either the federal government or by state and local governments enjoy some employment protection as a consequence of statutes and judicial decisions that place stricter limits on the right of a public employer to hire and fire.[14] Public actions must be consistent with the due process procedural restrictions of the U.S. Constitution and hence must be "fair." Due process requires that a public employer show a "nexus" between employment decisions and their rationale. Since governments have not been able to show any rational nexus between an employee's sexual orientation and his or her job performance, public agencies are limited in their formal ability to practice discrimination.

Other possible protections offered gay employees are found in union contracts that require "just cause" for employer actions[15] and in new legal trends which are eroding the "employment at will" doctrine. However, in general, gay employees live with the constant possibility of job loss because of their sexual orientation.

To be sure, discrimination also exists in many other areas. Persons have been evicted because they are gay,[16] denied entrance into the armed services,[17] excluded from immigration,[18] and denied security clearances.[19] Gay groups have been denied access to telephone yellow pages,[20] college facilities,[21] and other supposedly public forums. Gay lawyers and doctors have lost their licenses, and gay groups denied tax exempt status.[22] Not all these forms of discrimination exist so blatantly because in recent years gay litigants have increasingly been willing to fight for their rights in courthouses, legislative bodies, and elsewhere. However, it is against this background of sanctioned discrimination that gay parents have sought to assert their parental rights in court, often unsuccessfully.

SPECIAL PROBLEMS IN THE JUDICIAL ENVIRONMENT

Most legal battles involving the custody of children occur in state domestic relations courts. These courts are trial courts, courts of "first impression." In a trial court the facts must be ascertained and resolved before the legal issues are addressed. The finder of fact, either the judge or the jury, must decide who is telling the truth and what the facts are. In most domestic relations courts, judges are the fact finders. Only in Texas are juries used. Once the facts are "found," then the law must be applied to those facts.[23]

The legal standard applied in custody cases is very broad and vague. The decision of original custody is supposed to be "in the best interests of the child." This rather general statement is applied almost universally in the United States. When a judge decides what the facts are in a particular case, he or she must then decide, as a matter of law, what is in the "best interests of that child."[24] Some states have attempted to narrow the permissible range of judicial decisions by setting forth in statute a list of criteria that must be examined.[25] Unfortunately, these standards are themselves also often vague. One such criterion is that the judge should consider "the moral environment of the home."[26] As is easily seen by any practitioner of family law, such a criterion allows much room for the judge to impose his or her own "moral standards."

Once an original custody decision is made using the "best interests" standard, that decision is never final. Until the child reaches the age of majority, the noncustodian can attack the original decision. However, the legal standard applied to change-of-custody cases is higher, that is, more difficult to attain. To change custody, a noncustodian must show two things. First, he or she must show that "a change in circumstances" has occurred that affects the child, and second, he or she must show that a change in custody would be in "the best interests of the child." Without the threshold showing of "a change in circumstances," the "best interests" standard does not come into play in subsequent litigation.[27]

Unfortunately, courts have found that generally the discovery of the sexual orientation of the custodial parent constitutes a change in circumstances.[28] In fact, courts have gone quite far on this issue. Where the noncustodial parent knew at the time of the original custody hearing that his or her spouse was gay, one could argue quite plausibly that the noncustodial parent could never label the homosexuality of the other parent as a "change of circumstances." After all, he or she knew at the time of the original hearing, so no circumstances have changed. But courts have generally held that such knowledge by the other parent is irrelevant, that if the judge did not know, a subsequent allegation of homosexuality could constitute a change of circumstances.[29] Every divorced parent who has received custody lives under the threat of a new custody challenge. For gay parents, however, that threat is particularly real. At any time, if the noncustodial parent discovers or decides to reveal the custodial parent's sexual orientation, a custody challenge is possible.

Custody decisions are normally decided on the basis of the facts a judge chooses to consider rather than the application of some legal standard. Thus, the decision of the judge rests to a great extent on his or her perception of the "truth." Consequently, decisions made by trial judges in the domestic relations area are seldom appealed. Two basic reasons exist for the relative paucity of appellate decisions reviewing gay custody decisions. First, one can only appeal in the American judicial system if one can allege that "the law" has been misapplied to the facts. Facts are decided once and for all at the trial level and cannot be redecided at the appellate level. Since the standards applied in custody cases are so vague and open to interpretation, appellants can seldom convince an appellate court that the law has been misapplied. On rare occasions, appellate courts can reverse trial judges on factual issues. However, the standard applied is that a "gross abuse of discretion" has occurred. Again, such an abuse is seldom found. The second reasons that original custody decisions are seldom appealed is that appeals are extremely costly.[30] The whole trial record must be transcribed at great cost and a lawyer paid to review the record and write the brief. Parents who have gone through a trial seldom have money left for an appeal.

Appellate review comes only after an original custody trial, which is also especially costly for gay litigants. Generally, gay litigants have to present special kinds of evidence to the court that is difficult and expensive to obtain. First, they must convince the judge that gay persons are not per se incapable of parenting, are not per se immoral, and are not per se to be denied custody. Gay litigators attempt to "educate" the court through a series of expert witnesses to demythologize gay people.[31] The expert not only provides facts for the court but attempts to destroy myths and stereotypes about gay people that have adversely affected the gay litigant. Generally, such experts are psychologists, sexologists, and social workers. Each must be paid a witness fee and travel expenses. The most qualified witnesses and experts usually command a high fee. Secondly, the gay parent must convince the court that he or she is a good parent, that the child has not and will not be harmed by custody with the gay parent, and in some cases, that his or her life partner is not a bad influence in the home. To accomplish this task, usually the gay parent, his or her life partner, and all the children must be tested and evaluated by psychologists and the home environment investigated by a social worker. All these tests and evaluations cost money. Then these experts must also be paid witness fees and expenses. Aside from these costs, ordinary litigation costs are increasingly burdensome. Depositions, interrogatories, and pretrial motions are all expensive, as is the lawyer's fee. The costs associated with a well litigated gay custody case are frequently beyond the reach of many people.

Other special factors influence the case as well as the law and the costs. First and foremost are the judges. Most judges are over fifty, white, and male.[32] Few have had any association with openly gay people. There were few, if any, openly gay faculty in law schools thirty years ago and certainly no gay law student organizations. Most harbor the stereotypes of their gender and class. Moreover, trial level judges in most states are not, as a general rule, concerned with the finer points of legal reasoning. Often trial judges are put in office by local political organizations because of their political reliability. They are seldom willing to make decisions at the cutting edge of the law or that might bring local disapprobation, especially at the next election.

A second important factor is the paucity of lawyers who are willing and able to try gay custody cases. Many persons at the domestic relations bar are willing to try any case as long as they are paid. However, many persons who are willing to handle such a case are inappropriate. Many domestic relations lawyers are totally inexperienced with gay custody problems and tend to believe incorrectly that it can be tried like any other domestic matter. At the same time, many of these lawyers do not examine their true feelings toward homosexuality and hence do not zealously represent their client because they believe their gay client is in the wrong.[33] In recent years, the number of lawyers competent and willing to try gay custody cases has increased, but most of these professionals are located in large cities, often on either coast. Persons who do not live in those areas are hard pressed to find a lawyer who will try their case competently. If a gay parent retains such a lawyer, he or she faces another problem. In small towns and rural areas much resentment exists against a lawyer who is not a member of the local bar. In other words, one must decide whether it is better to have a local lawyer or an experienced out of towner. A compromise, of course, is two lawyers, but again the cost is usually prohibitive.

A final, institutional consideration that impacts gay custody cases is the imbalance between the pervasiveness of gay custody problems and the inability of the judicial system to "make" laws that adequately address those problems. Millions of lives are adversely affected by outmoded legal doctrines that surround gay parenting. We know by using Kinsey statistics that approximately 14 percent of all men and 4 percent of all women are predominantly homosexual for a significant portion of their lives.[34] Experts estimate that one-third of all lesbian women and one-fifth of gay men have children. In the United States, current fertility rates are 1.7 children per mother. Using these figures, we can estimate roughly 7.5 million children in this country have either a lesbian mother or a gay father.[35]

Not all of these children are the subject of litigation. Some gay parents choose not to divorce. Perhaps the nongay parent never realizes that his or her ex-spouse is gay, or perhaps they do not consider it relevant. Some nongay spouses are absent, either through death or abandonment. Some lesbian mothers never married or became pregnant through artificial insemination.

Thus, only a relatively small minority of gay custody cases ever enters the legal system. If they do, the prudent lawyer usually tries to avoid litigation if remotely possible, primarily because of the problems of prejudice we have already discussed. No statistics are available on the outcome of cases at the trial court level because the cases are not "reported" in the printed volumes which provide precedents for future litigants. Only the decisions of appeals courts are "reported," and the vast majority of trial court decisions are never appealed.

Probably the majority of such trial court opinions would be unfavorable. Because the equities in gay custody cases are generally in favor of the gay parent, many courts grapple with the issue of fairness and discover that there are few, if any, legitimate arguments against gay custody. When this happens, new, more responsive legal doctrines can be born. This response is the manner in which the common law has traditionally provided flexibility. The absence of such a mechanism in gay custody cases contributes to the maintenance of a profoundly inequitable legal system that affects not only the unfortunate parents and children who fall into the snares of that system but also those who never enter a courtroom but whose lives are unduly restricted by the harshness of antiquated legal doctrine.

The reader can see that litigating the issue of custody when one of the parents is gay takes on larger dimensions not found in other kinds of civil litigation or indeed in nongay custody cases. Those nonlegal dimensions profoundly affect the substantive issues raised by gay custody cases. Only when we have grasped these larger issues are we fully able to understand the substantive legal questions we are about to consider.

SUBSTANTIVE LEGAL ISSUES OF GAY AND LESBIAN PARENTING

Assume that the best efforts to avoid litigation are to no avail. What substantive, procedural, and strategic legal issues face the gay parent?

Who Are the Litigants?

This issue will affect procedural aspects of the case as well as its outcome. The most likely set of litigants is the natural father and mother. They usually face off in a custody case brought on by divorce. Obviously, either parent can be the gay litigant. By far the greater number of cases involve gay mothers, a phenomenon which is a feature of American family life rather than a commentary on gay litigants. Until the mid-eighties, mothers traditionally were the custodians of children.[36] Fathers seldom fought for custody regardless of their sexual orientation. Most states had statutes or rules that presumed that children in "their tender years" were best left with their mothers.[37] Because change of custody required a "change of circumstances" which was difficult to prove, most children remained with their mothers. Hence, most gay custody cases involve nongay fathers who seek to remove children from the custody of their lesbian mothers, a trend decidedly contrary to mainstream custody litigation. More recently, the tender years presumption has been abolished,[38] and many states have statutes that obligate the courts to strict neutrality between mothers and fathers as custodial litigants.[39] Gay fathers have sought custody more frequently in the eighties, but they have fought not only a residual prejudice against fathers but also the current prejudice against gay parents.

The second most likely set of litigants is the state versus a parent. Such cases arise when one parent has abandoned the family or died, and the state seeks to remove the child from the remaining parent. These cases are usually brought as "neglect" cases and are tried under a different standard than divorce custody cases. In a neglect action, the state must show that the custodial parent is unfit.[40] To show that a change of custody is in the child's best interest is not enough; the parent must in fact be unfit. This standard is ordinarily a tough one to meet for the state. However, since gay persons are often presumed to be unfit parents, the state is more likely to prevail.

The third set of litigants is a gay parent versus some third party, usually grandparents or aunts and uncles. The standard to be applied will depend on whether the issue arose from a divorce setting or a neglect setting. Looking at precedent, this last combination should produce the easiest case to decide. A substantial body of law supports the right of a natural parent against the world for custody of his or her child.[41] However, the issue of homosexuality of the parent has created decisions that fly in the face of precedent. A particularly disenchanting situation arises where the gay parent's own parents (for example, the paternal grandparents where dad is gay) fight for custody of their grandchild on the grounds of their own child's homosexuality.[42] If the courts truly believe that environment causes homosexuality in children, then awarding a grandchild to grandparents who have already raised one gay child seems incongruous; however, a number of courts have done so.[43] Apparently, the courts are only concerned with the heterosexuality of the current caretakers.

Is the Homosexuality of the Parent Known?

Before proceeding to set this issue in the context of the gay custody trial, one must consider that the label of homosexual/gay for an individual by a court has little relationship to any scientific or objective standard. For the purposes of making judicial decisions, courts have generally found that "once is enough" to label an individual for a lifetime.[44] While Kinsey and other sex researchers have found infinite variety in human sexual behavior, the courts of the United States have tended to label a person "homosexual" in a rather fixed way. If you have admitted to one sexual experience with another person of the same sex, you are apparently branded for life. With that label come all the problems of discrimination.

Assuming for the moment that our litigant considers himself or herself to be gay, what role does this fact have in the litigation? If the gay parent can "pass" and secure custody without raising the issue of sexual orientation, perhaps he or she can have the child for a sufficient length of time to establish the stability of a home environment. However, the possibility of a suit for change of custody on the grounds of change of circumstances always hangs over the parent's head. One strategy is to try to postpone the issue as long as possible. In effect, the gay parent will probably have to live a single life and relay on clandestine sexual outlets. (This posture of course will not guarantee safety.) Such a choice often results in lack of help in child raising and perhaps a less happy parent and child. Another tactic is to stipulate (that is, admit) to the parent's homosexuality before trial. The reason for such a stipulation is to allow the court to focus on the best interest of the child and not on the sexuality of the parent.[45] By stipulating to the issue, the gay parent hopes to avoid the patent voyeurism that occurs in many gay custody trials. In numerous trials opposing counsel joined by the bench have spent hours questioning the gay parent and his or her partner about their intimate sexual lives.[46] One appellate court held that a trial judge who had engaged in such behavior "was only trying to better understand the gay life style of the mother."[47]

In many cases, the gay parent will have little choice over the openness of the issue of sexual orientation. A frequent problem for the lawyer arises when the gay parent, in the exuberance of honesty and sharing, tells the soon to be ex-spouse of his or her newly recognized sexual orientation. Such revelations are almost always counterproductive and are often used against the gay parent. Most litigators advise their gay clients to guard that information so that its release can be controlled to the advantage of the child or children's well-being.

What Standard Will Be Applied?

When confronted with a gay parent, what weight will the judge give to this factor in making his decision? In 1981, a trial court judge in North Dakota commented on this issue. The judge in the *Jacobson*[48] case

indicated in his opinion that he had "extensively researched the issue."[49]
His conclusion was that the cases are divided into categories: "those in
which courts, without explaining the reasons for their conclusions,
determine that homosexuality is a factor to be considered in awarding
custody, [and] those in which, based upon expert testimony, the courts
conclude that the subject is irrelevant."[50] Having reached this conclusion,
the judge in *Jacobson* said that sexual orientation of the lesbian mother
was only one factor in the total case. He determined that less disruption
would occur if the children remained with their mother.[51] However, the
trial judge was overruled by the North Dakota Supreme Court which held
that the homosexuality of the mother was "the overriding factor" in the
case.[52]

In many cases, the courts apply an irrebutable presumption that the
homosexuality of the parent is a conclusive factor against custody by the
gay parent. The courts of Missouri have reached this conclusion.[53] In
addition, Missouri rules of evidence say that expert evidence is not
binding on the trier of the fact, the judge.[54] Given this approach, little can
be done with legal doctrines or expert testimony to win a gay custody
case in Missouri. Another example of such an approach is the Iowa case
of *King v. King*[55] where the court said that "were it not for the lesbian
lifestyle chosen by [the mother] she would be awarded custody."[56]

A second approach used by judges is that homosexuality per se is not
a sufficient reason to deny custody. The court thus posits that in theory a
gay parent can win custody if other factors override the issue of
homosexuality. But a New Jersey court held that if other factors are
equal, a heterosexual home is preferred over a homosexual home.[57]
When gay parents win custody in court using this second standard, the
reason quite often is that the alternative custodian is so clearly
unacceptable that in the court's eyes the gay parent is the only viable
alternative.[58] Unfortunately, where a gay parent is given custody as a last
resort, the court often imposes severe restrictions on the life of the gay
parent.[59]

The third judicial approach is to use some form of a nexus standard.
In its purest form, this standard would require a showing that the
homosexuality of one parent would harm the child. Sometimes, the
statute which governs custody decisions in a state already requires such a
showing. The purest application of this standard in a gay custody case
occurred in the case of *Peterson v. Peterson*[60] where the judge applied
the Colorado statute. The judge said, "the court is not to consider the
conduct of a party that does not affect his relationship to the child."[61] He
examined the two sets of prospective custodians, the father and his new

wife, and the mother and her lesbian life partner. Since the father was unable to show potential harm to the child and since both couples were shown to be fit, the court ignored the sexual orientation issue, evaluated the best interests of the children, and chose the mother as the primary custodian.

However, even where a statute mandates a nexus between the parent's behavior (that is, homosexuality), and some harm to the child, not every case treats sexual orientation in such a rational manner. Technically some statutes require a showing of present harm and forbid speculation about future harm. In such a state, the chances of the gay parent receiving custody are greater. However, some statutes, or at least the judge's interpretation of them, allow the court to consider future harm. In those cases, the custody rights of the gay parents are often defeated by the judge's personal speculation of future harm or the speculation introduced by experts called by the nongay parent. One of the clearest examples of such a case is *Stevenson v. Stevenson*[62] decided in Kentucky in 1979. The trial court judge found in favor of the lesbian mother saying that no present harm was revealed by the record.[63] This finding was particularly interesting because the judge admitted that his own predisposition was against the lesbian mother.[64] The Kentucky Court of Appeals reversed[65] and said that the trial court judge had erred. The court said that the Kentucky statute used the word "may" with regard to harm and thus possible potential harm was admissible and relevant.[66] The Appeals Court pointed out that even though all the experts had found no present harm, one of the examining psychologists had testified that the child "might" be teased or embarrassed in the future.[67] The same psychologist also testified that the child "might" have trouble adjusting sexually in adult life. Based on this "potentiality of harm," the Appeals Court removed custody from the mother.[68]

TYPES OF HARM ALLEGED

Child Molestation

One type of future harm postulated by nongay parents and often accepted by courts is the allegation that a gay parent will molest his/her child. Even where such a claim is not stated, the belief in this popular myth lies just below the surface. In Missouri a judge who had listened to expert testimony on this subject of child molestation expressed his disbelief as follows: "Every trial judge . . . knows that the molestation of minor boys by adult males is not as uncommon as the psychological expert's testimony indicated."[69] Every expert will testify to a court that 85 percent of all molestation involves men who are heterosexually oriented and about 14 percent concerns men who are homosexually oriented.[70] (Note that Kinsey found that 13.9 percent of all men were homosexually oriented.)[71] Thus, men as opposed to women are child molesters, and their behavior is unrelated to their sexual orientation. Moreover, all experts today will testify that child molestation is unrelated to adult (mature) sexual orientation and results from a fixation on childishness as a sexual object. In fact, the gender of the child is unimportant.

At a minimum these figures should remove lesbian mothers from consideration as child molesters, but it has not. From the standpoint of a domestic relations lawyer, I have noted that courts are hysterical on the issue of child molestation by a gay parent yet ignore (and often implicitly condone) child abuse and incest charges leveled at natural fathers by ex-wives seeking to protect their daughters.[72] Judges seem willing to recognize that parents will do horrible things to their children only if that recognition conforms to ancient stereotypes.

Even when judges allow visitation with a gay parent, they often refuse to permit overnight visitation. One can only presume that the judge believes that child molestation occurs only in the dark of night.

The Child Will Become Gay

In terms of rationality this claim probably is the most ludicrous. Who are the parents of gay human beings? Heterosexuals hold that distinction, in the great majority of cases. Obviously, the way to prevent homosexuality is to prevent heterosexual childbearing or childrearing. An overstated humorous remark to be sure, but after hours of testimony on the etiology of homosexuality, courts still end up removing children from their parents in the mistaken belief that parental sexual orientation influences that of the child. Experts will tell judges that all the previous theories on why persons are homosexually oriented have been disproven. They will say that we have no idea why some persons are heterosexual and some homosexual.[73] Professor John Money of the Johns Hopkins Medical School will testify that regardless of the reason, sexual orientation is probably set in the earliest years, probably below three years of age.[74] (So if the children are over three, "it's too late"!) Many scientists now favor a genetic trait argument,[75] but all would say that regardless of parental or societal attitudes, 10 percent of the population will be predominately homosexual.

Often judges will ask gay parents while they are on the stand whether they want to have their child grow up to be gay. Almost universally they answer no.[76] I am unclear whether they really mean this or merely want the judge to be relieved. Most of my clients say something slightly different. "I want my child to grow up to be authentic and to be happy with themselves; heterosexual or homosexual is irrelevant." My clients also say, "Who would encourage their kid to be gay? For what purpose? To be harassed, discriminated against, to be hated . . . what are we nuts?"

Regardless of the testimony of experts or the pragmatism of gay parents, courts still buy the argument that gay parents can influence the sexual orientation of their children. In cases where the gay parent is given custody or allowed visitation, the judge often sets restrictions seemingly in response to their fears of parental influence. For example, a parent can have visitation but have no homosexual person present during the visitation, especially not their life partner.[77] Gay parents are often warned about displaying (flaunting) any open affection for another adult of the same sex in the presence of their child. Parents who are allowed to keep custody are often ordered not to live with their life partner or have any overnight visitors.[78] Presumably, the children would be affected adversely by seeing their parent express affection and love toward a same-sex individual. We are not talking about limits imposed on open sexual intimacy in front of children such as those implicitly imposed on even heterosexual couples. Rather, a gay parent who is allowed custody must in effect live an "ostensibly" celibate life presumably seeking sexual gratification in clandestine and furtive ways. Ironically, courts would thus force gay persons to live the kind of lives for which they are being condemned by society.

Current research indicates that decisions that force the gay parent to eject their life partner are counterproductive for the child's well-being. Dr. Jane Mandel, working with Dr. Richard Green under the auspices of National Institutes of Health, have conducted a longitudinal study of sixty lesbian mothers and their children.[79] The study's main focus was on the effect on the children of having a lesbian mother. The study shows that children brought up by gay mothers are statistically unremarkable as compared to offspring raised by heterosexual mothers. However, as an unexpected bonus the Green-Mandel study also indicated that children brought up in a two-adult home regardless of the gender of the adults are in better emotional health than those raised by single parents. Thus, by forcing the same-sex partner from the home, the judge is not acting in the best interests of the child.

A clear example of such a decision is the Virginia case of *Roe v. Roe*.[80] Here, the gay father and his life partner had raised his daughter for more than five years before the mother brought suit. The evidence showed the child to be normal in all respects, bright, happy and well-adjusted. The court not only removed custody from the father based solely on his homosexuality, but also limited visitation so that the father's life partner (who we should remember had coparented this child for five years) was not to be in the home when the child visited the father. (Note also that it was *also* the life partner's home.)

The Child Will Be Stigmatized and Embarrassed

This argument says that even if the child will not be molested or converted to homosexuality, the child will be stigmatized by society in general and by other children in particular because their mother or father is gay. They will be teased and harassed to such an extreme degree that the child should be placed with the nongay parent regardless of other factors. This claim often arises when all others fail. Even when no current evidence of any "teasing" exists, the nongay parent suggests and the court accepts the argument that such teasing and stigmatization is inevitable. One attorney pointed out to the court that regardless of who had custody, the child in question would still have a gay parent. The court agreed, but said at least the child would not have to confront this issue on a day-to-day basis.[81]

Gay litigators find this argument hard to confront by expert evidence. Children are no doubt teased, and much of society is indeed homophobic. Where possible, the lawyer points out that much of society is racist and that children of minorities are often teased, stigmatized, and harassed, yet no one suggests removing children for these reasons. Many parents harbor unpopular views of a religious or political nature, but again no one removes children for these reasons. The U.S. Supreme Court faced the issue in a case involving white children whose father sought to regain custody from the mother because she had remarried a black man.[82] The father alleged that the child would be stigmatized and teased. The

Supreme Court rejected that argument saying that just because society was bigoted the courts could not condone such behavior.[83] The Supreme Court of Alaska took the language of the U.S. Supreme Court and applied it in a lesbian mother case.[84] The father had alleged in his bid for custody that the child would be teased. The Alaska Supreme Court permitted the mother to retain custody and referred to the U.S. Supreme Court decision saying, "Simply put, it is impossible to rely on any real or imagined stigma attaching to mother's status as a lesbian."[85] In light of the recent *Hardwick* decision, one can suppose that the U.S. Supreme Court never thought that its words would be construed to protect the motherhood of a lesbian.

A New Jersey court had a similarly unusual approach to the teasing issue. The court said that the child would probably grow up to be a more tolerant person, more understanding of differences in our society.[86] The New Jersey Court implicitly seemed to regard this attitude as a virtue.

Immoral Environment Allegation

This claim is but another method of stating that homosexuality per se prevents custody. This claim says that it is against the best interests of a child to grow up in an immoral environment. Therefore, regardless of the child's health, emotional needs, or other issues, the child cannot be left with a gay parent. Such claims have been attacked on the grounds that a theocratic standard is being applied that violates the constitutional separation of church and state. However, domestic relations courts are prone to ignore constitutional issues. The recent *Hardwick* decision will lend great credence to such an argument, not only in the states that still criminalize adult consensual sex, but also in others because of the chilling effect of the majority's words.[87]

One method gay litigators use to overcome such claims is the expenditure of a great deal of time in the trial educating the court on homosexuality, demythologizing and demystifying gay people and their lives. They attempt to break down the US-THEM dichotomy and help the court to understand gay parents as multidimensional people whose sexual orientation is just one part of their personalities. Often clergy are used as witnesses to show judges that moral disapprobation is not as monolithic as the nongay parent would have the court believe. Most mainstream Protestant denominations and many individual clergy members of other denominations hold positive views of gay persons as individuals and parents. Litigators try to make the court see that there is more to a person's character (as a parent role model) than his or her choice of intimate sexual partner.

AIDS — The New Factor

With the advent of the disease AIDS, which strikes primarily gay and bisexual men, nongay parents have acquired a new weapon for their arsenal. Interestingly, the weapon is not just used against gay or bisexual fathers. This author's first experience as a litigator in this area was in the case of a lesbian mother who was forbidden to kiss her children or have them in her home because of the danger from AIDS. Since lesbians are not at risk for AIDS this use of the disease as a surrogate for homophobia proves its effectiveness.[88]

Obviously, gay fathers are the more affected group. In Chicago, a nongay mother, in the midst of a long term custody battle, has now petitioned the court to stop visitation with the father until he has taken an HTLV-III test.[89] In Puerto Rico, a gay father has been ordered not to kiss his children when they visit.[90]

Numerous other instances of the use of AIDS against gay parents will inevitably follow. This space does not permit a discussion of AIDS. Suffice it to say that expert testimony would indicate that a child is not at risk if cared for or visited by their gay father whether he has AIDS or ARC (AIDS Related Complex), is HIV-positive, or is perfectly healthy. AIDS is not transmitted by household contact.[91] Nonetheless, the fear in the general population, the low level of knowledge about AIDS, and the unfortunate connection between the disease and gay men have created a formidable obstacle for gay women and men who wish to parent their children.

SUMMARY

Reviewing this material, the reader may conclude that no gay parents can hope to win custody of their children regardless of their parental abilities. Certainly, the battle is uphill. However, dramatic changes have occurred since the first gay custody case was recorded until today. A study of the cases reveals that changes in judicial attitudes are governed both by time period and geographical location.[92]

Before 1950, only one published case dealing with gay custody appears in reports.[93] From 1950 to 1959, only three cases were published.[94] Only two cases during 1960 to 1969 were seen. [95] Starting in the 1970s the number of gay custody cases increased dramatically. Between 1970 and 1979, over fifty cases were found.[96] The significant historical event that accounts for this dramatic increase is, I believe, the Stonewall riot of 1969. This riot, which occurred on Christopher Street in New York City, was the first time that gay men and women fought back against police harassment. Historians credit this event as the beginning of the gay liberation movement and with it the growth of a positive gay consciousness.[97] Certainly, the litigiousness of gay men and women rose. More and more gay persons were willing to be out enough to contest their rights in the courts. Gay parents were not an exception.

Interestingly, but not surprisingly, most of these gay custody cases were in states on either coast, in particular California, Washington, and Oregon on the West Coast and New York, Massachusetts, and New Jersey in the East. Moreover, most of the victories for gay parents were in these same areas, and the greatest number of victories were in the last five years of the decade. Proportionally fewer cases were brought in the South and the Southwest, and fewer victories occurred there. Midwestern cases are less extreme and less easy to categorize. Such a pattern is not surprising because the growth of gay activist communities was greatest in San Francisco, Los Angeles, New York City, and Boston. When gay people began to feel some sense of confidence and power, they also brought lawsuits. Moreover, as those urban cultures adapted to more visible gay populations, the general population became more knowledgeable about and less fearful of gay men and women. As the coastal populations became more tolerant, as the issue of homosexuality became demystified and domesticated, the courts were less prone to apply stereotypes and more willing to use a rational nexus approach in gay custody cases.

Thus by the 1980s, definite patterns developed with East and West Coast states having the most progressive approach issues while the South and the Southwest were just beginning to experience significant numbers of gay custody cases. In the South and Southwest, the developing case law was virulently antigay and paralleled the decisions of the late sixties and early seventies in the East and West.

In the eighties, gay parents won significant victories in Delaware, Vermont, Maine, New Jersey, New York, and Massachusetts. California, Washington, Oregon, and Alaska were also the scenes of gay parental victories. For example, in *Bezio v. Patenude*[98] and *Doe v. Doe*,[99] the Supreme Court of Massachusetts held that "the State may not deprive parents of custody of their children simply because their households fail to meet the ideal approved by the community . . . or simply because the parents embrace ideologies or pursue life styles at odds with the average."[100] Moreover, the Massachusetts court placed great emphasis on the testimony of a clinical psychologist that "there is no evidence at all that the sexual preference of adults in the home has any detrimental impact on children."[101] In New York, an appellate court held in *Guinan v. Guinan*[102] in 1984 that "A parent's sexual indiscretions should be a consideration only if they are shown to adversely affect the child's welfare. Specifically, the mere fact that a parent is a homosexual does not alone render him or her unfit as a parent."[103] Another New York appellate court carried this approach further in the 1985 *Gottleib*[104] case, a landmark gay custody case. In *Gottleib*, the gay father who was not chosen as custodian saw the lower court impose severe restrictions on his visitation rights, not unlike restrictions placed on gay parents in many other states. The father was ordered to exclude his life partner and any other known gay persons from his home when his child was present and was forbidden to permit his child to have any kind of contact with his life partner or other gay people. Likewise, he was not allowed to take his child to any place where "known homosexuals" were present. Lastly, he was prohibited from involving the child in any "homosexual activities or publicity."[105] The appellate division struck down all of these restrictions except the last (the concurring judge said that the last restriction applied to the heterosexual mother as well).[106]

As we have seen, a New Jersey court issued a decision in 1979 which held that deciding a case on the basis of the parent's sexual orientation was impermissible.[107] The Alaska Supreme Court decided in 1985 to leave a child with its lesbian mother and specifically rejected the stigma argument.[108] Colorado has a statute that requires the showing of a nexus between harm and a parent's behavior. In the *Cabalquinto*[109] case, the Washington Supreme Court held that visitation rights must be determined with reference to the needs of the child rather than the sexual orientation of the parents.[110] California and Oregon have similar positive precedents.

These cases must be contrasted with cases in Missouri in the 1980s, where all the decisions went against the gay parents and are filled with every stereotype in the book, that is, molestation, stigma, immorality, and conversion or recruitment to "gayness." Similar cases are found in

Iowa and Oklahoma. The court in the *Potter* case said, "It is now time to draw the line in Oklahoma so that it can take its place in the columns [sic] where it stands on homosexual marriage and homosexual custody. . . ."[111] Southern cases have also been unhelpful to gay parents. Probably the clearest example comes in the *Roe*[112] case where the Virginia Supreme Court removed the custody of a child from her gay father who had had custody for five years. The court held that "as a matter of Law" the father was an unfit and improper custodian of his daughter.[113]

This pattern of cases would seem to suggest that in the future, as the rest of America learns to deal with its gay citizens, gay custody cases will be decided more on the merits of the case and less on homophobic responses. However, two events might slow or reverse this progress — the advent of AIDS and the *Hardwick* decision. *Hardwick* creates a "chilling" atmosphere and raises the specter of "criminality" based on sexual orientation; AIDS adds a new level of irrational fear. These events coupled with the resurgence of Christian fundamentalism, which teaches that gay people are pawns of Satan, will no doubt add to the obstacles of gay parents seeking custody of their children. The author is confident these obstacles will one day be overcome as long as gay parents are willing to face them and fight for their children.

NOTES

1. Rhode Island, for example, passed its first sodomy law in 1662. Some states had no criminal sodomy statutes, per se, but at the time of the ratification of the Bill of Rights they adopted the common law of England, and sodomy was a criminal offense at common law. *Bowers v. Hardwick*, 54 U.S.L.W. 4919, 4921 n. 5 (U.S. June 30, 1986).

2. *Wolfenden Report, Report of the Committee on Homosexual Offenses and Prostitution* (1957).

3. In 1961, Illinois adopted the American Law Institute's Model Penal Code, which decriminalized adult, consensual, private, sexual conduct. The law took effect Jan. 1, 1962. Criminal Code of 1961, §§11-2, 11-3, 1961 Ill. Laws 1985, 2006 (codified as amended at Ill. Rev. Stat., ch. 38, ¶¶11-2, 11-3 (1983)(repealed 1984). American Law Institute, Model Penal Code § 213.2 (Proposed Official Draft 1962).

4. Alaska, California, Colorado, Connecticut, Delaware, Hawaii, Illinois, Indiana, Iowa, Maine, Nebraska, New Hampshire, New Mexico, North Dakota, Ohio, Oregon, South Dakota, Vermont, Washington, West Virginia, Wisconsin, Wyoming.

5. Massachusetts, New Jersey, New York, Pennsylvania. *Commonwealth v. Sefranka*, 382 Mass. 108, 414 N. E. 2d 602 (1980); *State v. Saunders,* 75 N. J. 200,

381 A.2d 333 (1977); *People v. Onofre*, 51 N. Y. 2d 476, 415 N. E. 2d 936, 434 N. Y. S. 2d 947 (1980), cert. denied, 451 U.S. 987 (1981); *Commonwealth v. Bonadio*, 490 Pa. 91, 415 A.2d 47 (1980).

6. Massachusetts: void for vagueness. New Jersey: violates right of privacy. New York: violates both equal protection and right of privacy. Pennsylvania: violates equal protection.

7. See Ala. Code § 13A-6-65 (a) (3) (1982) (1-year maximum); Ariz. Rev. State. Ann. §§ 13-1411, 13–1412 (West Supp. 1985) (30 days); Ark. Stat. Ann. § 41–1813 (1977) (1-year maximum); D.C. Code § 22-3502 (1981) (10-year maximum); Fla. Stat. § 800.02 (1985) (60-day maximum); Ga. Code § 16–6–2 (1984) (1 to 20 years); Idaho Code § 18–6605 (1979) (5-year minimum); Kan. Stat. Ann. § 21–3505 (Supp. 1985) (6-month maximum); Ky. Rev. Stat. § 510.100 (1985) (90 days to 12 months); La. Rev. Stat. Ann. §§ 14:89 (West Supp. 1986) (5-year maximum); Md. Code Art. 27, §§ 553–554 (1982) (10-year maximum); Mich. Comp. Laws §§ 750.158 (15-year maximum), 750.388(a)-(b) (1968) (5-year maximum); Minn. Stat. § 609.293 (1984) (1-year maximum); Miss. Code Ann. § 97–29–59 (1973) (10-year maximum); Mo. Rev. Stat. § 566.090 (1978) (1-year maximum); Mont. Code Ann. § 45–5–505 (1985) (10-year maximum); Nev. Rev. Stat. § 201.190 (1985) (6-year maximum); N. C. Gen. Stat. § 14–177 (1981) (10-year maximum); Okla. Stat. Tit. 21, § 866 (1983) (10-year maximum); R.I. Gen. Laws § 11–10–1 (1981) (7 to 20 years); S.C. Code § 16–15–120 (1985) (5-year maximum); Tenn. Code Ann. § 39–2–612 (1982) (5 to 15 years); Tex. Penal Code Ann. § 21–06 (1974) ($200 maximum fine); Utah Code Ann. § 76–5–403 (1983) (6-month maximum); Va. Code § 18.2-361 (1982) (5-year maximum).

8. Arkansas, Kansas, Montana, Nevada, Texas.

9. *Bowers v. Hardwick*, 54 U.S.L.W. 4919 (U.S. June 30, 1986).

10. See Rubenfeld, With Hardwick Lost, What Now? *The Washington Blade*, July 4, 1986, at 6. *See also*, Knocking on the Bedroom Door, *Time*, July 14, 1986, at 23, 24.

11. See Dailey V. Dailey, 635 S. W. 2d 391 (Tenn. Ct. App. 1981). In this case, the attorney for the ex-husband argued, "But Your Honor, this is the Bible Belt. This (a lesbian raising her children) might be okay in New York or California, but this is the Bible Belt." The lesbian mother's attorney attempted to educate the court with expert testimony about homosexuality; the opposing attorney argued that in Tennessee the mother was a criminal for engaging in lesbian sexual activity. The mother lost custody of her child, and visitation was severely restricted. See also Clark, Lesbian Mothers Lose Custody, *Gay Community News*, May 16, 1981, at 1. See also *Roe v. Roe*, 228 Va. 722, 324 S. E. 2d 691 (1985).

12. Rivera, Queer Law: Sexual Orientation in the Mid-Eighties — Part I, 10 U. *Dayton L. Rev.* 459 (1985) provides an extensive discussion of recent employment and related occupational discrimination.

13. Wisconsin passed the first statewide gay rights act in March of 1982, prohibiting discrimination based on sexual orientation in housing, employment, and public accommodations.

14. See *Norton v. Macy*, 417 F. 2d 1161, 1164 (D.C. Cir. 1969). *Norton* established that to discharge a federal civil service employee a "rational nexus" had to exist between the proscribed conduct of the employee, such as gay conduct, and the

"efficiency of the service." Seven states — California, New Mexico, New York, Ohio, Pennsylvania, Rhode Island, and Washington — now have executive orders that prohibit discrimination on the basis of sexual orientation in certain areas of state employment. Local ordinances protect some county and municipal workers.

15.   Most collective bargaining agreements require "cause" or "just cause" for discharge or discipline. F. Elkouri, *How Arbitration Works*, 652 (4th ed. 1985). " . . . [A]n employee's conduct when the employee is off duty and off company property is beyond the employer's disciplinary reach under the collective bargaining agreement, unless the conduct adversely affects the operation of the business. That must be no less true for homosexual than heterosexual conduct. Moreover, the employer has the burden of proving any such adverse effects. Management's disapproval alone does not satisfy the contractual standard of 'good cause.'" *Ralph's Grocery Company and Retail Clerks Union Local 770*, 77 Lab. Arb. (BNA) 867, 871 (1981) (Kaufman, Arb.).

16.   Two recent victories are worth noting. In *Two Associates v. Brown*, 502 N. Y. S. 2d 604 (N.Y. Sup. Ct. 1986), the landlord attempted to evict the surviving gay life partner of a deceased apartment tenant in Manhattan. The court first ruled for the landlord, but then reversed itself holding a gay life partner had the same right as a family member to a vacancy lease under the Rent Stabilization Law. The decision is being appealed. In *People of the State of New York, Joseph Sonnabend, M.D., et al. v. 49 West 12th Tenants Corp.*, No. 43604/83 (N.Y. Sup. Ct., Sept. 1984), an openly gay New York doctor was being evicted from his office because he treats AIDS patients. An injunction against the eviction was obtained and the case settled while appeal of the injunction was pending. Dr. Sonnabend won a new one-year lease and $10,000 damages.

17.   Discrimination against homosexuality in the military has a long history. In no other area of American life has discrimination against gays been so systematic and systemic as in the armed forces. Elimination of gay persons has been an official policy since 1943. DOD Directive 1332.14 § H.1.a. asserts "Homosexuality is incompatible with military service."

18.   See *In re Schmidt*, 56 Misc. 2d 456, 289 N.Y.S. 2d 89 (Sup. Ct., Dutchess County 1968); *In re Nemetz*, 485 F. Supp. 470 (E.D. Va. 1980).

19.   See *Adams v. Laird*, 420 F. 2d 230 (D.C. Cir. 1969); *Finley v. Hampton*, 473 F. 2d 180 (D.C. Cir. 1972). In some recent cases openly gay men and women who "dig in their heels" and fight the revocation or denial of their security clearances sometimes win after long battles. See *Doe v. Casey*, 601 F. Supp. 581 (D.D.C. 1985). See also A Gay Aerospace Worker Sues the CIA, *Newsweek*, Nov. 28, 1983, at 53, col. 1. However, recently a gay employee lost a battle for a security clearance in *Doe v. Weinberger*, No. 85–1996 (D.D.C. 1986). Also, Killian Swift, an openly gay recorder/transcriber of President Reagan's speeches and news conferences, was suddenly stripped of his security clearance and fired from his job. The White House refuses to tell him why his clearance was revoked. Walter, Gay Transcriber Sues White House Over Lost Job, Security Clearance, *The Advocate*, July 9, 1985, at 14.

20.   *Loring v. Bell South Advertising*, 177 Ga. App. 307, 339 S.E. 2d 372 (1985). In this Georgia state action a gay/lesbian bookstore challenged a decision by the Yellow Pages to prohibit an advertisement with the word "gay" in it. The court

held Bell South Advertising is a "private enterprise" that does not perform an essential public service, and thus has no duty to accept particular advertising.

21.   Gay student groups have been denied recognition by college officials. It may take years of litigation before a gay organization is recognized as an official student group. See *Gay Activists Alliance v. Bd. of Regents of Univ. of Oklahoma*, 638 P. 2d 1116 (1981). As an unrecognized group they could not put notices in the student newspaper, have meeting rooms, a faculty sponsor, or use university facilities. See also Lacey, Gay Rights Coalition v. Georgetown University: Constitutional Values on a Collision Course, 64 *Or. L. Rev.* 409 (1986); Barol, et al., The Fight Over Gay Rights, *Newsweek On Campus,* May 1984, at 4; Stanley, The Rights of Gay Student Organizations, 10 *J. College Univ. Law* 397 (1983–84).

22.   *McLaughlin v. Bd. of Medical Examiners* , 35 Cal. App. 3d 1010, 111 Cal. Rptr. 353 (1973); *Florida Bar Ass'n v. Kay* , 232 So. 2d 378 (Fla.), cert. denied, 400 U.S. 956 (1970). But see In re *Florida Bd. of Bar Examiners (Eimers)*, 358 So. 2d 7 (Fla. 1978). The Mississippi Attorney General's office rejected the Mississippi Gay Alliance's application for a corporate charter (the first step toward tax exempt status). The AG's office said that for the state to grant the group a charter "would ostensibly give official legal status to an organization dedicated on its face to subverting the criminal statute" (Mississippi's sodomy law). After months of pressure and an impending federal lawsuit the charter was granted. Victory in Mississippi, *Lambda Update,* Nov. 1984, at 6. Not until 1977 did the IRS reverse its policy of denying charitable tax exempt status to gay charities. See also comment, Tax Exemptions for Educational Institutions: Discretion and Discrimination, 128 U. *Pa. L. Rev.* 849 (1980).

23.

[A] judge agonizes more about reaching the right result in a contested custody issue than about any other type of decision he renders.

The lives and personalities of at least two adults and one child are telescoped and presented to him in a few hours. From this capsule presentation he must decide where lie the best interests of the child or, very often, which parent will harm the child least. The judge's verdict is distilled from the hardest kind of fact-finding. From sharply disputed evidence, he must predict the future conduct of parents on his appraisal of their past conduct. And his decision is disturbingly final. Since it is based fundamentally on factual findings, an appellate court will rarely disturb it. B. Botein, *Trial Judge* 273 (1952).

24.   This theory was originally advanced by Justice Cardozo who observed that "[the judge] is not adjudicating a controversy between adversary parties, to compose their private differences. He is not determining rights 'as between a parent and a child' or as between one parent and another . . . Its concern is for the child." *Finlay v. Finlay,* 240 N.Y. 429, 433–4, 148 N.E. 624, 626, 211 N.Y.S. 429, 434 (1925).

25.   For example, the Michigan Child Custody Act of 1970 says,

"Best interests of the child" means the sum total of the following factors to be considered, evaluated, and determined by the court:

(a) The love, affection, and other emotional ties existing between the * * * parties involved and the child.

(b) The capacity and disposition of the parties involved to give the child love, affection, and guidance and continuation of the educating and raising of the child in its religion or creed, if any.

(c) The capacity and disposition of the parties involved to provide the child with food, clothing, medical care or other remedial care recognized and permitted under the laws of this state in place of medical care, and other material needs.

(d) The length of time the child has lived in a stable, satisfactory environment, and the desirability of maintaining continuity.

(e) The permanence, as a family unit, of the existing or proposed custodial home or homes.

(f) The moral fitness of the * * * parties involved.

(g) The mental and physical health of the * * * parties involved.

(h) The home, school, and community record of the child.

(i) The reasonable preference of the child, if the court deems the child to be of sufficient age to express preference.

(j) The willingness and ability of each of the parents to facilitate and encourage a close and continuing parent-child relationship between the child and the other parent.

(k) Any other factor considered by the court to be relevant to a particular child custody dispute.

Mich. Comp. Laws Ann. § 722.23 (3) (West Supp. 1986).

26. See Ohio Rev. Code Ann. § 3109.04 (B) (1) (c) (Page Supp. 1985).

27. See Hunter and Polikoff, Custody Rights of Lesbian Mothers: Legal Theory & Litigation Strategy, 25 *Buffalo L. Rev.* 691, 700–03 (1976). See also, *Schuster v. Schuster* and *Isaacson v. Isaacson*, 585 P. 2d 130 (Wash. 1978) applying the Washington statute, Wash. Rev. Code § 26.09.260 (1) (1975).

28. See *Newsome v. Newsome*, 42 N.C. App. 416, at 425, 256 S.E. 2d 849, at 854 (1979); *Dailey v. Dailey*, supra note 11.

29. See *Newsome v. Newsome*, supra note 28. In this case the trial court made no finding of fact on the issue of the mother's alleged homosexuality, but removed the child from her custody. On appeal the mother argued that there had been no evidence presented of a substantial change of circumstances sufficient to warrant a change of custody to the father. One reason the court of appeals did not adhere to the normal standard of review was that facts pertinent to the custody issue (allegations of lesbianism) had not been disclosed to the court at the time the original decree was rendered. Therefore the prior decree was not res judicata as to those facts not before the court.

30. See D. Hitchens, *Lesbian Mother Litigation Manual*, § 4.4 (1982).

31. See Hitchens and Price, Trial Strategy in Lesbian Mother Custody Cases: The Use of Expert Testimony, 9 *Golden Gate*, 451, 461–463 (1978–79).

32. Ninety-six percent of state trial judges are white, 98 percent male, and the average age of judges in this survey was 53.4 years. J. P. Ryan, *American Trial Judges* 128 (1980).

33.   The mother's lawyer is quoted as saying that even though his client lost he was glad that the state's highest court had at last established a guideline to be used by Oklahoma courts in dealing with gay custody cases. *The Advocate*, Mar. 18, 1982. at 1. See *M.J.P. v. J.G.P.*, 640 P. 2d 966 (Okla. 1982).

34.   The Institute for Sex Research at Indiana University now estimates that 13.95 percent of males and 4.25 percent of females have had more than incidental homosexual experience. The combined figure is 9.13 percent of the total population of the United States. Letter from Paul Gebhard, Director, Institute for Sex Research, Indiana University, March 18, 1977.

35.   See Harris and Turner, Gay and Lesbian Parents, 12 (2) *J. of Homosexuality* 101, 102 (1985/86). See also, Hunter and Polikoff, supra note 27.

36.   See Orthner and Lewis, Evidence of Single-Father Competence in Childrearing, in *Child Custody Disputes* 283 (1985), indicating in the 1970s, the mother gained custody 90 percent of the time.

37.

> Mother love is a dominant trait in even the weakest of women, and as a general thing surpasses the paternal affection for the common offspring, and, moreover, a child needs a mother's care even more than a father's. For these reasons courts are loathe to deprive the mother of the custody of her children, and will not do so unless it is shown clearly that she is so far an unfit and improper person to be entrusted with such custody as to endanger the welfare of the children. *Freeland v. Freeland*, 92 Wash. 482, 483, 159 P. 698, 699 (1916)

See Roth, The Tender Years Presumption in Child Custody Disputes, 15 *J. Fam. L.* 423 (1976–77). See also 2 *Family Law and Practice* § 32.01 (A. Rutkin ed. 1985).

38.   See Foster and Freed, Life with Father, in *Child Custody Disputes* 127, 152–172 (1985).

39.   For example, Ohio's law states parents "shall stand upon an equality as to the care, custody and control of such offspring, so far as parenthood is involved." Ohio Rev. Code Ann. § 3109.03 (Page 1980).

40.   "In . . . neglect proceedings the standard is statutory, but the language is often imprecise . . . it usually is not limited to physical neglect or cruelty, and considerations of parental fitness come into play. In order to remove the child from the parent, the state may be required to show that the child lacked proper care or that the parent is 'depraved.' Hunter and Polikoff, supra note 27, at 693.

41.   The leading case is *Stanley v. Illinois*, 405 U.S. 645 (1972), which held the state was barred from taking custody of the children of an unwed father without giving him a hearing and without finding he was an unfit parent.

42.   *DeBoise v. Robinson*, No. C-9104 (Del. Fam. Ct., New Castle County Nov. 17, 1980) involved a contest between a lesbian mother and her parents. The court said "the grandparents are devout and fundamental Christians and the mother is not, and in addition the mother's sexual preference is female." The court followed the recommendations and awarded custody to the mother. But in *Bennett v. Clemens*, 230 Ga. 317, 196 S.E. 2d 842 (1973), the Georgia Supreme Court upheld an award of custody to the paternal grandparents of their eight-year old

grandaughter. The majority made no mention of the rights of a natural mother over those of a nonparent.

43. See *Chaffin v. Frye*, 45 Cal. App. 3d 39, 119 Cal. Rptr. 22 (1975). See also note, Parent and Child: *M.J.P. v. J.G.P.*: An Analysis of the Relevance of Parental Homosexuality in Child Custody Determinations, 35 *Okla. L. Rev.* 633, 658 (1982) which discusses *N.A.T. v. M.G.T.*, Cause No. 54084 (Opinion not for official publication). In *N.A.T.* the trial court found both parents unfit and awarded permanent custody to the paternal grandparents. The gay father appealed arguing the award was based solely on his sexual orientation. The father was awarded legal custody.

44. For example, the following persons have been labeled as homosexual and treated as such by courts: a married father who engaged in same-sex behavior in his late teens, *Dew v. Halaby*, 317 F. 2d 582 (D.C. Cir. 1963); a man with a single conviction for a same-sex crime, *United States v. Flores-Rodriguez*, 237 F. 2d 405 (2d Cir. 1956); a woman whose friends were bisexuals, *Bennet v. Clemens*, supra note 42; a man who said he was a homosexual, but never admitted any overt same-sex behavior, *Gaylord v. Tacoma School Dist.*, 85 Wash. 2d 348, 535 P. 2d 804 (1975); women in mannish attire, *Nikola v. Munro*, 162 Cal. App. 2d 449, 328 P. 2d 271 (1958); persons who exhibited characteristics and mannerisms which evidenced homosexual propensities, *Kerma Restaurant Corp. v. State Liquor Auth.*, 27 App. Div. 2d 918, 278 N.Y.S. 2d 951 (1967).

45. See *Mitchell v. Mitchell*, No. 240665 (Cal. Super. Ct., Santa Clara County June 8, 1972). See also D. Hitchens, *Lesbian Mother Litigation Manual* § 4.2, § 5.7 (1982).

46. *Towend v. Towend*, No. 639 (Ohio Ct. App., 11th Dist. Sept. 30, 1976), was as blatant a case of judicial homophobia as one is likely to find; the mother lost custody to the paternal grandmother. In *Nadler v. Nadler*, No. 177331, reporter's transcript at 20 (Cal. Super. Ct., Sacramento County Nov. 15, 1967) the judge asked the mother "Ma'am, will you explain to the court exactly what occurs — we talk here generally of a homosexual act. Just what does this entail? What do you do?"

47. *M.J.P. v. J.G.P.*, supra note 33, at 969.

48. *Jacobson v. Jacobson*, 314 N.W. 2d 78 (N.D. 1978).

49. Ibid. at 79.

50. Ibid.

51. Ibid.

52. Ibid. at 80.

53. See *N.K.M. v. L.E.M.*, 606 S.W. 2d 179 (Mo. Ct. App. 1980); *L v. D*, 630 S.W. 2d 240 (Mo. Ct. App. 1982); *J.L.P. (H) v. D.L.P.*, 643 S.W. 2d 865 (Mo. Ct. App. 1982). For a discussion and analysis of these cases, see Rivera, Queer Law: Sexual Orientation Law in the Mid-Eighties — Part II, 11 *Dayton L. Rev.* 275, 335–39 (1986).

54. See *J.L.P. (H) v. D.L.P.*, supra note 53 at 868. See also, note, "Visitation," 22 *J. Fam. L.* 185, 187 n. 14 (1983–84).

55. No. 3–66091, Mills No. 342 (Iowa Sup. Ct. Sept. 22, 1981).

56. Brief for Appellant at 24–25, *King v. King*, No. 3–66091, Mills No. 342 (Iowa Sup. Ct. Mar. 9, 1981).

57. *Belmont v. Belmont*, 6 *Fam. L. Rep.* (BNA) 2785 (N.J. Super. Ct., Hunterdon County July 22, 1980).

58.   See *King v. King*, supra note 55, where the mother remained the physical custodian of the children while the absent father remained the legal custodian. See also *A v. A*, 15 Or. App. 353, 514 P. 2d 358 (1973) where the gay father was allowed to keep his two sons, but his life was considerably restricted. The mother had not had any contact with the boys for over ten years.

59.   These restrictions are discussed infra at 22.

60.   No. D–66634 (Colo. Dist. Ct., Denver County May 3, 1978).

61.   Ibid. slip op. at 4.

62.   No. 220098 (Jefferson Cir. Ct., Jefferson County, Ky., May 3, 1979).

63.   Ibid. slip op. at 22.

64.   Ibid. slip op. at 21.

65.   *S v. S*, 608 S.W. 2d 64 (Ky. App. 1980).

66.   Ibid. at 65.

67.   Ibid. at 66.

68.   Ibid.

69.   *J.L.P. (H) v. D.L.P.*, supra note 53 at 869.

70.   Pedophilia, a sexual preference for children, is distinct from homosexuality. See D. J. West, *Homosexuality Re-Examined* 212–17 (1977); D. J. West, *Homosexuality* 118–19 (1967); Comment, Private Consensual Homosexual Behavior: The Crime and Its Enforcement, 70 *Yale L. J.* 623, 629 (1961). Homosexual men primarily prefer men of their own age rather than children. *Institute for Sex Research, Sex Offenders* 639 (1965); M. Schofield, Sociological Aspects of Homosexuality 147–55 (1965), *cited in* W. Barnett, *Sexual Freedom and the Constitution* 129–30 n. 51 (1973). In fact, child molesters tend to be heterosexual in orientation. Schofield, supra; *Institute for Sex Research*, supra at 277–79, 303–34, 332–34. Moreover, child molesters are almost never female, either heterosexual or homosexual. West, *Homosexuality*, supra at 115; *Institute for Sex Research*, supra at 9.

71.   Letter from Paul Gebhard, supra note 34.

72.   A psychiatrist testified as follows: "Incest or child molestation within the family essentially is primarily an issue involving stepfathers and fathers, and their daughters. Child molestation, victimization of children sexually is not an offense or a crime that is reported for females. It is almost non-existent." *Ranson v. Ranson*, No. 477051–8 (Cal. Super. Ct., Alameda County, Nov. 9, 1977), Reporter's transcript at 18.

73.   A. Bell, *Sexual Preference* 183–84 (1981).

74.   R. Green, Sexual Identity Conflict in Children and Adults (1974). See also the evidence indicates both that the majority of lesbians had heterosexual parents and that the children of lesbian parents were heterosexual. Green, Sexual Identity of 37 Children Raised by Homosexual or Transsexual Parents, 135 *Amer. J. Psych.* 692 (1978). (Of the 37 children studied, 36 were heterosexually oriented.)

75.   Bell, supra note 73 at 220.

76.   See Brief for Appellant, supra note 56 at 20, 24–25. Sheila King testified it was "her duty" to bring the children up as heterosexuals, but the trial court denied her custody stating that "were it not for the lesbian lifestyle chosen by [the mother] she would be awarded custody." See also *Whitehead v. Black*, Nos. CV–76–422, CV–76–426 (Me. Super. Ct., Cumberland County June 14, 1976) where the lesbian mother obtained custody. The court noted that "she was aware that her homosexual

lifestyle could have an impact on her children and was intelligently seeking to minimize, if not totally eliminate, that impact." But see *J.L.P. (H) v. D.L.P.*, supra note 53 at 872, where the gay father said he wanted his son to be gay. The court warned the father whose visitation had already been severely restricted that if he persisted in this position and harm resulted to the child, even greater restrictions were in store for him.

77. See, e.g., *L. v. D.*, supra note 53; *N.K.M. v. L.E.M.*, supra note 53; *Dailey v. Dailey*, supra note 11.

78. See, e. g., *Irish v. Irish*, 102 Mich. App. 75, 300 N.W. 2d 739 (1980); *M.J.P. v. J.G.P.*, supra note 33.

79. Hotvedt, Green, and Mandel, The Lesbian Parent: Comparison of Heterosexual and Homosexual Mothers and Their Children, presentation at the Annual Meeting, American Psychological Association, Sept. 4, 1979. See also Green, Mandel, Hotvedt, Gray, and Smith, "Lesbian Mothers and Their Children: A Comparison with Solo Parent Heterosexual Mothers and Their Children," 15 *Archives of Sexual Behav.* 167 (1986).

80. *Roe*, supra note 11.

81. *Jacobson*, supra note 48 at 81.

82. *Palmore v. Sidoti*, 466 U.S. 429 (1984).

83. Ibid. at 433.

84. *S.N.E. v. R.L.B.*, 699 P. 2d 875 (Alaska 1985).

85. Ibid. at 879.

86. *M.P. v. S.P.*, 169 N.J. Super. 425, 438, 404 A.2d 1256, 1263 (App. Div. 1979).

87. The majority states, "No connection between family, marriage, or procreation on the one hand and homosexual activity on the other has been demonstrated either by the Court of Appeals or by respondent." *Bowers v. Hardwick*, supra note 1 at 4920. The law's failure to recognize the formation and existence of gay family units belies the existence of the large number of gay people involved in long-term relationships and raising children. The Court may have fallen prey to the myth that gay people lead lonely, isolated lives, condemned to promiscuity. See Rivera, *Queer Law: Sexual Orientation Law in the Mid-Eighties — Part II*, supra note 53 at 372–98, for a discussion of gay families.

88. "The AIDS issue has now spawned a second epidemic — a wave of hysteria whose symptoms include ostracism, discrimination, and violence. As with other communicable maladies, we'll give this hysteria a name: Acute Fear Regarding AIDS or, more simply, AFRAIDS." AFRAIDS, *The New Republic*, Oct. 14, 1985, at 7.

89. In re *Doe*, No. 78–D–5040 (Ill. Circuit Ct., Cook Cty. Dom. Rel. Div., May 28, 1986). As I write, the order has been temporarily vacated pending a full hearing on the meaning of the test results.

90. See *Lambda AIDS Update*, No. 8, July, 1986, at 6.

91. See Friedland, Saltzman, Rogers, Kahl, Lesser, Mayers, and Klein, Lack of Transmission of HTLV-III/LAV Infection to Household Contacts of Patients with AIDS or AIDS-Related Complex with Oral Candidiasis, 314 *N. Eng. J. of Med.* 344 (Feb. 6, 1986).

92. This analysis of litigation with respect to time and geographic location is discussed in two previous articles: Rivera, Book Review, 132 *U. Pa. L. Rev.* 391

(1984) (reviewing J. D'Emilio, *Sexual Politics, Sexual Communities: The Making of a Homosexual Minority in the United States, 1940–1970* (1983); and Rivera, *Queer Law: Sexual Orientation Law in the Mid-Eighties — Part II*, supra note 53 at 335. The latter article analyzes cases and explains why courts are currently more homophobic in the central and southern regions of the United States than they are on the East and West Coasts.

93.   *Holland v. Holland*, 49 Ohio Law Abstracts 237, 75 N.E. 2d 489 (Ohio Ct. App. 1947).

94.   In re *Mara*, 3 Misc. 2d 174, 150 N.Y.S. 2d 524 (Fam. Ct. 1956); *Commonwealth v. Bradley*, 171 Pa. Super. Ct. 587, 91 A.2d 379 (1952); *Immerman v. Immerman*, 176 Cal. App. 2d 122, 1 Cal. Rptr. 298 (1959).

95.   *Nadler v. Superior Ct.*, 255 Cal. App. 2d 523, 63 Cal. Rptr. 352 (1967); *Commonwealth v. Cortes*, 210 Pa. Super. 515, 234 A.2d 47 (1967).

96.   The fifty cases are discussed in Rivera, Book Review, supra note 92, and Rivera, Queer Law: Sexual Orientation Law in the Mid-Eighties, supra note 53 at 330–71.

97.   See generally, Rivera, Book Review, supra note 92. D'Emilio's book documents the creation of the homosexual minority from its days of unawareness to 1981, when gay rights became a minority plank in the Democratic Party national platform. The book review compares legal events with D'Emilio's socioeconomic observations of each historical period.

98.   381 Mass. 563, 410 N.E. 2d 1207 (1980). The custody issue in this case involved a natural parent versus a guardian, so the stricter "fitness of the parent" standard was applied.

99.   16 Mass. App. Ct. 499, 452 N.E. 2d 293 (1983). The Doe court, relying on *Bezio* left standing a joint custody arrangement for a lesbian mother.

100.   *Bezio*, supra note 98 at 579, 410 N.E. 2d at 1216 (quoting custody of a minor (No. 2), 378 Mass. 712, 719, 393 N.E. 2d 379, 383 (179).

101.   *Bezio*, supra note 98 at 578, 410 N.E. 2d at 1215.

102.   *Guinan v. Guinan*, 102 A.D. 2d 963, 477 N.Y.S. 2d 830 (1984).

103.   Ibid. at 964, 477 N.Y.S. 2d at 831.

104.   *Gottlieb v. Gottlieb*, 108 A.D. 2d 120, 488 N.Y.S. 2d 180 (1985).

105.   Ibid. at 122, 488 N.Y.S. 2d at 181–82.

106.   Ibid. at 123, 488 N.Y.S. 2d at 182 (Kassal, J., concurring).

107.   *M.P. v. S.P.*, 169 N.J. Super. Ct. App. Div. 425, 404 A.2d 1256 (1979).

108.   *S.N.E. v. R.L.B.*, supra note 84.

109.   *Cabalquinto v. Cabalquinto*, 100 Wash. 2d 325, 669 P. 2d 886 (1983). The Washington Court of Appeals recently held that the father's homosexual relationship cannot justify restricting the visitation order. The court commented that parents come in all shapes and sizes, and while there are some restraints society may place upon parents, they are few in number, and do not include sexual preference.

110.   Ibid. at 329, 669 P. 2d 888.

111.   *M.J.P. v. J.G.P.*, supra note 33 at Record 302–5. The trial judge's statement is contained in Note, supra note 43 at 657.

112.   *Roe v. Roe*, supra note 11.

113.   Ibid. at 727, 324 S.E. 2d at 694.

V
EPILOGUE

13

GAY AND LESBIAN PARENTS: FUTURE PERSPECTIVES

Frederick W. Bozett

As editor of this volume it has been my intention to create both a new perspective within the field of family studies to include the gay and lesbian family, as well as to expand the horizons of gay studies to include families. Traditionally, researchers have shackled gay men and lesbians to their sexual orientation with the implicit assumption that they are either sterile or that parenting is outside their purview. Nongays have no purchase on parenthood. These facts can no longer be ignored by educators, researchers, or practitioners. A body of knowledge is now developing on gay men and lesbians who are or who want to parent and who live within family constellations. There is no such thing as *the* gay or lesbian family. There are single custodial families, stepfamilies, coparental and communal families, and others. Increasingly, gay and lesbian parents are coming out of the closet and are therefore known about by the population in general. Thus it is also imperative that professionals in many different disciplines become knowledgeable about these families so that depth research can be carried out in order to understand them more completely and accurately, and so that professional assistance, based upon facts rather than stereotypes and implicit assumptions, can be provided with objectivity and sensitivity.

There are several obstacles to achieving full-fledged parenthood by gay men and lesbians. First, and most important, is that homosexuality is not acceptable in the United States, and certainly gay and lesbian parenthood is anathema. Our culture is a highly homophobic one. But it is also an error to equate lack of education or factual knowledge about homosexuality with homophobia. It is likely that many people have

231

negative viewpoints solely out of not knowing the facts or having misinformation rather than holding deeply internalized pejorative attitudes. Thus, continued education at all educational levels and in multiple forums is crucial. Moreover, one of the most viable means of dispelling the many myths which surround homosexuality is for individual gay men and lesbians to come out to their significant others. This is likely an especially valuable tactic for gay and lesbian parents.

Another obstacle is the absence of legal recognition for same-sex marriages. Although the actual legal advantages may be limited (Harry & DeVall, 1978), there are serious advantages for gay and lesbian parents and their children. The most important advantage is that both parents would have legal rights to their children: Adopted children or those conceived through artificial insemination (or conceived naturally if the father gave up his legal rights to the child), would be legally related to both parents. The advantage is that if a parent were to die the other parent would be assured of custody of the children. Likewise, the children would have a guarantee of remaining in the custody of one parent in the event of divorce. As it now stands, if the biological or adoptive parent becomes incapacitated or dies, the child has no assurance of remaining in the custody of the parent who is left. Grandparents and other relatives have been known to seek and obtain custody of children, even when their involvement in the children's lives has been peripheral, when the remaining parent is known to have been most adequate in the parental role, and when the children have voiced their desire to live with the remaining parent. Even so, it is highly unlikely that marriages between same-sex individuals will be legalized in any state in the foreseeable future. However, as pointed out in Chapter 6, two joint adoptions by openly lesbian couples occurred in 1986 in California. While such actions by the court bode well for the future it is unlikely that such favorable decisions will become commonplace.

Another obstacle yet to be overcome is "parentophobia" on the part of many gay men and lesbians who not only seem unable to understand why homosexually oriented individuals would want children, but who also denigrate those who do. Often gays seem unaware of the painful process so many gay and lesbian parents have gone through to arrive at the point of openly acknowledging themselves as gay or lesbian parents. In preceeding chapters it has been pointed out that it is frequently very difficult to give up one's selective self-representation and secret half-lives, and that divorce and separation with the resulting isolation, especially if the children live with the other parent, is often exquisitely painful. Gays often assume that the freedoms gained make up for the losses. Sensitivity, understanding, and support by the gay community in general and individuals in particular through all phases of gay/lesbian parenthood is needed. Gay and lesbian parents choose not to have the economic and other freedoms characteristic of singlehood, and other gays must accept that without negative value judgments. In 1975 Mager made the point that "gays in general should be more open and understanding of the special problems of gay parents" (p. 132), and the admonition is as fitting today as it was then.

One of the most pressing needs in the study of the gay/lesbian family is the need for theory development. The content of this volume attests to this need: No chapter is tied to another by any conceptual or theoretical formulations. This is not to say that none of the research to date has been based on established theory or has as its intent theory development. Examples of the former are research on the children of lesbian mothers which has tested elements of psychoanalytic theory. Representative in the current work is the original research of Steckel on separation-individuation of children in lesbian mother stepfamilies. Examples of the latter are the middle range theories of *adult sexual identity resocialization* by Miller (1978, 1986), and of *integrative sanctioning* by Bozett (1981). Likewise, the inductively derived findings of McCandlish reported in the present work provide a beginning upon which further theoretical conceptualizations and propositions can be constructed.

Several assumptions will underlie the development of gay and lesbian family theory. First is that the gay/lesbian family is, in fact, a legitimate family form, and that it is deserving and in need of study in its own right. Closely related to this is the assumption that the gay/lesbian family is unique, that it varies sufficiently from other family forms that current family theory, developed from and tested on the heterosexual norm, may not fit the gay/lesbian family. It would be a serious mistake to attempt to analyze and understand the dynamics of the gay/lesbian family through the use of models formulated from a dissimilar population. An analogy to this would be the attempt to evaluate the effectiveness of therapy with the gay stepfamily against the heterosexual stepfamily model. There is no evidence to support their comparability.

It is likely, however, that theory in this substantive area of family studies will be generated from elements of preexisting theory, amplified or refined, and from original formulations deductively and/or inductively constructed, into one or more new and novel eclectic theories. The theories need to be characterized by maximum scope and generality so they are not limited to time or place, nor should they specify household composition, except that the adults would be self-identified as homosexual. Also, I do not mean to imply that the research on gay fathers and lesbian mothers already reported, much of which has been reviewed in this volume, is to be disregarded. However, while it adds to our understanding of individual or dyadic behavior, it does not fill the gap for which gay/lesbian family theory is intended. Hence, theory development at both the micro and macro levels, both substantive and formal theory, middle range and grand is needed.

Readers may question the need for a separate theory for gay/lesbian families. In some respects what may be needed is only a refinement of existing family theory that takes into consideration same-sex sexual relationships and gay/lesbian culture. While formal theories such as exchange, systems, or symbolic interactionism are sufficiently generalizable to be used to study the gay/lesbian family, other theories that are closer to the data and that are more narrow in scope and generality, and that are easily tested and easily revised (Holman & Burr, 1980) are more urgently needed. Others may question the viability of the notion of gay/lesbian family theory as a single entity, believing that the two family forms, gay father and lesbian mother, differ sufficiently so that two, not one, theories will be needed in order to explain the phenomena. I think this might be the case. Researchers must be alert to all of these considerations as their work progresses.

Although many of the chapters in this book have contained recommendations for further research, several additional suggestions are in order. Top priority should be given to cross sectional and longitudinal study of the gay/lesbian family to identify the (1) family life-cycle stages; (2) developmental tasks of the families as a unit and of their individual members; (3) effect of parental homosexuality on children beyond the pre-oedipal and oedipal phases of development and into their adulthood; (4) effect of parenthood on the adult development of the parents through middle age and into old age taking into consideration the context of gay culture; and (5) the intergenerational effects of gay/lesbian parents, that is, the effects of gay/lesbian grandparenting. Moreover, research is needed to ascertain "normal" gay/lesbian parenting behaviors and determinants of the "healthy" gay/lesbian family so that aberrant behaviors and family pathologies can be identified. Certainly, gay/lesbian families are more like than not like nongay families. But it cannot be assumed they are identical. What is true for one may not be true for the other. There is also a critical need for the study of gay father and lesbian mother families of different ethnic origins and socioeconomic backgrounds. The contents of this volume are based almost solely on research on middle and upper-middle class Caucasians. Likewise, research on gay/lesbian families from rural areas, rather than urban centers, is needed. In general there is also need for sample size to be larger, and for multiple methodologies to be employed. To begin to accomplish these research needs, interested researchers from several disciplines need to network. Although isolated investigations with small sample sizes are of value, large, more comprehensive studies should receive priority attention. The research of Eiduson and colleagues (1982) in which they studied the relationship between family lifestyle and child development in single-mother families, in communal living groups, and social-contract couples is an example of one form of research that needs to be undertaken.

I am also advocating the development of a new specialty, that of gay/lesbian *family* studies within existing departments of family science, psychology, sociology, departments of family nursing and medicine, or other academic units of universities concerned with families. Scholars in this specialty would come from varied disciplines and would be expert in the area of gay studies as well as family science. The time has arrived for serious study by qualified professionals of this family form — as family — in its multiple variations.

In conclusion, although much research yet needs to be conducted, this volume attests to a solid and rich foundation upon which to build further knowledge. Moreover, it attests to the fact that the family is not dead. Family is a universal that is not bounded by sexual orientation nor by society's rigid sex role assignments and stereotypes. What gay men and lesbians long for (and are beginning to achieve) is to lead an ordinary life without hiding their sexuality (Goldstein, 1986). This, too, is what many gay/lesbian parents want. Based upon the research to date, it can be stated with some confidence that, in general, gay/lesbian parents are highly committed as parents, and that they have a high emotional investment in the parent-child relationship. Homosexuality is neither incompatible nor incongruent with parenting. As Harry and DeVall (1978) point out, as preoccupation with the sex lives of gays and lesbians has diminished, interest in other aspects of their lives has expanded. It is now time to get on with the job of conducting much needed research on this highly viable family form.

REFERENCES

Bozett, F. W. (1981). Gay fathers: Identity conflict resolution through integrative sanctioning. *Alternative Lifestyles, 4*, 90–107.

Ediuson, B. T., Kornfein, M., Zimmerman, I. L., & Weisner, T. S. (1982). Comparative socialization practices in traditional and alternative families. In M. E. Lamb (Ed.), *Nontraditional families: Parenting and child development* (pp. 315–346). Hillsdale, NJ: Lawrence Erlbaum.

Goldstein, R. (1986, July 1). The gay family. *Village Voice,* pp. 19, 21–22, 24, 26, 28.

Harry, J., & DeVall, W. B. (1978). *The social organization of gay males.* New York: Praeger.

Holman, T. B., & Burr, W. R. (1980). Beyond the beyond: The growth of family theories in the 1970s. *Journal of Marriage and the Family, 42*, 7–19.

Mager, D. (1975). Faggot father. In K. Jay and A. Young (Eds.), *After you're out.* New York: Links.

Miller, B. (1978). Adult sexual resocialization: Adjustment toward a stigmatized identity. *Alternative Lifestyles, 1*, (2), 207–234.

Miller, B. (1986). Identity resocialization in moral careers of gay husbands and fathers. In A. Davis (Ed.), *Papers in honor of Gordon Hirabayashi.* Edmonton, Alberta, Canada: University of Alberta.

ADDITIONAL REFERENCES

Abbitt, D., & Bennett, F. (1979). Being a lesbian mother. In B. Berzon & R. Leighton (Eds.), *Positively gay*. Millbrae, CA: Celestial Arts.

Bigner, J. (1986). *Attitudes toward parenting and the value of children: Straight versus gay fathers*. Manuscript submitted for publication.

Brown, H. (1976). Married homosexuals. In H. Brown, *Familiar faces, hidden lives*. New York: Harcourt Brace Jovanovich.

Campbell, S. M. (1980). *The couples journey*. San Luis Obispo, CA: Impact.

Curry, H., & Clifford, D. (1984). *A legal guide for lesbian and gay couple s*. Berkeley, CA: Nolo Press.

Feminist Self-Insemination Group. (1979). *Self-Insemination*. Feminist Self-Insemination Group, 27 Clerkenwell Clse, London WC1, England.

Fishel, A. H. (1983). Gay parents. *Issues in Health Care of Women, 4*, 139–164.

Gantz, J. (1983). *Whose child cries*? Rolling Hills Estates, CA: Jalmar Press.

Hanscombe, G. E. (1983). The right to lesbian parenthood. *Journal of Medicine Ethics*, (9), 133–135.

Hitchens, D. (1980). Social attitudes, legal standards, and personal trauma in child custody cases. *Journal of Homosexuality, 5*, 89–95.

Humphreys, L., & Miller, B. (1980). Identities in the emerging gay culture. In J. Marmor (Ed.), *Homosexual behavior: A modern reappraisal*. New York: Basic Books.

Hunt, S. P. (1978). Influence of a homosexual father (Question and answer). Medical Aspects of Human Sexuality, 12, 103–104.

Klein, F. (1978). *The Bisexual Option*. New York: Arbor House.

Kohn, B. & Matusos, A. (1980). *Barry & Alice: Portrait of a bisexual marriage*. New York: Prentice-Hall.

Loulan, J. (1986). Psychotherapy with lesbian mothers. In T. S. Stein, & C. J. Cohen (Eds.), *Contemporary perspectives on psychotherapy with lesbians and gay men*. New York: Plenum.

Miller, B., & Humphreys, L. (1980). Lifestyles and violence: Homosexual victims of assault and murder. *Qualitative Sociology, 3,* 169–185.

Ostrow, D. (1977). *Gay and straight parents: What about the children?* Unpublished manuscript, Hampshire College.

Richardson, D., & Hart, J. (1981). Married and isolated homosexuals. In J. Hart & D. Richardson, *The theory and practice of homosexuality*. London: Routledge & Kegan Paul.

Riddle, D. (1977). *Gay parents and child custody issues*. (Report No. C6–012–219). Tucson, AZ: University of Arizona. (ERIC Document Reproduction Service No. ED 147 746).

Robinson, B. E., & Skeen, P. (1982). Sex-role orientation of gay fathers versus gay nonfathers. *Perceptual and Motor Skills, 55,* 1055–1059.

_____. (1984). Family backgrounds of gay fathers: A descriptive study. *Psychological Reports, 54,* 999–1005.

_____. (1985). Gay fathers' and gay nonfathers' relationship with their parents. *The Journal of Sex Research, 21* (1), 86–91.

_____. (1986, July). *Gay fathers: Victims of both the heterosexual and homosexual worlds*. Paper presented at the Groves Conference on Marriage and the Family, London, England.

INDEX

ABOUT THE AUTHORS

ROBERTA ACHTENBERG is Directing Attorney of the Lesbian Rights Project, a San Francisco-based public interest legal center specializing in public education and litigation of issues of sexual orientation discrimination and the lesbian and gay family. Ms. Achtenberg is the editor of *Sexual Orientation and the Law* (Clark Boardman Co., Ltd., 1985), the first lawyers' treatise on the representation of lesbian and gay clients. Former Dean of New College of California School of Law, Ms. Achtenberg was also a Teaching Fellow at the Stanford Law School. She received her B.A. from the University of California at Berkeley and her J.D. from the University of Utah College of Law.

DAVID A. BAPTISTE, JR. received his B.A. from Howard University and his Ph.D. from Purdue. He has served as a family therapist in the Massachusetts Department of Corrections and is currently a counseling psychologist at New Mexico State University. He also has a private practice in marital and family therapy. His principle areas of interest in psychotherapy are stepfamily systems — heterosexual and homosexual, single-parent family systems, racial and cultural minority family systems, and adolescent pregnancy. He has articles in these areas published in a variety of professional journals.

FREDERICK W. BOZETT received his Doctor of Nursing Science degree from the University of California, San Francisco. His bachelor's and master's degrees are from Teachers College, Columbia University. He has taught at the University of San Francisco, University of California, San Francisco, and is currently a Professor of Nursing in the graduate program at the University of Oklahoma. He is coeditor of *Dimensions of Fatherhood* (Sage, 1985), and has written extensively on gay fathers. His primary research interest is in gay-father families. He has recently completed a study of the children of gay fathers, and he is currently undertaking a grounded theory study of gay grandfathers.

G. DORSEY GREEN received her A.B. from Dickinson College and her Ph.D. from the University of Washington. She is in private practice as a psychologist in Seattle. Her professional interests are in procrastination and lesbian couples with and without children.

DAVID R. MATTESON received his Ph.D. from Boston University. He has taught at Boston University, Marietta College, The Royal Danish School of Higher Education in Copenhagen, and is presently a University Professor of Psychology and Counseling at Governors State University. His research areas include adolescent identity, family dynamics, sex roles, and alternative lifestyles. He is a founding member and on the Council of the National Organization for Changing Men.

BARBARA M. MCCANDLISH received her Ph.D. in clinical psychology from Harvard University. She has eighteen years of clinical training and experience and is now in private practice in Santa Fe. Her current clinical, research, and teaching interests are in the areas of gender development and lesbian relationships, and families from a feminist development perspective. She has also taught and trained graduate students in psychology and counseling at Antioch University since 1978.

BRIAN MILLER received his Ph.D. from the University of Alberta. He has a private psychotherapy practice in West Hollywood and writes a regular mental health column for the Los Angeles magazine, Edge. His Ph.D. dissertation is a longitudinal study of the identity development of gay husbands and fathers, and he has published widely on the subject.

SARALIE BISNOVICH PENNINGTON studied social work at Howard University and the University of Pittsburgh where she received her M.S.W. She coordinates the family therapy program at Operation Concern, a gay and lesbian out-patient psychotherapy clinic in San Francisco. She is also in private practice.

CHERI PIES received her B.A. and M.P.H. from the University of California, Berkeley, and her M.S.W. from Boston University. She has been leading groups for lesbians considering parenthood since 1977, and is currently an AIDS educator for the Department of Public Health in San Francisco. Her principle areas of interest are maternal and child health, women and AIDS, and the social and ethical implications of reproductive technologies. She is author of *Considering Parenthood: A Workbook for Lesbians*, Spinsters Ink, 1985.

WENDELL RICKETTS is a freelance writer living in San Francisco. Formerly the manuscript editor of the *Journal of Homosexuality*, he received his B.A. from the Human Sexuality Studies Program at San Francisco State University and has studied in the Graduate School of Social Work Program for the Study of Sex at the University of Hawaii. He is currently writing a book on the Boston foster care case.

RHONDA R. RIVERA received her B.A. (cum laude) in Economics from Douglass College, Rutgers University; her M.P.A. from Syracuse University; and her J.D. (magna cum laude) from Wayne State University Law School. She also holds certificates in Applied Urban Economics from the Massachusetts Institute of Technology, and Law and Economics from the University of Miami Law School. She is currently a candidate for a Master's Degree in Theology. She is a Professor of Law, The Ohio State University College of Law. She is nationally known for her publications on homosexuality and the law.

AILSA STECKEL received her Ph.D. in clinical psychology from the Wright Institute. She is currently in private practice in San Francisco and Oakland. Her major research interests are in the areas of object relations and early childhood development.